AF248550

THE REBELLIOUS GALILEAN

THE REBELLIOUS GALILEAN

by

JOHN BONFORTE

Philosophical Library
New York

Library of Congress Cataloging in Publication Data

Bonforte, John.
  The rebellious Galilean.

  1. Jesus Christ—Biography. 2. Christian biography—Palestine. I. Title.
BT301.2.B558   232.9′01   81-82691
ISBN 0-8022-2391-5   AACR2

Manufactured in the United States of America

Overseas distributor: George Prior Associated Publishers Ltd.
Lower Ground Floor, High Holborn House, 52-54 High Holborn,
London WC1V 6RL England

Contents

PREFACE

The Encyclopedia Britannica states that, "Any attempt to write a 'Life of Jesus' should be frankly abandoned. The material for it certainly does not exist. It has been calculated that the total number of days in his life regarding which we have any record does not exceed fifty."

In spite of this admonition, many men have written books on the life of Jesus and it is safe to assume that many more will continue to do so. This is natural since the life of Jesus is the single most important event that has ever occurred in the life of mankind. His thoughts and his words have affected everyone, including those persons who have gone to extreme lengths to blot out his teachings. Undoubtedly, the Encyclopedia Britannica is correct in one respect, and that is that no one will ever write an adequate life of Jesus.

The approach adopted in this book has been to assemble the material from the four gospels into individual stories of each event as it occurred in its approximate chronological order, and then to tie these separate events together with assumed stories which appear logical from the action that preceded and followed the recorded events. The King James translation of the Bible has been used as the source of the material for this book. For the convenience of the reader, the references from the Old and New Testaments that have been used in this book are placed at the beginning of each chapter.

I gratefully acknowledge the tremendous help and encouragement that I have received in writing this book from E. J. Sprague (Mrs. Marshall Sprague) and Father Wilbur of the Church of Our Saviour.

John Bonforte
Colorado Springs

Matt. 27 (26-56) John 19 (16-37)
Mark 15 (15-41) Ps. 23
Luke 23 (26-49) Deut. 21 (22-23)

Chapter 1

The Crucifixion

Captain Giovanni Ditalo, serving with the Roman Legion in Judaea, was a simple old soldier who had fought in all the major wars that Rome had waged in Greece, Gaul and Italy, from the time that he was a boy of twelve. As a boy he had entertained the Roman Legionnaires stationed in his Sicilian village, singing native folk songs while playing on his home-made bagpipes. When the soldiers were ordered to leave the village, they adopted the homeless orphan as a mascot and took him with them wherever they went.

The young boy travelled with the Legionnaires to many strange countries and when he grew older fought with them, sharing in their hardships and triumphs. With the passage of time, he was entrusted with greater and greater responsibilities, until finally he had been promoted to centurion, a company commander. Now, in compensation for his long years of faithful service, he had been rewarded with a supposedly easy assignment in a civilized country where he could live in comfort with his wife and family.

At first, Captain Ditalo, who was an easy-going, friendly person, had enjoyed his assignment in Judaea. He liked to relax in the afternoon sun because it helped relieve the pain that wracked his shoulder, where an enemy's poisoned spear had pierced him many years ago. He still enjoyed the semitropical climate of the country, because it was so similar to that of his native village, but unlike his friend, Captain Paolo Catania in Galilee, he was disappointed in his inability to make friends with the people of Jerusalem, who viewed him with undisguised hostility.

As a soldier, Captain Ditalo had early learned the most important of all soldierly lessons of obeying without question all military orders, no matter how distasteful those orders might be. Never in all the years that he had been a Roman Legionnaire had he ever questioned an order that had been given to him; but now, he was seriously troubled. His brow was wrinkled in deep thought, which was quite unusual for the easy-going captain. He had killed many men in the heat of battle, but those deaths had never bothered him, because they had occurred in the excitement of human encounter, where only the laws of the jungle prevailed—kill or be killed. Now, there was no enemy before him, only a pathetic, dedicated individual with a strange philosophy of life about the brotherhood of man. Yet his orders were to execute that man in the most brutal way humanly conceivable.

When Captain Ditalo received the dread order to crucify Jesus, he had stiffened subconsciously, because he could not erase from his mind the events he had witnessed that morning. He had heard the governor's wife speak highly of the man's spirituality and plead with the governor to save the man's life. His good friend, Captain Catania, had testified to the man's supernatural powers, and the governor himself had publicly proclaimed the innocence of this Jesus of Nazareth. Why execute such a man?

Bitterly, Captain Ditalo reflected upon the misfortune that had befallen him to be the executioner of this godly man who had done no harm either to him or to his country. Execution in itself was bad enough, he thought, but why did Rome have to adopt a method of execution invented by their hated enemies the Phoenicians? Captain Ditalo thought that only sadists and men who lived soft, corrupt lives could enjoy the brutality of the prolonged torture of crucifixion.

While Captain Ditalo was in the midst of his reveries, the screaming of the mob outside the fort for the blood of their innocent victim reached an ear-splitting crescendo. The sergeant of the guard approached the captain, saluted and asked, "What shall we do with the prisoners, captain?"

Dispiritedly, Captain Ditalo answered, "Release the murderer, Barrabas, and replace him with the Galilean. Then scourge the three prisoners."

The soldiers untied the thongs that bound Barrabas and released him. Jesus and the two remaining prisoners were stripped to the waist and faced against whipping posts constructed in the form of a tee. While their outstretched arms were being tightly bound to the horizontal bar, the captain heard Jesus fervently praying—

> "The Lord is my shepherd,
> I shall not want.
> He makes me lie down
> In green pastures."

Now the flogging of one of the two criminals began. As the whip fell relentlessly upon the tough, hardened body of the convict, his face became contorted with pain and he screamed in anguish. Soon, his entire body was a mass of bloody corrugated flesh. With each blow, Jesus winced and recoiled in horror as though he, himself, were being whipped. Meanwhile, he continued his anxious prayer to God, saying—

> "He restores my soul,
> And leads me into
> The paths of righteousness.
> His rod and his staff,
> They comfort me."

At the twelfth stroke, Captain Ditalo shouted, "Enough!"
Then the guard approached the second convict and methodically resumed the whipping until the second prisoner was another horrible bleeding example of man's inhumanity to man. Once again Jesus winced and trembled as the whip fell painfully upon the back of the second helpless prisoner. Continuing his fervent prayer, Jesus said—

> "Even tho I walk
> Through the valley of death,
> I shall fear no evil,
> For God is with me."

Once again, at the twelfth stroke, Captain Ditalo shouted, "Enough!"
As the guard approached Jesus with his whip already dripping with the blood from the bodies of the other two prisoners, he devoutly prayed—

> "Surely goodness and mercy
> Shall follow me
> All the days of my life,
> And I shall dwell
> In the house of the Lord,
> Forever and ever."

The last words were barely out of his mouth before the first cruel lash of the whip curled around his weakened body and quickly drew a spurt of blood. By the time the guard had completed six strokes, Jesus' body hung limply at the post, held in place only by the thongs that bound his wrists to the horizontal cross-bar. For the third time, Captain Ditalo jumped up and shouted, "Enough! Cut him loose and give them all a drink of spiked wine; then take them to their crosses!"

The soldiers cut Jesus free and offered him a drink of drugged wine, which he rejected, even though his slender body was wracked in pain. After Captain Ditalo left the courtyard to confer with Pontius Pilate the soldiers, seeing the expensive robe hanging on Jesus' shoulders, mockingly saluted him as the king of the Jews. To add to the merriment of the occasion a soldier made a crown of thorns, which he placed upon Jesus' head as an imitation crown, while another soldier cut a reed and placed it into the hands of Jesus as an imitation kingly scepter. The soldiers then took turns at marching up to Jesus, sallaaming deferentially and saying, "Hail, O mighty king of the Jews!"

Captain Ditalo returned just in time to see one of the soldiers strike Jesus over the head with the reed. Blazing with anger, Captain Ditalo shouted, "Enough of this nonsense! Take each prisoner to his cross-piece and march them out the gate. Step lively!"

The two husky convicts easily shouldered their cross-pieces and walked out the gate behind the marching soldiers, but Jesus was so weak that he could scarcely move. Repeatedly, he stumbled and fell in his effort to carry the heavy cross-piece and keep up with the other prisoners. As soon as the prisoners and soldiers were outside Fort Antonia, Captain Ditalo ordered the first burly person that he saw to carry the cross-piece for Jesus.

The soldiers marched their prisoners through a winding

street which has become appropriately known as Via Dolorosa, because it means the Road of Agony in Latin. The Via Dolorosa is in the northern part of Jerusalem and leads to the Gennareth Gate in the western wall of Jerusalem. A short distance beyond it there was a small mound known to the people of Jerusalem as Golgotha, because its shape resembled that of a skull.

Outlined against the skyline above Golgotha were the grim reminders of past crucifixions, the vertical pieces of numerous crosses firmly set in the ground. Each vertical piece was from twelve to fifteen feet high and equipped with a wooden projection about two inches wide and twelve inches long, set into the vertical post about eight feet above the ground. At the top of the vertical posts were a series of holes set about two inches apart.

When the soldiers arrived at Golgotha, they offered their three prisoners another drink of spiked wine, and then quickly and in a business-like manner proceeded with the crucifixion of the three prisoners. Four soldiers were assigned to each prisoner. Skillfully and forcefully, they dropped each prisoner on his back across the horizontal cross-piece. Two soldiers kneeled on the prisoner's shoulders and arms; the third soldier sat across the prisoner's knees; while the fourth soldier nailed the prisoner's hands to the cross-piece.

Each prisoner was then raised up on the vertical post until his crotch rested on the wooden projection of the cross. Another soldier climbed a ladder behind the cross and helped raise each prisoner and his cross-piece until his body was stretched at full length. This soldier then pushed the angle bolt in the vertical post through the holes in the horizontal cross-piece, thereby securely fastening both pieces of the cross together. To complete the crucifixion, one of the soldiers nailed the prisoner's feet to the bottom of the cross.

The torture of crucifixion was caused by alternately creating excruciating pain in the crucified person's hands and feet. A fiendish addition to this torture was created by the fact that the crucified person could momentarily relieve the pain in either his hands or his feet by transferring the weight of his body, either to his crotch or to his feet. When the crucified person pushed down on the spikes driven through his feet, the pain in his hands and arms was momentarily relieved and he could draw a full breath of air. However, this effort created such tremendous pain in the crucified person's feet that he would quickly slump down again and rest his body on the wooden projection provided at his crotch, thus re-creating the intense pain in his hands and arms. Since no vital organ was injured during crucifixion and since the loss of blood of the crucified person was minor, crucifixion could last for many hours, depending upon the physical strength of each individual. Some crucified persons lived for more than twenty-four hours.

After Jesus had been raised up on his cross, he raised his eyes to heaven and said, "Father, forgive them, for they know not what they do."

There was one last act remaining to make the crucifixion official and that was the nailing of the official notice of the crime committed by each prisoner at the top of his cross. So, once again one of the soldiers climbed to the top of the ladders at the backs of the three crosses and nailed over the head of each prisoner the official accusation against him. The scroll containing the charges against Jesus had been written by Pontius Pilate himself, in Latin, Greek and Hebrew. It simply read, "Jesus of Nazareth, King of the Jews."

By simply stating Jesus' name and title, Govenor Pilate was again proclaiming to the world that he found Jesus guilty of no crime. Off to one side, attentively watching the crucifixion of Jesus, were Chief Rabbi Caiaphas, Rabbi Ahab and other temple personnel. When they saw the Roman soldier nailing the scroll above the head of each prisoner, they walked over to the foot of Jesus' cross to read the official accusation against him.

When the Chief Rabbi read the inscription that Pontius Pilate had written, his sadistic pleasure quickly changed to one of bitter anger. Between gritted teeth, he said to Rabbi Ahab, "Stay here until I get back. I am going to Fort Antonia to see the governor. He must change that accusation against the rebel Galilean at once."

The Chief Rabbi was soon back at Fort Antonia, demanding to see Pontius Pilate. When the governor learned who his caller was, he strolled reluctantly to the balcony and looking down at the Chief Rabbi said, "What do you want?"

Caiaphas replied, "Honorable governor, the accusation against the Galilean must not say that he is the King of the Jews, but only that he *claimed* to be the King of Jews."

Pilate coldly replied, "What I have written, I have written," and curtly turned on his heel and re-entered the fort. Fuming with anger, Chief Rabbi Caiaphas returned to Golgotha, just in time to hear Rabbi Ahab shout at Jesus, "You, who boasted that you could destroy the temple and rebuild it in three days, let's see you save yourself."

The Chief Rabbi next strode up to Jesus and shouted at him, "If you want us to believe that you are the Messiah and the King of Israel, let us see you come down from the cross."

Rabbi Ahab sarcastically said, "You know he said, 'I am the Son of God.' Since he trusts in God, let us see if God will save him; that is if God wants him."

One of the criminals shouted at Jesus, "If you are the Messiah, why don't you save yourself and save us?"

The other criminal cried out, "Don't you fear God, knowing that you will die at the same time that this man does? You and I have been condemned to death justly but this man has committed no crime."

Then, turning to Jesus, this criminal said, "Lord, remember me when you come into your kingdom."

Jesus answered, "Today, you shall be with me in heaven."

Clustered around the foot of the cross were his mother, Mary, and John and Mary Magdalen. Turning to his mother, Jesus said, "Henceforth, let John be as a son to you."

Then, turning to John, he said, "Take my mother and let her be as your own mother to you."

Jesus continued his slow upward and downward painful motions and then said, in great agony, "I am thirsty."

One of the soldiers put a sponge on the tip of his spear, dipped it into the drugged wine and raised it to the lips of Jesus, but he barely touched it. It was now almost three hours past high noon. Chief Rabbi Caiaphas looked toward the setting sun and then looked back at Jesus and said to Rabbi Ahab, "That Galilean will live beyond sundown, and as a result, defile our Passover. He must die before sundown."

Rabbi Ahab asked, "How can we do that?"

Chief Rabbi Caiaphas grimly answered, "By having his legs broken. Then he won't be able to push himself upward to get a breath of fresh air, and so he will quickly die in his own blood."

Rabbi Ahab asked, "Do you think the Roman governor will agree?"

The Chief Rabbi growled, "He must. Otherwise, we will threaten to riot again."

Rabbi Ahab asked, "Shall I come with you?"

The Chief Rabbi answered, "No, remain here and make sure that no one interferes with the crucifixion of the Galilean. We can't trust these Gentiles to do it."

While Chief Rabbi hurried to the Roman fort on his evil errand, Jesus was so weak he could no longer force his body upward to exhale and get a breath of fresh air. He had suffered the agonies of crucifixion for about three hours, and with his last breath, he prayed, speaking the first line of the psalm that he and his disciples had sung at their last supper—

"My God, my God, why have you forsaken me?"

This psalm, written hundreds of years before the birth of Jesus, predicted in almost exact detail his crucifixion. However, some persons at the foot of the cross who heard Jesus' last words thought that he was calling upon the prophet Elijah for help, so one of them said, "He is asking Elijah to help him."

One of the soldiers went to get Jesus another sip of spiked wine, and as he did so Rabbi Ahab growled at him, "Let him be. Let us see whether or not Elijah will come and take him down from the cross."

With one last effort, Jesus said, "Father, I commit my soul into your hands."

And so, Jesus died.

While Jesus was dying on the cross, Chief Rabbi Caiaphas arrived at Fort Antonia and once again demanded to see Pontius Pilate. When the Roman governor was told who it was that wished to see him, he strode out to the balcony, looked down at the loathsome figure below him and angrily said, "What do you want now?"

The Chief Rabbi tried to adopt the sly, crafty tone of his father-in-law, as he said, "Honored sir, it is growing late. The prisoners still live and the sun will soon set. At sundown, our Passover begins, and our people believe that evil will befall our nation if the prisoners die during our sacred Passover."

Pontius Pilate growled, "What is that to me?" Chief Rabbi Caiaphas answered, "Please sir, have the prisoners' legs broken, so that they will die before sundown." Pontius Pilate reflected a moment and then, glaring coldly at the evil man before him, said, "So let it be."

Chief Rabbi Caiaphas gleefully waited at the fort until a soldier was sent to Golgotha to carry out the order to break the legs of the three crucified men. The Chief Rabbi followed him happily back to Mount Calvary. At Golgotha, the soldier swung a heavy club and broke the shin bones of both the convicts. The bodies of the two men immediately slumped down on the cross and they died quickly for lack of fresh air.

When the soldier approached the body of Jesus, he found that Jesus was already dead, so he did not bother to break his legs. Another soldier, wondering whether or not Jesus was actually dead, pierced his side with a spear. The spear pierced Jesus' lungs so when the soldier withdrew it, clear body fluid and blood flowed out.

When Chief Rabbi Caiaphas and Rabbi Ahab saw that Jesus was dead, they embraced each other in happiness that their mission of witnessing the death of Jesus was successfully accomplished. They returned to the temple, prepared to give the Great Sanhedrin a detailed account of the death of Jesus.

Chapter 2

Jewish History

As Jesus was a devout religious Jew, it is necessary to know some basic facts about Judaism at the time that he lived in order to understand those things that motivated him. The earliest known record of Judaism begins with Abraham, a nomadic Semite who lived on the west bank of the Euphrates River about the year 1900 B.C. It is interesting to note that the Arabs also claim and honor Abraham as one of their famed ancestors. When Abraham was about seventy-five years old, he and his family and a number of their relatives moved to Canaan, which included all the land around the Dead Sea, the Jordan River and the Sea of Galilee, or more correctly, Lake Tiberias.

About 180 years later, about 1730 B.C., one of Abraham's descendants named Joseph was sold into slavery by his brothers. The slave-traders took Joseph into Egypt where he prospered, married into a prominent family, and became one of Egypt's leading citizens. Before the arrival of Joseph into

Egypt, the Hyksos, a semitic people from the land now known as Syria, Lebanon, Iraq and Turkey, conquered Egypt and ruled it. This means that Joseph married into and became influential with the Hyksos, the conquerors of Egypt, and did not establish cordial relations with the Egyptians themselves.

After Joseph was settled in Egypt, his father, his brothers and their families joined him there, and created a large and thriving Jewish community. As long as the Hyksos remained in power, that Jewish community grew and prospered. However, in the year 1580 B.C. the Egyptians rebelled, overthrew the Hyksos, and thereafter, the lot of the Jews changed abruptly from that of prosperity to one of adversity.

About 280 years later in the year 1301 B.C., Ramases II became the ruler of Egypt, and he was responsible for the construction of many large imposing structures that required an enormous amount of manual labor. In order to construct these national monuments, Ramases II made virtual slaves of the Jews. The hardships and the suffering they endured caused them to seek a leader through whom they could unite and rebel. They found such a leader in the palace of the king, a Jew named Moses, who had been adopted while he was still an infant by the daughter of the king.

Moses tried repeatedly to persuade the Egyptian king to allow the Jews to leave Egypt, but Ramases II refused every request that Moses made. Moses then prayed to Jehovah, the Jewish God, to curse the Egyptians with a plague, which Jehovah promptly granted causing great suffering among the Egyptians; but still the king refused to allow the Jews to leave Egypt. Thereafter, Moses prayed to Jehovah to punish the Egyptians with one plague after another and Jehovah granted all of his prayers. Even though the Egyptians suffered severely from these plagues, Ramases II refused to grant the Jews permission to leave Egypt.

While these disagreements between the Jews and the Egyp-

tians were taking place, Ramases II died and he was succeeded by Minepteh, who became so fearful of the power of
Moses and his God, Jehovah, that he allowed the Jews to
leave Egypt. Fearing that Minepteh might change his mind,
Moses quickly led his people eastward across the sea toward
Canaan, the land that Jehovah had promised to give to the
Jews. The direct route from Egypt to Canaan was along the
pleasant southern coast of the Mediterranean Sea, but that
route required crossing heavily populated areas, which Moses
knew would require fighting hostile inhabitants every foot of
the way. Consequently, he led his people over the far longer
route around the Sinai Peninsula through sweltering hot deserts and over difficult mountainous terrain.

Many Jews became so discouraged by the difficulties they
encountered along this route they decided to return to Egypt.
Iron-fisted Moses ordered them to continue the journey to
Canaan and when they refused, a fight took place in which
all the rebellious Jews were killed. As a result, a journey
that could have been comfortably made in several weeks,
stretched out into forty years. However, Moses never arrived
at Canaan, the goal he had set for himself, because he died
before the final battle for Canaan took place.

Before he died, Moses firmly established the basic laws of
Judaism in the numerous commandments that he laid down
for the Jews in the first five books of the Old Testament,
called the Torah, or the Law. The names of these five books
are Genesis, Exodus, Leviticus, Numbers and Deuteronomy.
None of the Jewish leaders after Moses made any important
changes in these basic laws. Modifications in them have occurred during the many centuries that have passed since then,
but these modifications have come about very slowly, because
the Jewish rabbis have resisted all changes in the Mosaic laws
for as long a period as possible. Consequently, the modifications that have occurred have been of an evolutionary character, rather than revolutionary ones; and these changes have

come about so slowly that they have been barely perceptible in any one generation.

The basic philosophy of Judaism is contained in the following address that Moses made to the Jews prior to their arrival in Canaan. This is the address:

"When the Lord, thy God shall bring you into Canaan and shall deliver that nation into your hands, you shall smite them and utterly destroy them. You shall make no agreement with them, nor show them any mercy, nor shall you marry any of them, for they will turn your children away from me. If you do marry any of them, the anger of the Lord will be turned against you and destroy you. You are a holy people to God. He has chosen you to be a special people unto himself, above all the people that are on the face of the earth."

In this address there are the basic teachings of Judaism, which are—

1. Jehovah is the god of the Jews and of the Jews only.
2. The Jews are his chosen people and are to be favored above all others.
3. Jews must not intermarry with non-Jews.
4. All Jews must abide by a strict set of laws that govern their daily lives from birth to death.
5. Jews must maintain a high standard of morality toward each other, but they were free to behave toward Gentiles as circumstances required.

In summary, Judaism is both a religion and a nationality and the two are indivisible. In order to administer the laws that he established, Moses created a perpetual group of administrators from the tribe of Levi. These men were related to each other by blood ties and transmitted their authority to administer the Mosaic laws to their sons. The strict administration of these laws effectively set the Jews apart from all other people.

A secondary result of the strict administration of these Mosaic laws was that the Jews developed a dual morality, one that was concerned with their relationship toward each other and a separate morality that was concerned with their relationship to Gentiles. Therefore, from its inception, Judaism had a dual nature—one was spiritual; the other was pragmatic and materialistic. Another noticeable division among Jews was that some tended strongly toward the religious side while others were attracted toward the nationalistic side of Judaism.

After the death of Moses, Joshua beame the leader of the Jews and under his leadership the Jews quickly conquered large sections of Canaan. After Joshua died, the Jews elected no new leader, but preferred to be ruled by a group of men known as Judges. Under the numerous Judges, the Jews suffered many military defeats until they again accepted individual leadership under Saul, David and Solomon. These men were given the exalted title of King.

After the death of King Solomon, there occurred one of the worst periods in Jewish history because the Jews became divided between Israel, the kingdom of the north, and Judah, later call Judaea, the kingdom of the south. During this period the Jews fought disastrous civil wars which were worse than their wars against foreign enemies. Thereafter, the Jews were ruled by one foreign invader after another until, by the time of Jesus, the Romans were the rulers of Palestine.

On the religious and spiritual side of Judaism there was an ancient prophecy that some day a Messiah, the Son of God, would come to judge the quick and the dead and, according to this Jewish prophecy, the messiah would be a descendant of David and a native of Bethlehem. His coming would signify the end of the world. Few Jews living during the lifetime of Jesus gave serious consideration to the possibility of the messiah arriving among them during their lifetime.

While the temple rabbis were primarily concerned with the physical existence of Judaism, the devout Jews such as John the Baptist and Jesus were basically conerned with the preservation of the moral principles of Judaism. These men who were the conscience of Judaism were revered by the Jews as their prophets. It was inevitable that the men representing these two opposing views of Judaism would eventually clash.

Briefly then, this is the background of Judaism at the time that Jesus lived. The reforms that Jesus tried to make in Judaism are these:

1. The Jewish conception of a god who was concerned solely with the welfare of Jews should be replaced by a universal God concerned with the welfare of all mankind.
2. The brotherhood of man should not be considered solely as a blood relationship, but as a spiritual relationship that binds all men together on spiritual and moral grounds.
3. Spiritual matters and wordly matters should be kept strictly apart, because God is concerned with man's spiritual welfare and not his material welfare.

In a religion as tradition-bound as Judaism, it was only natural to the Jewish rabbis that they must vigorously oppose the reforms that Jesus tried to make. The life of Jesus is the story of the conflict between Jesus, the spiritual leader of Judaism, and the temple rabbis, concerned with the physical existence of Judaism. In the chapters that follow, this book attempts to tell the story of that conflict simply and truthfully.

Matt. 3 (1-17)   Mark 1 (1-11)   Luke 7 (11-23)
Matt. 11 (1-6)   Mark 6 (18-20)   John 1 (6-8)
Matt. 14 (3-5)   Luke 3 (1-22)   John 1 (15-36)

Chapter 3

Birth to Manhood

Before continuing with the story of the life of Jesus, it is necessary to know what events had occurred in Palestine between 6 BC and 28 AD, the years between the birth and death of Jesus and John the Baptist. Before the two evangelists were born the Romans had made Herod, the son of the Jew Antipater, king of all Palestine, including Judaea, Samaria, Galilee and some other adjacent areas. Initially, Herod ruled Palestine so successfully that the Romans continually increased his domain, so that during the latter years of his life he was called King Herod the Great.

King Herod died in 4 B.C. when both John the Baptist and Jesus were about two years old. In his will, the king gave Judaea and Samaria to his elder son, Herod Archelaus; Galilee to his younger son, Herod Antipas; and the remaining portion of his empire to his youngest son, Herod Philip, the half-brother of the aforementioned sons. None of these three sons had the ability to rule adequately so that by the year 25

A.D., when both John and Baptist and Jesus were in their early thirties, the Romans had replaced both Herod Archelaus and Herod Philip with the Roman governor, Pontius Pilate; while they still allowed Herod Antipas to remain as the nominal ruler of Galilee.

It is notable that when the Romans took over the rule of Judaea, they did not make Jerusalem the headquarters of their governor, but chose instead the small town of Caesaria on the coast of the Mediterranean Sea for the Roman headquarters. The reasons for making this choice appear to be that in Jerusalem the Roman forces could be surrounded and destroyed by the very hostile Jews; whereas in Caesaria the Roman forces could withstand an attack for an extended period and they could be reinforced from Rome or other nearby Roman bases by sea. This fact is important to bear in mind because it means that when Jesus was condemned to death and crucified in Jerusalem Pontius Pilate was there on a temporary visit.

By 29 A.D. both John the Baptist and Jesus are dead, and a brief review of their background is necessary to understand the events that led up to their deaths. John the Baptist was the son of Rabbi Zacharias and his wife Elizabeth. Both his parents were the children of rabbis which meant that the rabbi and his wife were descended from upper class educated Jews. They lived in the hill country about four miles southwest of Jerusalem, where Rabbi Zacharias was a member of the clergy that directed the operation of the newly reconstructed temple.

Elizabeth beame unexpectedly pregnant late in life. To assist her during this pregnancy she sent for her young cousin, Mary, who lived in Nazareth, a village in Galilee, almost a hundred miles away. Mary went to Jerusalem and stayed with her elder cousin during the final months of her pregnancy. The child born to Rabbi Zacharias and Elizabeth was a boy whom they named John. When Mary returned to Nazareth she married a carpenter named Joseph.

In December of 6 B.C. when King Herod the Great was still the ruler of Palestine, the Roman emperor, Caesar Augustus, ordered all Roman governors to take a census in their provinces for the purpose of taxation and administration. In order to carry out this instruction, Quirinus, the Roman governor of Judaea, ordered all persons living within his province to return to the point of origin of the head of each family. As Joseph was descended from the house of David and their point of origin was Bethlehem, about six miles south of Jerusalem, Joseph and Mary set out for Bethlehem from Nazareth, a distance of almost one hundred miles. At this time Mary was heavy with child, so she and Joseph traveled very slowly. When they arrived in Bethlehem, they found the village already overcrowded with numerous travelers who had come to register for the census. The village inn was wholly inadequate to take care of the large influx of visitors, and as there were no accommodations available anywhere, Joseph asked the innkeeper to allow him and his wife to occupy a stall in the stable. The innkeeper readily agreed and Joseph and Mary made themselves as comfortable as they possibly could in one of the stalls in the stable. During the night, Mary gave birth to her first-born child, a son, whom they named Jesus.

The gospels tell us little more about Jesus and John the Baptist until both are in their early thirties. The Roman emperor is now Tiberius Caesar in the fifteenth year of his reign and the Roman governor of Palestine is Pontius Pilate and the ruler of Galilee is King Herod Antipas. Roman rule had little direct effect upon the daily lives of individual Jews because Roman authority was limited to the maintenance of law and order and keeping open the channels of international trade.

The real ruler of the people was the Jewish council known

as the Great Sanhedrin, which directly influenced the lives of the Jews from the day of their birth to the day of their death. It was presided over by a Chief Rabbi named Caiaphas, who lacked the essential qualities of leadership for that important post. Consequently, the real power of the office of the Chief Rabbi was exercised by his father-in-law, Rabbi Annas, the former Chief Rabbi.

Then, as now, the Jews were divided into various religious groups depending upon their individual philosophies and their beliefs in Judaism. The four major groups were the Essenes, the Zealots, the Pharisees and the Sadducees. The Essenes were a comparatively small group of extremely orthodox Jews, who withdrew from the main body of Judaism and lived a strictly ascetic life along the shores of the Dead Sea. The Essenes not only believed in the resurrection, in life in the hereafter, and the coming of the Messiah, but in addition, they expected some of these events to occur at any time and possibly during their own lifetime. To the Essenes, all other Jews appeared irreligious, particularly the Sadducees, whom they rated as being little better than Gentiles.

At the other extreme were the Zealots who were intensely nationalistic and whose primary purpose in life was to fight for the political independence of Judaism. To achieve this end, they were willing to compromise on religious principles and even form alliances with Gentiles. In between these two extremists groups were the Pharisees and the Sadducees who looked upon Judaism in a more practical way than either the Essenes or the Zealots.

The Pharisees were more orthodox than the Sadducees, and they had a larger following, particularly among the poorer Jewish people. From the Greeks, the Pharisees had acquired a belief in resurrection and in life in the hereafter. The Sadducees, who drew their strength from the upper classes and the businessmen, had no belief in the life in the hereafter. The controlling power in the Great Sanhedrin was

Pharisaic, primarily because the Mosaic traditions required a large number of Pharisaic rabbis to perform the numerous detailed religious rituals. The Pharisees got along well with the Sadducees because the Sadducees were practical business men who acted as the Jewish representatives in the necessary negotiations with the Romans.

Whether or not Jesus or John the Baptist belonged to any one of the four groups mentioned above, we do not know. It does seem probable that John the Baptist was an Essene because his way of life and his beliefs closely paralleled those of the Essenes. In addition, John the Baptist followed the Essene practice of baptism, as an outward indication of personal repentence and the cleansing of sins.

Since there was little cooperation among the above-mentioned four groups, their divisions weakened their opposition to the Romans, and this was a particular source of worry to the Pharisees. In addition, the Jewish temple authorities were constantly worried by the meteoric rise of false prophets, who created religious splinter groups and thus weakened them further.

Jewish belief in God's personal intervention in their daily lives through the appointment of prophets made it comparatively easy for a person with a strong personality and a persuasive tongue to obtain a very large following in a comparatively short period. Because Jewish scriptural writing included the prophecy of the coming of a Messiah who would bring all Jews both living and dead together into the Kingdom of God, Jews readily accepted new prophets. What the Jewish authorities wanted most was a military leader such as Joshua to lead them to victory against the Romans, and not another religious leader who would create more divisions amongst them. Therefore, whenever John the Baptist preached, Chief Rabbi Caiaphas kept a group of spies at his meetings to report on his activities. Some of these spies mingled with the crowd as ordinary townspeople, while others openly wore their clerical garb which readily distinguished them as members of a special group of religious persons from the great temple in Jerusalem.

John the Baptist was now about thirty-five years old. He lived in the wilderness, probably about ten miles west of the Jordan River and about thirty-five miles northeast of Jerusalem. His clothing was crude and primitive, consisting of the skins of animals, and his food was limited to what he could find in nature, mostly locusts and wild honey. His mode of living, his fervent teaching and his complete immersion of his followers into the waters of the Jordan River all implied a rejection of orthodox Jewish life and the formation of another Jewish splinter group. Hence, he became widely known as John the Baptist, and his fame as a fiery evangelist spread throughout Judaea, Samaria and Galilee.

At the time that the following event occurs, it is apparent that deep-rooted hostility had already developed between the evangelist and the temple rabbis.

Following his usual custom John the Baptist was preaching to a large crowd adjacent to the Jordan River when he said, "When you come to God seeking forgiveness for your sins, come to Him with repentance in your souls and a record of good behavior to justify your salvation."

Someone asked, "What shall we do to achieve salvation?"

He answered, "Let him who has two coats give one to him who has none; and let him who has food in excess give part of that food to him who is hungry. And now those of you who are truly repentant of your sins, come forward to be baptized."

First came the tax-collectors, who said to John the Baptist, "Master, what must we do to achieve salvation?"

The evangelist answered, "Collect from the people only a fair tax."

Next, came a group of soldiers who asked, "Master, what must we do to achieve salvation?"

John answered, "Do violence to none. Don't accuse people falsely and don't abuse them."

When all those persons seeking salvation were in the water, John the Baptist raised his hands and said, "I baptize you with water, but another who is greater than I, and whose shoelaces I am not worthy to touch, will come after me and he will baptize you with the Spirit of the Holy Ghost."

The temple rabbis and their agents watched these proceedings with disdain and contemptuous condescension. Finally, the rabbi in charge of the group said to John the Baptist, "Who do you claim to be? Do you claim to be the prophet Elijah?"

The great evangelist answered, "No, I am not the prophet Elijah."

The rabbi scornfully asked, "Well then, who *do* you claim to be? Do you claim to be the Messiah?"

"No, I am not the Messiah," John replied.

The rabbi now sneeringly asked, "Well, are you any other prophet?"

John the Baptist replied, "No, I am not any other prophet. I am simply myself, John the Baptist."

The rabbi petulantly said, "Well, then, if you are neither the prophet Elijah, nor the Messiah, nor any other prophet, by what divine right do you baptize these people and forgive them of their sins? Tell us who you are, so that we can report that fact back to the Chief Rabbi in Jerusalem."

John the Baptist slowly answered, "I am the voice in the wilderness predicted by the prophet Isaiah, and like Isaiah, I come now to prepare the way for him who is to follow me. At this very moment, that man is amongst you, but you do not recognize him nor do you acknowledge him, just as you do not recognize nor acknowledge me. Remember the words of Isaiah—

"A voice cries out in the wilderness,
Prepare the way for the Lord,
Build straight the highway to God
And fill all the valleys with rock.
Remove all the hills and the trees,
Then smooth and straighten that road
So that all men may seek and find
The pathway to the kingdom of God."

When John the Baptist finished this quotation, and saw many Pharisees and Sadducees clustered around the rabbi, he said, "And now, you generation of vipers! Go back and tell your masters who I am!"

The rabbi and his agents sullenly walked away.

Although John the Baptist had heard of his cousin, Jesus, preaching the gospel of God, he still wondered whether or not Jesus was the true Messiah whom the Jews sought. Because of his uncertainty on this vital question, he sent two of his disciples to question Jesus on this matter. At this time, Jesus was preaching in Nain, a village about ten miles southeast of Nazareth in Galilee.

When John the Baptist's two disciples arrived in Nain, there was a funeral procession moving through the village streets and out through the village gate toward the cemetery. A large crowd was following the open coffin, containing the body of a young man. Immediately behind the coffin walked the dead man's grieving, sobbing mother. Those around the weeping woman tried their best to comfort her; but in spite of their best efforts, the sorrowing mother periodically broke out into uncontrollable sobbing.

As the two disciples watched this sad funeral procession move through the walled gates of Nain, they saw Jesus suddenly walk from the shadow of the portal of the gate up to the weeping mother and say to her, "Weep no more. Your son shall live."

Jesus then walked over to the coffin, touched the young man's forehead and said, "Young man, arise!"

To the amazement of the mourners and the onlookers, the young man arose and spoke to his mother. The first reaction of those present was fear of the unknown and of the supernatural, but their next reaction was one of thankfulness that God had restored the young man to life. The young man's mother turned to Jesus and said, "Glory be to God! A great prophet has risen amongst us and God has visited his people."

As Jesus walked slowly away from the crowd John's two disciples quickly followed after him. When they had caught up with Jesus, one of them said to him, "Master, John the Baptist believes that King Herod will have him killed, because he has preached so often about the adulterous marriage of the king to his niece, Herodias. Before he dies, John the Baptist wants to know whether or not you are the prophet whom God has promised to send to the Jewish people to bring them to salvation. If you are, he will advise his disciples to follow you after his death. So, we have come to ask you a direct question, 'Are you that prophet, or must we seek another?' "

Jesus answered, "Go back and tell John what you have seen and heard. Tell him that the blind have received their sight; that the lame do walk; that the lepers have been cleansed; that the gospel is preached everywhere; and that the dead have been raised from their coffins. Blessed are they who accept me."

John's disciple replied, "Thank you, master. We will tell John what you said."

The two disciples returned to the Jordan River and reported to John the Baptist their conversation with Jesus. A short time later when John the Baptist had completed his sermon to a group of his followers, he saw Jesus walk out of the crowd toward him. Beaming with pleasure, the evangelist turned toward the crowd and said, "This is he, of whom I said, 'After me comes another who is greater than I.' When you see the Holy Spirit descending upon a certain man and remain there, that man is the one who has been baptized by the Holy Ghost. Behold! This is the Lamb of God, who taketh away the sins of the world."

Stepping up to John and quietly bowing his head, Jesus said, "Please baptize me."

The great evangelist hastily drew back and replied, "It is I who have need to be baptized by you; so why do you ask me to baptize you?"

Jesus answered, "Let it be so for now, so that each of us may fulfill our duty to God."

And so, John the Baptist baptized Jesus.

Matt. 4 (12-25)   Mark 1 (14-22)   Luke 5 (27-39)   Luke 10 (1-12)
Matt. 8 (18-22)   Mark 2 (14-22)   Luke 6 (13-16)   Luke 15 (1-2)
Matt. 10 (1-20)   Mark 3 (13-20)
                  (31-35)   Luke 8 (19-21)   John 1 (35-51)
Matt. 12 (46-50) Mark 6 (7-13)   Luke 9 (1-6)   Hos. 6 (6)
Luke 5 (1-11)   Luke 9 (57-62)

Chapter 4

The Twelve Disciples

One day while Jesus was walking along the shore of Lake Tiberias followed by a large crowd, he stopped when he saw four fishermen drying out their nets at the lake shore. He had been looking for a place where he could stand above the crowd in order to address them. Finding none, he asked one of the fishermen, "Would you mind letting me use your boat as a platform so that I may speak to these people who are anxious to hear me preach?"

The fisherman cordially replied, "Of course, you can use my boat. In fact, I'll row the boat a short distance from shore and my brother and I will steady it for you while you speak."

Jesus answered, "Thank you very much. That is very kind of you."

After Jesus finished his sermon, the two fishermen rowed him ashore and he thanked them both for the help they had given him. The elder fisherman said to Jesus, "My name is Simon and my brother's name is Andrew. We were both very well rewarded for the use of our boat by being able to listen to you preach. You remind us a great deal of John the Baptist."

Jesus replied, "I am glad that you liked my sermon, and I thank you again for the use of your boat. I know I couldn't have gotten along without it."

"Well," Simon replied, "I am glad that you could make better use of our boat than my brother and I could last night."

"Why is that?" Jesus asked.

Simon replied, "Well, we were out fishing all night and even though the weather was perfect and we cast our nets repeatedly in those places where we normally make a good catch, we couldn't catch enough fish to make a decent meal."

Jesus asked, "Why don't you try again?"

"We will," Simon replied. "We'll fish again tonight and we'll hope for better luck."

"Why don't you fish again now?" Jesus asked.

Andrew looked up at Jesus and said to him with a considerable air of incredulousness, "Now? Don't you know that no true fisherman ever fishes in the daytime? Night time is when the fish bite. It's plain to see that you are no fisherman."

Jesus quietly answered, "No, I am not a fisherman, but even so, why don't you try fishing again?"

Simon said, "Come on, Andrew. Let's try fishing just once more. What have we got to lose except a few hours' sleep?"

Andrew looked skeptically at his brother and dryly said, "All right. If you say so. But you know as well as I do, that it's just a waste of time."

Reluctantly, Andrew rolled up the net while Peter got the boat ready for another fishing trip. The two brothers hauled their net into the boat and once again rowed out to their favorite fishing ground. Throughout these preparations, Andrew acted as though he were humoring this strange preacher and hoped that none of his neighbors would think that he and his brother had lost their senses by going out fishing in the middle of the day.

When the two brothers reached their favorite fishing place, they lowered their net into the water, and after a short period of time began to haul it in again, expecting that it would come up empty. However, after they had pulled in only a small portion of their net, they found it so heavy with fish that they knew that unless they got some help either their net would break or their boat would capsize. So the two brothers yelled to their friends ashore, James and John, to row out and help them.

James and John answered with a mighty roar and then quickly rowed out and helped Simon and Andrew haul in their large catch of fish. When the net was all hauled in, the fishermen found there was enough fish to fill both boats to capacity. As soon as Simon and Andrew reached the shore, Simon dropped to his knees before Jesus and said, "Lord, forgive me for not knowing who you are. I am a sinful man!"

Jesus answered, "Simon, son of Jona, follow me. From now on you shall be a fisher of men and your name shall be Peter, because you are as sturdy as a rock."

Peter replied, "Thank you, Lord. I shall follow you wherever you go."

Before Jesus could reply, Andrew said, "Wherever my brother goes, I go too."

Jesus said, "I will be very happy to have you both as my disciples."

Watching this scene were the other two brothers, John and James, and John smilingly said to Jesus, "Don't forget about my brother and me. We also helped to bring in that large catch of fish."

With a twinkle in his eye, Jesus said, "With those powerful voices you two brothers have, you could scare people into becoming my followers whether they wanted to be or not. I think I will call the two of you the Sons of Thunder."

All five men laughed heartily and then Jesus said seriously, "Now let us go to the synagogue and pray that God will help and guide us in our work."

Jesus and his disciples walked along the shore of Lake Tiberias toward Capernaum, where they passed by the post of a tax collector named Levi, who collected a toll from all travelers who went by his post. Under the Roman system, taxes were paid directly to Rome by the tax collectors in a lump sum and they in turn collected what taxes they could from the public. The difference between the amount the tax collectors paid to Rome and the amount they collected from the public constituted their pay and their profit for the collection of the taxes. This system of taxation obviously led to many abuses and, as a consequence, the Jews referred to tax collectors and sinners in the same breath. In the eyes of Jews, the Jewish tax collectors were traitors and, therefore, worse than sinners.

Jesus and Levi engaged in a conversation which the evangelists did not record; but apparently it was of such an agreeable nature that Jesus ended it by saying to Levi, "Follow me."

Levi answered, "Very well, I will; but first, let us meet tonight in my house in Capernaum for supper. I shall give a farewell supper to all of my friends, both old and new, and all of you are cordially invited to come."

Jesus answered, "Good. We'll be there. A good supper after our long tiresome journey from Nazareth will be welcome."

That night after all the invited guests had eaten heartily of a very fine meal, Levi stood up and said, "Let us drink a toast to my guest, Jesus of Nazareth, and to his disciples."

After that toast was drunk, Jesus stood up and said, "Now

let us drink another toast to our host, Levi, whom I hereby re-name Matthew to signify the change from his old way of life to his new way of life."

After everyone had drunk this toast, Levi gravely bowed his head and said, "Master, I am greatly honored. In giving me a name meaning the gift of God, you place upon my shoulders a grave responsibility. I shall do my best to be worthy of this great name."

Of all the disciples, Matthew was probably the best educated and the richest, so when he gave his farewell supper that night signifying the end of his old life and the start of his new life, he apparently gave the disciples a feast that they never forgot. Matthew is an extremely important disciple of Jesus because his story contains accounts of many events in the life of Jesus that are not told by any of the other evangelists. His lengthy account of the Sermon on the Mount alone makes Matthew's book, written in Aramaic, outstandingly important.

After the supper Levi, now renamed Matthew, and his guests sat around the open doorway, reminiscing of days gone by and conjecturing about the days to come. Since practically every one in Capernaum was a friend, a relative, or an acquaintance of everyone else, practically every passerby waved a greeting or shouted some salutation as they went by the open doorway. When the town rabbi passed by and saw Jesus, he angrily walked up to him and said, "Why do you eat with tax collectors and sinners?"

Jesus answered, "Do you recall the words of the prophet Hosea, who said, 'I desire repentance from my people and not punishment for them.' It is only the sick who need the services of a physician, not those who are well. Remember, I have come to call the sinners to repentance, and not the righteous ones."

During the weeks that followed Jesus selected seven other disciples, who became the final twelve who followed Jesus until the day of his death. Among them were Thomas, whose skeptical frame of mind earned him the world renowned title of "the doubting Thomas," and Judas Iscariot who became the treasurer, paymaster and purchaser of supplies for Jesus and his twelve disciples. In this capacity, he probably spent most of his time away from Jesus and the other disciples in places and under circumstances that led him into temptations to which the other disciples were not exposed. Jesus' earliest instructions to his disciples are noteworthy, because they reveal the mind of a provincial Jew. These are his instructions to his twelve disciples:

"Go nowhere among the Gentiles and do not enter into any city of the Samaritans. Instead, seek out the lost sheep of the house of Israel and tell them that the Kingdom of God is at hand. Take no gold, silver or any kind of money with you. In whatever city or village you may be, stay in the home of a worthy person and bless that home. I send you forth as sheep in the midst of wolves. Therefore, be as wise as a serpent and as harmless as a dove.

"Heal the sick, cleanse the lepers, raise the dead and cast out evil. Freely give of yourselves to others, as freely as I have given of myself to you. But, beware of certain men who will deliver you up to the judges and flog you in their synagogues. Have no fear of these men because he who has faith in God will be saved. He who values his life, shall lose it; but he who loses his life for my sake, shall save it."

Matt. 19 (16-30)   Mark 10 (17-31)
Matt. 20 (1-16)   Luke 18 (18-30)

Chapter 5

The Kingdom of God

Jesus had already discovered a certain amount of unfriendliness in his home town of Nazareth and found a more receptive audience to his missionary message particularly in Capernaum, Peter's home town. So gradually, he remained there more often and eventually made it the base of his operations. On one occasion while he was resting at Peter's home, one of Capernaum's wealthiest men came to see him and asked, "Good Master, what must I do in order to obtain eternal salvation?"

Jesus looked at the man questioningly and said, "Why do you call me good? There is only one who is really good and that is God Himself. The answer to your question is this—the way to obtain eternal salvation is to keep God's commandments."

The wealthy man asked, "Which ones?"

Jesus answered, "All of them. Certainly you must know

God's commandments: 'Do not kill, do not steal, do not commit adultery, do not bear false witness, honor thy father and thy mother, love thy neighbor as thyself,' and so on."

The wealthy man said, "I have obeyed all of these commandments all the days of my life, what else must I do?"

Jesus answered, "There is one thing more that you must do to gain eternal salvation and that is, sell all your possessions and distribute to the poor the money that you receive from the sale of these possessions. Then when you have placed your faith and your treasure in God, come and follow me."

When the wealthy man heard these words, he bowed his head sorrowfully, and silently got up and left the house. Jesus watched the slouched, departing figure of the wealthy man and turning to his disciples, said, "Truly it will be very difficult for a rich man to enter the Kingdom of Heaven. In fact it will be easier for a camel to go through the eye of a needle than for a rich man to enter the Kingdom of God."

All the disciples looked at Jesus in surprise and several felt a sense of consternation, because while none were wealthy, several came from well-to-do families. Sensing the reaction of several of the disciples, Peter asked, "Master, we have left everything we had to follow you—our homes, our families and all our possessions. What more must we do?"

Jesus answered, "There is no one who has left his home, or his family or his possessions for my sake to preach the gospel who shall not be rewarded a hundred times over in the world to come for the sacrifices he has made upon this earth."

Peter gratefully said, "Master, it is good to hear you say this, because several of our disciples have been severely reprimanded by their families for sacrificing the comforts of their homes to follow you. And now in addition to these physical hardships, they have earned the animosity of the temple rabbis, who threaten them with expulsion from the synagogue. It will hearten all of us to know that we will be rewarded in heaven for the sacrifices we have made upon this earth."

Jesus thoughtfully replied, "There is one thing that all our disciples should beware of."

Peter asked, "What is that?"

Jesus answered, "God does not reward all persons on the same basis of their individual contributions to the kingdom of heaven. Otherwise, the widow's mite would be unimportant to Him, when compared to the rich man's gold. Whereas, the reverse is true; because the widow's mite is a contribution from her insufficiency, while the rich man's gold is a contribution from his superfluous abundance. Therefore, God recognizes the widow's mite as the greater contribution and will reward her accordingly."

Peter asked, "What reward can our disciples expect from God for their sacrifices?"

Jesus answered, "Peter, before I answer your question, let me tell you a parable to explain my answer to you. God may be likened to a farmer, who owned a very large vineyard. One day in the fall, this farmer needed many laborers to harvest his crop; so he went out before sun-up to hire all the men he could find. At that early hour, there were only a few men in the market-place looking for work, and the farmer hired all of them to work for him for twelve hours from sun-up to sundown for ten shekels.

"Several hours later, the farmer returned to the market place and when he saw several idle laborers standing there, he said to them, 'Go to work in my vineyard for the rest of the day, and at sun-down I will pay you whatever is right for your work.' So, these laborers joined the first group of men who were already at work in the vineyard. About noon and again at about the ninth hour, the farmer again hired more laborers to work in his vineyard without setting any price with them for their labor. About an hour before sundown, the farmer again returned to the market place, where he saw several laborers loitering about. The farmer said to them, 'Why do you stand here all day idling your time away?' One of the laborers answered, 'Because no one has hired us.' The farmer said, 'Even though there is only one hour of daylight left before sundown, go to work in my vineyard and I will pay you what is fair for your work.' So these laborers also went to work in the farmer's vineyard.

"At sundown, all the laborers stopped work and went to the farmer to collect their pay. The farmer said to his fore-man, 'Pay each of the laborers ten shekels for his work, beginning with those who were hired last.' Following the farmer's instructions, the foreman paid each of the laborers who were hired last ten shekels. When the laborers who had been hired first saw that those who had been hired last received ten shekels for their one hour's work, their eyes bulged in expectation of receiving far more for their work than the ten shekels the farmer had promised them at sun-up. However, when these laborers came to get their pay, the foreman paid each of them only ten shekels. Bitterly disappointed with their pay, these men complained to the farmer, 'The laborers you hired last only worked for you one hour at the end of the day when it was cool. We worked for you a full twelve hours through the scorching heat of the day and we did the major share of the work. Why do you pay us the same amount that you paid these late-comers?'

"The farmer replied, 'Friend, I have done you no wrong. Did you not agree to work for me for twelve hours for ten shekels? Have I not paid you the ten shekels I promised you? If I decide to pay other laborers ten shekels for one hour's work, am I not allowed to do what I will with my own money? Why are you angry with me, because I am generous to others? Take what belongs to you and go.' "

After Jesus finished his story, a long silence followed, as each of the disciples tried to understand the full meaning of this parable. Finally, Peter said, "Master, I am sure it would help all of us if you explained this parable to us."

Jesus answered, "Peter, the final judgment of man is God's

alone. The same rules of reward and judgment cannot be applied to all men alike, because the circumstances of the life of each person are different. Therefore, each person should be thankful for those blessings he receives, without comparing them to the benefits received by others. Otherwise, people will spend their lives in bitterness, envying the benefits their neighbors have received which they have not."

Peter humbly answered, "Thank you, Master. I am beginning to understand you."

Chapter 6

Nicodemus

The Jewish council in Jerusalem known as the Great Sanhedrin was composed of seventy-one members, including the most prominent temple rabbis and a number of the leading citizens of Judaea. Among them were several who were secretly in sympathy with Jesus and the gospels record the activities of two of them, who openly showed their sympathy for him. Their names were Nicodemus and Joseph of Arimathea.

Nicodemus' first recorded visit to Jesus was made secretly and at night, and this is understandable because Nicodemus jeopardized his position in Jerusalem by visiting Jesus. From the following conversation, it is apparent that Nicodemus greatly respected Jesus, but he also had certain reservations about Jesus' belief in life in the hereafter. Nicodemus was a Pharisee, but during the conversation that follows, he sounds like a Sadducee. Nicodemus said, "Master, I know that you are a teacher sent to us by God, because no man could perform the miracles that you have, unless he had God within him. However, please explain one thing to me."

Jesus asked, "What is it that you would like to know?"

Nicodemus replied, "How do you explain the rebirth of man?"

Jesus answered, "Truthfully, I say to you that unless a man is born again, he cannot enter into the Kingdom of God."

Nicodemus incredulously asked, "But how can a man be reborn when he is old? Can he re-enter his mother's womb a second time so that he may be reborn?"

Jesus answered, "That which is born of the flesh is flesh and dies; but that which is born of the Spirit of God is spirit, and lives forever. Therefore, I say to you that unless a man is born of the Spirit of God, he cannot enter into the kingdom of God."

Nicodemus' face was a study in puzzled doubt as he said, "I am sorry, Master, but I can not follow your line of reasoning."

Jesus quietly replied, "Do not be surprised because I say to you that man must be born again before he can enter the kingdom of heaven. There are many events that happen in this world of which man is not given the knowledge to understand. The winds blow from all directions, but where they come from and where they go, no man knows. So it is with those born of the Spirit of God."

Nicodemus' face was still clouded in doubt as he said, "I am sorry, Master, but I must admit that your explanation does not help me understand your statement about the rebirth of man."

Jesus asked, "Have you become one of Judaea's leading citizens without knowing certain basic facts of the material world as contrasted to those of the spiritual world? If you do not understand earthly matters, how can you possibly understand the heavenly matters that you ask me about?"

Nicodemus replied, "Master, you still have not answered

my original question which was, 'How can a man be born again?' "

Jesus patiently answered, "Nicodemus, you are thinking of physical and bodily rebirth, while I am speaking to you about spiritual rebirth. God is a spirit and we can only worship Him in spirit. When we dedicate our lives to God, He enters within us and in that spiritual sense, we are reborn. I say reborn, because without the Spirit of God, man is already dead. By physical standards a man may be said to be alive; but without the Spirit of God, man is only an animated lump of clay. It is only when a man contains the spirit of God within himself that it may be said that he is truly alive."

While Jesus was speaking, Nicodemus' clouded face gradually cleared up, and then smiling brightly, he said, "Thank you very much, Master. Now, I understand you."

Jesus replied, "Nicodemus, God so loved the world that he sent his only begotten Son into the world, not to condemn it, but that the world through him might be saved."

Matt. 9 (13)   Luke 13 (11-17)   Luke 18 (9-14)
Matt. 18 (15-35)   Luke 15 (11-32)   Is. 15 (22)
Mark 11 (26)   Luke 17 (3-5)   Ho. 6 (6)

Chapter 7

The Prodigal Son

The disciple Peter was greatly distressed because he had a younger brother named Sharon who lived a dissolute and riotous life. Sharon had caused Peter and his parents considerable sorrow because he repeatedly continued on his evil ways after faithfully promising his parents and Peter that he would repent and behave himself. On a Sabbath day, while Peter and Jesus were on their way to the synagogue, Peter told Jesus of the difficulties that he was having with Sharon and how depressed he felt to see his brother waste his life so foolishly. Jesus tried his best to cheer Peter up, but Peter's spirits were so low that nothing that Jesus could say could comfort him.

Finally, Jesus said, "Peter, let me tell you a parable about a king who decided to settle all of his accounts with his debtors. One of these debtors was a man named Achan who owed the king ten thousand silver pieces. When Achan was brought before the king to pay his debt, the man was found to be bankrupt. The king ordered that Achan, his wife and all his children be sold into slavery in compensation for the money he owed the king.

"Achan fell down upon his knees and begged the king not to sell him and his family into slavery. He promised that if the king would have patience with him, he would work hard and eventually pay the king all the money he owed him. The king was so impressed with Achan's piteous pleading that instead of simply granting his request for an extension of time to pay his debt, the king generously cancelled the entire debt.

"As Achan was leaving the palace he met one of the king's servants who owed him a hundred shekels. Achan grabbed the king's servant by the collar and snarled, 'Pay me every shekel that you owe me at once, or I will have you thrown in jail!' The king's servant fell to his knees and pleaded with Achan for more time to pay his debt. Achan ignored his plea and had him thrown into jail.

"When the king was informed that Achan had a palace guard jailed for failure to repay Achan, the king summoned Achan to the palace and said to him, 'You wicked man, could you not have forgiven a measly debt of a hundred shekels to one of my servants, after I had forgiven you your debt to me of ten thousand silver pieces? Now, you shall go to prison and you shall rot there until you pay me my entire debt in full.' "

Jesus paused at the end of his parable and when he found that Peter remained morosely silent, he said to him, "The moral of this parable is this—my heavenly Father will punish you for your trespasses, unless you forgive your brother his trespasses."

Peter replied, "Master, I agree with everything you say, but I have forgiven my brother over and over and over again. In fact, I have forgiven him on seven different occasions. Isn't seven times enough?"

Jesus quietly answered, "No, Peter, seven times is not

enough. It may be necessary that you will have to forgive your brother seventy-seven times seven."

Peter answered, "Well, supposing that I do forgive him seventy-seven times seven and he still continues on his wild ways. Then what?"

Jesus replied, "Peter, the first thing that you must do is to go to your brother privately and explain to him quietly and dispassionately all the grievances that you have against him. If he listens to you and mends his ways, you have gained a brother. But, if he will not listen to you, the next time you speak to him take two witnesses with you, who can confirm the statements that you have made to him. If your brother still continues to lead a sinful life, tell your problem to your rabbi and ask the rabbi to speak to your brother. If your brother refuses to listen to the rabbi, thereafter treat him as a stranger."

Peter nodded his shaggy head and said, "Yes, master, I know that you are right and I shall do my best to follow your advice; but there are times when my brother sorely tries my patience."

Jesus replied, "Peter, let me warn you against adopting the self-righteous attitude of the hypocrites who sanctimoniously pray to God in the synagogue and then spend their time persecuting us."

Peter reverently replied, "God forbid!"

By this time, Jesus and Peter had arrived at the synagogue, and as they entered, they found it was already filled with an overflow crowd. From previous experience, Jesus knew that a capacity crowd in the synagogue meant that the agents of the Chief Rabbi would be present to heckle him. In accordance with Jewish custom, the men prayed standing up in various parts of the synagogue, with the more prominent townsmen standing in the front and center of the building where they could be easily seen and heard. As Jesus and Peter quietly prayed in a dimly lit corner of the synagogue, a member of the wealthy, religious Jews stood up before the rostrum and prayed in a loud and blatant voice. He was richly dressed and clothed in a religious cloak that had been painstakingly embroidered with biblical mottoes.

Near Jesus and Peter, in the darkened corner of the synagogue, stood a tax collector who was meekly praying in a low undertone. His head was sunk low on his chest and the entire appearance of the man was one of pathetic dejection. While Jesus and Peter were looking at these two vastly contrasting types of men, they could hear the voice of the wealthy Jew boom out, "God, I thank you that you have not made me as other men are, unjust, greedy and impure. And, I particularly thank you that you have not made me like that contemptible tax collector mumbling over there in the shadows of this temple. I fast twice a week, I obey all the Mosaic laws, and I give to the temple one tenth of all my income. Thank you, Lord, for my many blessings."

During this boastfully loud prayer, the tax collector shrank down lower and lower in an attempt to make himself as inconspicuous as possible. Then, he dejectedly beat his breast and mournfully said, "God, be merciful upon me, a sinner."

Jesus walked up to the rostrum and addressing the congregation, said, "You have just seen and heard two men praying. One is so self-righteous in his own sight that he needs no help from anyone, not even from God. The other man, a self-confessed sinner, prays to God and asks Him for His mercy. Believe me when I tell you that the one who will be rewarded in heaven is the repentant sinner and not the self-righteous, pious person; because he who exalts himself upon this earth shall be humbled in heaven and he who humbles himself upon this earth shall be rewarded in heaven."

The wealthy merchant angrily retorted, "By what right do you speak of me in this insolent manner?"

Jesus camly replied, "I have no desire to offend you, sir, but as I listened to you and to the tax collector praying, I was reminded of a story of two brothers."

The wealthy man snapped, "What story?"

Turning to the congregation, Jesus said, "There were once two brothers, Reuben and Asher. Reuben, the elder brother, was pious, hard-working and self-righteous; Asher, the younger brother, was handsome, lazy and sinful. One day, he said to his father, 'I don't want to wait until you are dead to enjoy my rightful inheritance. Give me my share of the inheritance now, so that I may enjoy it, while I am still young.'

"With a heavy heart, the father divided his property and gave Asher his share of the inheritance. With his newly acquired wealth, Asher went to a foreign land, where without the restraint of family ties or of familiar faces, he lived more riotously then he had ever lived before. In a very short time, he had squandered his entire inheritance.

"While Asher was foolishly squandering his wealth in that foreign land, a severe famine spread throughout that nation. Thousands of persons became destitute and many of them died of starvation. When Asher was penniless, he tried to find employment, but he was fit for no gainful labor. Before long, Asher was as ragged, dirty and destitute as the most lowly of the poverty-stricken peasants in that foreign land. Finally, in his desperate need for food, he took a job as a swineherd, the guardian of pigs!

"Even though Asher worked hard and consciously, his pay was so small and the food he received was so meager that he was always hungry. One day while he was feeding husks to the swine, he reflected bitterly that he would gladly eat those husks himself, if his stomach could digest them. Then he said to himself, 'Here, I work and live like a slave and yet, I starve; while at home, the lowliest of my father's servants has more than enough to eat. It is time that I ended my foolishness and returned home. I shall go to my father and beg him for forgiveness.'

"So Asher left that foreign country and returned to the land of his father. As he was approaching his father's home, his father saw him coming and ran out of the house to meet him. The father embraced his son fervently and thanked God for his safe return. Asher was so overcome with joy and gratitude at the warmth of his father's greeting, that he dropped to his knees and humbly said, 'Father, forgive me. I have sinned against you and against God. I am no longer worthy to be called your son. Hereafter, treat me as you would one of your hired servants.'

"The father ignored Asher's words and said to one of his servants, 'Quick, get my best robe and some decent shoes and put them on Asher.' To another servant, the father said, 'Get the fatted calf and kill it, because today we shall eat, drink and be merry. This, my son who was dead, is now alive again. He who was lost, is now found. Thank God for this great blessing.'

"Before long, the father, Asher and all the household servants were feasting, singing and dancing in celebration of Asher's return. Meanwhile, Reuben was still hard at work in the field. At the end of the day when Reuben was returning from his work, he heard the singing and the dancing in the house, and asked one of the servants what all the merriment was about. The servant told Reuben that his younger brother, Asher, had returned home and that his father had killed the fatted calf to celebrate his safe return.

"In bitter anger and resentment, Reuben turned on his heel and strode away from the house. The father, who had seen Reuben approaching and then turn away, ran after him and begged him to come back and join in the celebration. Reuben turned angrily on his father and in a voice filled with bitterness said, 'Father, all my life I have worked hard for you and

I have never displeased you. Yet you never gave me a fatted calf to kill so that I might have a feast and be merry with my friends. Now, when this wastrel, Asher, returns home, you kill the fatted calf in honor of his home-coming. And all that he has ever done is to waste his inheritance and ruin himself with riotous living. Where is the justice in all this?'

"The father quietly said, 'Reuben, my son, everything you say is exactly true. You have always been a hard-working, dutiful son to me. Everything that I have left is yours. However, it is still fitting and proper that we rejoice at Asher's safe return, for he who was dead is now found. Just as a shepherd rejoices when a lost sheep is found, so does God rejoice when a lost soul is returned to heaven. Therefore, let us rejoice with God that Asher is safely returned to us.' "

When Jesus had completed his long parable, there was a prolonged silence as each person pondered over its full meaning. As no one spoke, Jesus said, "The moral of the story is this. Just as anyone of you would rejoice at the return of any lost thing, whether it is a sheep, an ox, or any other object; so it is in heaven. There is more joy in heaven over the redemption of one lost sinner who repents, than there is in the arrival in heaven of ninety-nine good persons who never strayed from the fold. That is why God says, 'I would rather have mercy upon my people than to punish them.' That is my mission upon earth—to save the sinners of this world. Please remember, that it is the sick persons who need a physician and not the healthy ones."

When Jesus finished speaking, a woman who was so crippled that her face was no higher than her hips, walked over to Peter and said, "Blessed be your master. He speaks with the voice of God."

Jesus walked over to her and said, "What has been the nature of your illness?"

The woman looked painfully up at Jesus and said, "I don't

know, master, but it all started eighteen years ago when I arose from my bed one day and found that I could not stand erect. Ever since, my infirmity has become progressively worse, and someday, I am afraid that I won't be able to stand up at all."

Placing his hand upon her head, Jesus said, "Woman, you shall be cured."

The woman was immediately cured and thanked Jesus sincerely for her miraculous cure. The rabbi of the synagogue, who had been watching Jesus intently, rushed over to him and said, "By what right do you heal on the Sabbath?"

Before Jesus could answer, the rabbi turned to the congregation and indignantly said, "There are six days in the week in which men can work. If you want to be healed by this man, come to him on a weekday and not on the Sabbath."

Turning to the rabbi, Jesus said, "You hypocrite! Don't you release your ass and your ox from their stall on the Sabbath and lead them to water? And if it is proper for you to release your ass and your ox from their stalls on the Sabbath, should not this woman, a daughter of Abraham, who has been held in the clutches of the devil for eighteen years, also be released on the Sabbath?"

From the loud muttering of the congregation, the rabbi knew that the sympathy of the congregation was on the side of Jesus, and consequently he decided it was best to remain discreetly silent. On their return home, Peter said, "Master, that was a wonderful parable you told today. I think that hereafter I can deal with my brother with more understanding and more sympathy."

Jesus answered, "Good, Peter, I know that you can. All men should remember that they must do unto others as they would have others do unto them."

Peter walked silently beside Jesus, nodding his large head in agreement. After a long pause, Jesus said, "This world being what it is, it is impossible that there should not be a certain amount of evil in it. But, woe be to those from whom this evil comes! It would have been far better for them if they had never been born, rather than become the instrument of evil. That is why I say to you, Peter, that if your brother commits evil, never let that evil become part of you."

Chapter 8

The Gentile's Daughter

The total time that Jesus spent on his missionary work upon earth probably did not exceed thirty months. At the time the following event took place, he had been preaching for perhaps twelve to fifteen months, which means that he had already spent about half his missionary life upon earth. To date, he had accomplished little, beyond effecting some cures. Yet he had already incurred the deadly enmity of the Jewish religious authorities; and as a result, he was under the constant surveillance of the agents of Chief Rabbi Caiaphas. Jesus was quite discouraged.

In such a mood, he decided that he must get away for a little while to think things over. He particularly wanted to get away from the clamoring throngs who were forever demanding the performance of another miracle. He also wanted to get away from the agents and the spies of the Chief Rabbi who were constantly trying to trick him into making some statement that would get him into serious trouble with the Jewish or Roman authorities.

In this time of indecision, Jesus decided to go to the seashore of Phoenicia, the land now called Lebanon, a journey that would take about two days from Capernaum. Jesus had never been to the shores of the Mediteranean before, but he had heard a good deal about it from the Jewish merchants, who went there to buy foreign merchandise. The people of Phoenicia were Semitic, but the traders and the culture were Greek. It sounded like the perfect place to go for a rest and meditation.

Upon arriving in the Phoenician city of Tyre, Jesus and his disciples were the guests of one of Jesus' followers. Jesus spent most of his time walking along the seashore; it was relaxing and refreshing to him to walk barefooted along the shore at the water's edge and watch the water ebb and flow as it trickled through his feet.

As Jesus gazed at the endless expanse of greenish blue water, he tried to view his problem of preaching the Gospel of God to the Jews objectively. But he knew that if he dared preach the Gospel of God in Judaea or Galilee, the land of the Jews, he risked persecution; whereas in Samaria and Phoenicia he could preach unmolested. Yet at this stage in his missionary life he had no desire to preach salvation to the Gentiles or to the Samaritans, because his primary purpose in life was to bring salvation to the Jews.

The following is a story of the conflict that took place in the heart of Jesus when he was faced with the implicit faith of a Gentile. One day, while he and Peter walked along the seashore, they were approached by a Grecian woman who ran after them screaming, "Master, master, save my daughter!"

Jesus was quite surprised to hear this cry for help in this foreign land, because he thought that no one in Phoenicia would recognize him. He was also annoyed by it, because it was the very thing that he had tried his best to get away from by coming to this foreign land. The obvious fact that the woman was not Jewish added to the annoyance that he felt toward the screaming, pleading woman. Therefore, Jesus and Peter continued walking straight ahead trying to ignore her. But as she kept screaming and running after them, Peter finally turned to her and said with considerable irritation, "Woman, be on your way and leave our master alone."

The woman whose face was bathed in tears, cried out, "No, no! no! My daughter is desperately sick and only your master can save her."

Peter curtly answered, "If your daughter is sick, get yourself a Gentile healer. Now go!"

The woman dashed past Peter and grabbing Jesus by the shoulders, pleaded, "Please, master, please! My daughter is dying and only you can save her."

Jesus looked at the woman coldly and said, "I have been sent by God to help the lost sheep of Israel, and not the lost sheep of the Gentiles. Now, leave me alone. Please go away."

The Grecian woman dropped to her knees, kissed both Jesus' feet and begged, "Please! Lord God! Help me and save my daughter!"

Continuing to ignore the woman's pitiful pleas, Jesus stared straight ahead and said, "It is not right to take away the children's food and give it to the dogs until we have first fed the children of Israel."

The woman's face was now streaming with tears as she cried, "Yes, Lord, yes, you are right; but even the dogs under the table eat the crumbs on the floor that the children dropped there."

Jesus paused, looked down sympathetically at the weeping woman at his feet, and placing a gentle hand upon her head, said, "Arise, woman, you have great faith. Go home to your daughter; because of your faith, she has been cured."

The woman got up, thanked Jesus profusely and hurried home and found her daughter cured.

Chapter 9

The Samaritan Woman

We are indebted to John for the following story. It is a very important one because it shows a number of important changes taking place in the mind of Jesus. In sharp contrast to his attitude toward the Grecian woman in Phoenicia, whom Jesus initially ignored, he now associates with and preaches to non-Jews and for the first time he announces that he is the Messiah.

Jesus and his disciples were traveling north from Judaea to Galillee and had stopped in the village of Sychar in Samaria where Jacob's well is located. It was here that Jacob had dug a deep well and found refreshing water and it was also at this place that Jacob had given a plot of this ground to his son, Joseph. The Samaritans, being descendants of Jacob, considered this place holy in the same spirit that the Jews did.

Upon their arrival at Jacob's well the disciples went into the village to buy some food leaving Jesus sitting alone beside the well. Before long, a Samaritan woman came to the well to draw water and as Jesus was very thirsty, he said to her, "Please give me a drink of water."

In surprise, the Samaritan woman drew back and said to him, "How is it that you, a Jew, ask me, a woman of Samaria, to give you a drink of water, when normally you Jews will have nothing at all to do with us Samaritans?"

Jesus answered, "If you knew of the gifts that God can bestow upon you and if you knew who it is that says to you, 'Please give me a drink of water,' you would be asking me for a drink of the water of life that I have."

The woman eyed Jesus skeptically and said, "Sir, this well is very deep and you have nothing to draw water with. How will you get your water? Are you greater than our ancestor, Jacob, who drew water from this well the same way that we do?"

Jesus answered, "Whoever drinks the water of this well will soon be thirsty again, but whoever drinks of the water that I give, will never be thirsty again; because the water that I give is the living water of everlasting life that continuously replenishes itself."

The woman completely misunderstood Jesus and thought that he was speaking of some magical water possessing some supernatural power of rejuvenation, so she said to him, "Sir, give me a drink of this living water of life, so that I will never be thirsty again and will never have to come back to draw water from this well."

Jesus quietly said, "Go home woman and get your husband and then come back and I will tell you more about the water of life."

The woman answered, "I have no husband."

Jesus replied, "You are right in saying that you have no husband; because even though you have had five husbands, you are now living with a man who is not your husband."

The woman looked at Jesus in shocked amazement and

said, "How do you know all these things about me? Are you a prophet of God?"

Jesus replied, "Yes, I am."

The woman answered, "Since you are a prophet, will you stay here and preach to us Samaritans?"

Jesus answered, "I would like to stay and preach to you, but I must go on to Jerusalem, because it is the only proper place to worship God."

The woman said, "I will not dispute what you say. However, our ancestors worshipped God in these mountains and, if it was proper for them to worship God here, it is also proper for us to worship Him here."

Jesus answered, "You Samaritans do not know whom you are worshipping. Only we Jews know whom we are worshipping, because the salvation of mankind will only come through us Jews."

The woman replied, "All matters concerning God are beyond my understanding. All that I can do is worship God in these mountains just as my ancestors did."

Jesus quietly answered, "That may be well enough for now. But remember this, the time is coming when people will not be worshipping God, either in these mountains or in Jerusalem, because the true worshipers of God will worship Him in spirit, and not physically, from any earthly location."

With a troubled look, the woman answered, "I do not understand such things, nor do I understand about the living water of life; but I am sure that when the Messiah comes he will explain everything to us."

Almost inaudibly, Jesus replied, "I am the Messiah!"

When the woman heard these words, she looked at Jesus with open-mouthed amazement and then turned and ran into town to tell everyone that she met of her astounding conversation with Jesus. In her excitement and hurry to spread the news of her meeting with Jesus, she even forgot to take the jar of water with her.

Just before the woman ran excitedly away, the disciples returned and saw, from a distance, Jesus and the woman engaged in deep conversation. While they were surprised to see Jesus talking to a Samaritan, none of them questioned him about it.

Later, the disciples sat down to eat and urged Jesus to eat with them. Jesus declined the food offered him, saying, "I have food to eat that you don't know about."

One of the disciples asked, "Did anyone give some food to our master?"

Jesus who overheard the question, said, "My food is to do the will of God and to do His work."

A short time later, the Samaritan woman returned with a group of the leading citizens of Sychar, including the mayor of the town. The mayor urged Jesus to remain and preach to the townspeople. The remarkable thing is that Jesus accepted the Samaritan's invitation and remained two days in Sychar preaching the gospel of God to them. This is a notable occasion, as it marks the first time that Jesus preached to non-Jews.

When Jesus was saying farewell to his new Samaritan friends, the mayor of the town said to him, "At first we doubted what we had been told about you, but now that we have heard for ourselves, we know that you are truly the Messiah and the Saviour of the World."

Matt. 17 (24-27)   Mark 9 (33-37)   Luke 9 (46-48)
Matt. 18 (1-10)   Mark 10 (13-16)   Luke 18 (15-17)
Matt. 19 (13-15)   Mark 10 (35-45)

Chapter 10

Children and Heaven

After his return to Capernaum, Jesus went fishing with Peter and some of the other disciples. Upon his return from one of those fishing trips, Jesus dropped into a chair and said, "Peter, what were you and several of the other disciples talking about on our way back home? I heard a few fragments of your conversation but I was too far ahead of you to understand what was said."

Peter casually answered, "Oh, it was nothing very important, just a little gossip."

Jesus replied, "Really? I thought I heard heaven mentioned several times. That sounds very important to me."

Peter flushed slightly as he answered, "Well, master, we were discussing one question that you might call important."

Jesus asked, "What was that?"

Peter slowly answered, "Well, we were debating the question as to who is the most important person in heaven."

Jesus arched his eyebrows skeptically as he asked, "Is there any question about that? Do you have any doubt as to who is the most important person in heaven?"

Peter, who was now completely flustered, blurted out, "Truthfully, master, we were arguing among ourselves as to which one of us will be the most important person in heaven."

Jesus nodded his head knowingly and said, "Thank you, Peter, that is what I thought you were talking about."

While they were speaking, two of Peter's grandchildren entered the room and jumped up on the seat beside Jesus, where they continued tussling, as each tried to be seated closest to Jesus. Peter scolded them saying, "Run along and play some place else, don't annoy the master."

Jesus said to Peter, "Let the children be. I enjoy having them come close to me, for of such is the Kingdom of God."

In the meantime, several other disciples entered the room and Jesus looked up and said to them, "Unless you too become as these little children, you shall not enter the Kingdom of heaven. Therefore, the one who becomes as innocent as these little children shall become the most important person in heaven. Whoever receives one child in my name, receives me. But whosoever causes one of these little ones to sin, it would be far better for that person to have a millstone tied around his neck and be drowned in the middle of the ocean. If one of these children does commit some mischief, do not punish the child, but try to help that child find the path back to righteousness. That is my most important work upon this earth, because it is the will of God that not one of these little ones shall perish."

While Jesus was still speaking, the mother of James and John entered the room and, finding no empty chair, she stepped in front of the disciples and seated herself at the feet of Jesus. Turning to her, Jesus said, "It is very nice of you to come and join us this evening. To what do we owe the pleasure of your company?"

She replied, "Master, I have a special favor to ask of you."

Jesus asked, "What is it?"

Looking up at Jesus, she begged, "Before I answer, you must promise to grant me whatever request I ask."

Jesus answered, "I cannot do that until you first tell me what it is you want me to do for you."

Taking a deep breath, the woman replied, "Promise me that when you go to heaven, that you will place one of my sons on the seat at your right hand side and that you will place my other son on the seat at your left hand side."

Jesus was so amazed by this bold request that he hesitated momentarily before answering, "You do not understand what it is that you are asking of me."

Turning to James and John, Jesus asked, "Can you two drink of the cup that I must drink? Can you two bear the punishment that I must bear?"

Both disciples nodded their heads vigorously and answered, "Yes, master, we are sure we can."

Jesus replied, "Then you both must drink of the cup that I must drink and you both must bear the punishment that I shall bear. However, when it comes to your sitting on each side of me in heaven, that is something that is not within my power to grant. Only my Father has that power and he will allocate the seating in heaven in accordance with his own plans."

The faces of James, John, and their mother drooped sorrowfully and showed their deep disappointment at Jesus' candid reply. A long embarrassing silence followed and soon the room was buzzing with the angry resentment of the other disciples. When Jesus became aware of the irritated reaction of the ten other disciples, he raised his hands and said, "Silence, please! You have seen how foreign rulers lord it over the people whom they govern, taking for themselves the best of everything and leaving their people in want and poverty. Favoritism for the few results in discrimination for the many. That relationship must never exist among you. I came among you to serve and not to be served. I also came among you to give my life in order to set others free. So must it be with you. He who would be first among you must be the last among you. That is the will of God."

The disciples looked sheepishly at one another and no one dared speak because they all knew that Jesus had given them a justifiable rebuke. During the pause that followed, there was a loud knock on the door and Peter went to see who it was that was knocking. When Peter opened the door, he found that the caller was the treasurer of the local synagogue, who said to him, "Is your master in?"

"Yes," Peter replied.

The man said to Peter in a loud and indignant voice, "Why doesn't your master pay the temple tax? Heaven knows he uses the temple often enough."

Peter answered, "Just wait a moment and I will speak to him about it. However, I feel sure that he will pay the temple tax."

Peter went back into the adjoining room and said to Jesus, "The treasurer of the local synagogue is at the door. He wants to know if you will pay him the temple tax. What shall I say to him?"

Jesus answered, "What do you think I should say to him, Peter?"

Peter replied, "I told him that I felt sure that you would pay the tax."

Jesus said, "Peter, from whom do the kings collect their tribute and their taxes? From their own people or from foreigners?"

Peter answered, "From foreigners."

Jesus replied, "Then we, who are the children of the church, should not be required to pay this tax. However, I

have no desire to give offense to your local rabbi for refusing
to pay this tax. Therefore, open the mouth of the largest fish
that we caught today and in it you will find a silver coin. Take
it and give that coin to the treasurer of the synagogue for the
temple tax for you and for me."

Matt. 8 (1-4)
Matt. 9 (1-8)
Mark 1 (39-45)
Mark 2 (1-12)
Luke 5 (12-26)

Chapter 11

Jesus Heals

The earliest part of Jesus' ministry was mostly spent in healing the sick and the crippled persons. Jesus would have much preferred spending his time in saving men's souls rather than in healing their bodies, but it was only natural that his earliest fame was derived from the miraculous cures that he made. The result of this fame was that Jesus was followed everywhere by large crowds seeking his help to cure them of their various physical ailments.

Several of the stories of the cures that Jesus performed are worth noting because they bring out Jesus' attitude toward these physical cures and they also mark the beginning of the conflict between Jesus and the Jewish religious authorities. As Jesus was leaving a village of Galilee, a leper approached him, knelt before him and said in a pleading voice, "Lord, if thou will, thou can make me clean."

Jesus promptly stretched forth his hand, placed it upon the leper's head and said, "I will. Be thou clean."

The leper was immediately cleansed and thanked Jesus profusely for his miraculous cure. Jesus said to him, "Tell no one how you were cured, but go to the synagogue and show yourself to the rabbi. Thank him for your cure and give him those gifts required by Mosaic law for your recovery."

There are three points to note in this story. The first is that the leper dared approach Jesus, which was a violation of the Mosaic law; second, that Jesus touched the leper which was contrary to normal custom; and lastly, that Jesus asked the leper to report to the local rabbi and give him those gifts required by the Mosaic law in appreciation for his recovery. From this story, it is apparent that Jesus is still trying to maintain friendly relations with the Jewish temple authorities.

However, the leper did not remain quiet about his miraculous cure. Instead, he broadcast the story of his recovery around the whole countryside, so that Jesus' fame grew and grew. The result was that immense crowds followed Jesus everywhere he went demanding the performance of more miracles. In desperation, Jesus left Capernaum in the middle of the night for the peace and quiet of the desert country north of the village.

After Jesus had rested for several days in the desert, he returned just before daybreak to the home of James and John in order to avoid being seen and followed by the usual pleading mob. However, soon after sun-up when people were up and about attending to their daily chores, the news of Jesus' return to the village spread rapidly, and soon there was a large crowd gathered around the home of James and John patiently waiting to get a glimpse of Jesus. Some of them unceremoniously crowded into the house in order to see Jesus. In self-defense, he preached to the crowd gathered

around him as best he could, under those difficult circumstances.

While he was preaching, four brothers arrived carrying another brother on a stretcher, who was paralyzed. The four
brothers tried desperately to get through the crowd in order
to get their crippled brother before Jesus; but every one in
that crowd was just as determined to see Jesus as the four
brothers were; so no one moved. Being unable to get through
the crowd, the four brothers circled the house seeking another
entrance into it. Finding none, two of the brothers climbed
up on the tiled roof.

The two brothers on the ground raised their paralyzed
brother on the stretcher to the two brothers on the roof and
then climbed up on the roof themselves. The four men now
carefully crawled over the roof listening intently for the
voices of those inside the house. When they located the room
where Jesus was preaching, they removed the roof tiles over
that room until they had created an opening large enough to
pass the stretcher with their brother upon it, through the
opening. Gently, the four brothers lowered the stretcher with
four thongs attached to each corner of the stretcher, directly
in front of Jesus.

Jesus looked up at the four anxious faces of the men on the
roof and then down at the pleading face of the paralyzed
young man before him, who said, "Master, forgive my brothers for intruding upon you in this manner, but it was the only
way they could get me before you. Forgive me for my sins,
master, and help me to walk again."

Initially, Jesus was very annoyed by the disturbance created by the removal of a portion of the roof, but now he was
so moved with sympathetic compassion for these five brothers
who had demonstrated their complete faith in him as one of
God's healers, that he said to the crippled brother before him,
"Son, arise and walk; thy sins have been forgiven."

Unknown to Jesus, there were agents of the Chief Rabbi

present in the room who heard the conversation between Jesus and the paralyzed man. When these temple agents heard Jesus forgive the sins of the crippled brother, they angrily shouted, "Blasphemy! Who can forgive sins except God himself? How dare you utter such blasphemy?"

Jesus turned to them and said, "Why do you think evil in your hearts? Which statement is easier to make to this paralyzed man, 'Thy sins are forgiven thee' or 'Arise and walk'? But in order to prove to you that the Son of Man does have the power on earth to forgive sins, I say to this paralyzed man, 'Arise and walk.' "

The paralyzed young man immediately arose, thanked Jesus profusely, took up his stretcher and walked away. The news of the performance of this new miracle quickly spread throughout Galilee and beyond its borders into Samaria, Judaea and in all the surrounding lands. When this news reached the ears of Chief Rabbi Caiaphas and his father-in-law, Rabbi Annas, they noted it with grave displeasure. Jesus was now marked by the Chief Rabbi as a man who defied the highest Jewish authority and as a man who would bear careful watching.

Matt. 13 (54-58)   Luke 4 (16-31)   Is. 61 (1-3)
Mark 6 (1-6)   John 4 (43-44)   2 K. 5 (1)

Chapter 12

A Prophet Without Honor

In Capernaum, Peter's home town, Jesus had some unpleasant experiences which turned his thoughts to his own
home town of Nazareth, which he had not visited in many
months. Like many a person before him and like many a
person after him who has had some unpleasant experience in
a strange place, the remembrance of his home town with its
familiar faces and its well-known places had an unusually
strong, sentimental appeal to him. Therefore, he now turned
his thoughts and his footsteps back to Nazareth.

However, if Jesus expected to find peace and quiet and
friendly faces in Nazareth, he was in for a bitter disappointment. His fame had preceded him to Nazareth; but the
townspeople who had seen him grow up in their midst for
over twenty five years as the meek apprentice-carpenter, son
of Joseph and Mary, could not bring themselves to believe
that one of their local carpenters, whose family they had

known for generations, could possibly be a nationally famous prophet.

The logical meeting place between Jesus and the curiously doubting townspeople who wanted to see and hear him preach was the synagogue. The meeting occurred on the first Sabbath after Jesus arrived in Nazareth. When he went up to the rostrum to preach, the synagogue was overflowing with skeptical townspeople. As Jesus faced his hostile audience, he acutely felt the questioning eyes of his former neighbors critically turned upon him. For the first time in his missionary life, Jesus felt reluctant to preach his usual stirring sermon. During this moment of hesitation, Jesus slowly looked around the synagogue, then turned to the rabbi seated directly in front of him and said, "May I have your book of the Scriptures, please?"

The rabbi handed Jesus his book of the Scriptures which was opened to Chapter 61 of the Book of Isaiah. From it Jesus read,

> "The Spirit of the Lord is upon me.
> He has directed me
> To preach to the meek,
> To heal the broken-hearted,
> To comfort those who mourn
> And to free the prisoners
> Because he has appointed me
> To preach his gospel."

Then closing the book, Jesus handed it back to the rabbi and turning to the congregation, said, "At this very moment, this prophesy of Isaiah has been fulfilled before your very own eyes."

He quietly sat down, and for several minutes the congregation sat silent and motionless while the full implication of Jesus' words that he was one of God's chosen prophets sank into their minds. The congregation was astonished not only by the fact that Jesus, one of their own local carpenters, dared claim to be one of God's great prophets; but that, in addition, he dared claim that the great prophet, Isaiah, foretold his coming. The long silence that followed this bold claim was no indication of the angry uproar that was to follow. Soon there were hostile mutterings rising from all parts of the synagogue, culminating in a series of derisive shouts. Above the angry roar came voices shouting, "Isn't this the carpenter son of Joseph and Mary and the brother of James, Juda, Simon and Joses?"

"Aren't those women sitting here amongst us his very own sisters?"

"How dare he claim that he is God's prophet?"

When the angry hubbub partially subsided, Jesus stood up, motioned for silence, and slowly said, "Knowing me as you do, I can understand your doubts about me. There are obviously many among you who want some proof that I am a prophet of God."

A burly man jumped up and shouted, "That's right! If you are one of God's prophets, prove it."

Calmly Jesus replied, "I cannot give you the proof that you ask for, because you have no faith in me. You are bearing out the truth of the ancient proverb which says, 'A prophet is not without honor, except in his own country, among his own people and in his own home.' But remember that in the days of Elijah there was a drought that lasted three and a half years, and the famine that followed impoverished the entire country. Many persons died and many women became widows in Israel. But the Lord did not send Elijah to help any of these Jewish widows. Instead, he sent Elijah to help a Gentile widow in Sidon. Again in the days of Elijah, there were a great many lepers in Israel, but the Lord did not heal any of them; he only healed Haaman, the Syrian leper."

Again Jesus sat down, but this time the angry mutterings

became a threatening roar. From many parts of the synagogue came angry shouts of, "Kill him! Kill him! Kill him!"

Several of the biggest and burliest men near Jesus grabbed him and carried him out of the temple into the city streets on their shoulders. The congregation quickly stormed out of the synagogue shouting curses and threats at Jesus and those persons closest to him pummelled him and spit on him. From out of the milling mob, one voice rang out loud and clear shouting, "Take this blasphemous impostor to the Crested Cliff and cast him down on the rocks below."

The raging mob quickly replied with an angry roar of approval and carried Jesus to a high cliff at the edge of town, known as the Crested Cliff, because its outlines resembled those of a warrior's helmet. The section nearest town rose in a gradual, upward rounded slope, while the opposite side ended abruptly in a vertical cliff. Numerous large boulders were scattered over the top of the cliff, giving it its crested appearance from a distance and its name—the Crested Cliff.

When the yelling mob reached the top of the cliff, they were compelled to let Jesus walk because of the narrowness of the trail leading to its abrupt edge. The leaders of the mob were pushing and pulling Jesus around the huge boulders, when suddenly five determined men hiding behind an enormous boulder stepped out and blocked their path. The leaders of the mob shouted angrily at the men to stand aside or be thrown off the cliff themselves; but the men stood defiantly across the trail. At the head and center of this little band of men stood a large, bearded, brawny man, who glowered manacingly at the mob before him. He was a stranger in Nazareth and so were the men beside him. The large bearded man was Peter and his companions were Andrew, James, John and Philip.

As Peter and the other disciples refused to move, the leaders of the mob rushed at them in rage and frustration. Peter easily cast aside the first man, but soon there was a second, a third and then a fourth. Before long, the crest of the cliff was the battle ground of snarling, angry, fighting men, who were grappling and tumbling over one another in hopeless confusion. It was now almost impossible to distinguish between friend and foe. While the brawling was at its height, no one paid any attention to Jesus, who slipped unobtrusively down the hill.

Luke 17 (20-21)   Matt. 16 (21-28)   Luke 9 (22-27)
John 7 (1-53)   Mark 8 (31-38)   John 8 (1-11)

Chapter 13

Sukkoth or the Feast of
the Tabernacles

Jesus' initial attempt to bring the word of God to the Jews gave him much to think about. In his hometown of Nazareth in Galilee, his mission had ended disastrously, in fact almost permanently. Repeatedly the words he used to describe his reception there kept recurring to him, "A prophet is not without honor, except in his own country, among his own people and in his own home."

Having made this admission to himself, Jesus apparently arrived at these decisions: He would avoid going to Nazareth; he would establish a home base in Capernaum; he would acquire a group of devoted followers.

Regretfully, Jesus had to admit to himself that he not only needed disciples to spread the gospel of God over a wider area, but he also needed disciples for self-preservation. In the fall of that year A.D. 28, the career of Jesus skidded to its lowest point. The combined effect of the repressive policy of Chief Rabbi Caiaphas added to the smearing campaign of

Rabbi Annas had taken its toll of the followers of Jesus and frightened people away from his meetings. Even Jesus' twelve closest disciples had left him and gone to their respective homes.

Jesus was now almost thirty-five years old. He had been preaching for about two years. Within six months, he would be dead. Had he died at this time, the world might never have heard of him. It is little wonder that under these circumstances, he felt extremely depressed.

Chief Rabbi Caiaphas had issued orders that anyone knowing the whereabouts of Jesus must immediately report this information to the nearest rabbi or agent of the temple on penalty of being excommunicated from the synagogue. With all doors closed against him, Jesus sought refuge in the home of his parents at Nazareth. Going to Nazareth at all was a bitter blow to Jesus, because it was in Nazareth that the Jews had made their first direct attempt to kill him. To add to the bitterness of living in Nazareth and hiding in the home of his parents, there was the unpleasant fact that one of Jesus' own brothers had no faith in him.

It was now the fall of the year and Jews everywhere in and out of Jerusalem were happily preparing to celebrate Sukkoth, or the eight-day Feast of the Tabernacles in their capital city. Sukkoth is a major Jewish holiday extending for eight days in September or October during which all work is explicitly prohibited. Originally this holiday was probably a Canaanite festival, which the Canaanites celebrated at the end of the harvest season in gratitude to the Giver of Fertility for a bountiful crop. During this festival, the Canaanites erected booths made of tree branches and leaves as reminders of the shelters they used as dwelling places during the harvest.

In adopting this Canaanite festival into their religion, the Jews referred to the booths as tabernacles, which reminded them of the temporary places of worship they used during their exodus from Egypt. The Jews decorated the booths with citrus and palm branches, and myrtle and willow twigs to commemorate both the harvest and their exodus from Egypt. Since the Feast of the Tabernacles was a harvest festival, it was an occasion for great rejoicing, accompanied by feasting, drinking and dancing. Therefore, it was a religious festival which all Jews anticipated with great joy.

All of Jesus' brothers and sisters excitedly prepared to make the trip to Jerusalem. The hustle and the bustle of all these exciting preparations only emphasized the pathetic lonesomeness of Jesus' position in his own home. When one of Jesus' brothers saw that he made no preparation to leave for Jerusalem, he taunted him for deciding to remain in hiding in Nazareth, saying, "Why don't you get ready to go to the Feast of the Tabernacles in Jerusalem?"

Jesus quietly answered, "I am not ready yet."

His brother sneeringly replied, "I can see that. But since you are the great miracle-maker and prophet, why don't you go to Jerusalem and perform your miracles and expound your prophecies there, where all the world can see and hear you, instead of hiding yourself here at home? No one will ever know what a great prophet you are unless you show yourself publicly and tell the whole world about it."

Jesus slowly replied, "My time has not yet come. For you time means nothing, because your life is without meaning and without purpose. People do not hate you and plan to kill you because you are part of the evil of this world. But there are many who hate me because I have spoken truthfully about their evil ways."

Another of Jesus' brothers sympathetically said, "Come to Jerusalem with us. We'll protect you."

Jesus quietly replied, "Thank you, but I am not yet ready to go. However, you go to the festival, and I am sure that you will all have a much better time without me."

Before long, all of Jesus' family were packed and left home on their happy pilgrimage to Jerusalem. As they traveled south toward Judaea, they were joined by many of their relatives and friends. As far as the eye could see, ahead and behind, the road was black with people and heavily laden donkeys travelling south toward Jerusalem.

After almost a week of slow, leisurely travel, Jesus' family arrived in Jerusalem where they found that the main topic of conversation centered around the question as to whether or not Jesus would dare come to the festival. There were some persons who were positive that Jesus would show up; but they were greatly out-numbered by those persons who were equally positive Jesus would not have the courage to openly challenge the Chief Rabbi by coming to Jerusalem.

The next main topic of conversation was the question as to whether or not Jesus was a prophet of God. On this subject, public opinion was more evenly divided, with some believing that Jesus was a man of God, while others claimed that he was only an impostor. However, all those who thought Jesus might be a man of God were extremely cautious about expressing their opinion publicly, because Chief Rabbi Caiaphas had his spies everywhere seeking information about anyone who dared speak favorably of Jesus. After three days of the festival had passed without Jesus showing up, it was commonly assumed that Jesus lacked the courage to come to Jerusalem; so the public anticipation of excitement concerning his arrival evaporated.

Meanwhile, back in Nazareth, Jesus quietly prepared himself for his pilgrimage to Jerusalem. Concealing himself in a long shepherd's cloak, he left Nazareth before dawn several days after his family had gone. Desiring to avoid recognition, Jesus circled around all villages and inhabited areas, and consequently he did not arrive in Jerusalem until the fourth day of the festival.

He went directly to the temple, walked up to the front of the altar and threw off his enveloping cloak. As soon as the congregation recognized Jesus, an excited buzz of whispering rumbled through the building. Unquestionably, the congregation was thrilled by Jesus' audacious courage in openly challenging the authority of the temple rabbis by being present in the temple. Slowly, he began to preach. The temple guards and rabbis were so stunned at seeing Jesus calmly preaching within arm's length, that no one moved to stop him. It was painfully evident that the entire congregation was intently enthralled with Jesus' sermon. Rabbi Ahab finally found his voice, stood up and said, "How does it happen that you who have never been to school know so much?"

Jesus answered, "My preaching is not my own, but that of Him who sent me. If any man here understands the will of God, he will know whether or not I perform the work of God."

Rabbi Ahab replied, "If you perform the work of God, why do you repeatedly break the laws of Moses?"

Jesus answered, "I do not break the laws of Moses. All that I do is to amplify those laws and bring them up to date. Now, you tell me, why is it that you temple rabbis break the laws of Moses by trying to kill me?"

Rabbi Ahab shouted back, "Because you have the devil in you."

This public admission on the part of one of the temple rabbis that they had been trying to kill Jesus aroused the sympathy of the entire congregation to such an extent that they responded with an angry roar. Realizing that he had made a serious error, Rabbi Ahab lamely added, "Who is trying to kill you? Not one of us rabbis. We are only trying to convince you of the error of your ways so that you will stop breaking the laws of Moses."

Jesus replied, "You temple rabbis have persecuted me because I do God's work on the Sabbath. Yet you circumcise children on the Sabbath; so why condemn me if I heal a man's body on the Sabbath?"

Noticing an obvious undercurrent of hostile antagonism,

and the crowd's apparent friendliness to Jesus, Rabbi Ahab deemed it best that he remain discreetly silent. During this pause Captain Shama walked over to him and said, "Chief Rabbi Caiaphas ordered me to arrest this Galilean. Shall I arrest him now?"

Rabbi Ahab growled back, "Not now, you fool. Can't you see that the Galilean has swung this crowd over to his side. Wait until after this meeting is over."

Meanwhile, throughout the congregation an excited hum of animated discussion was taking place over the dramatic turn of events. Evidently the daring appearance of Jesus in the temple at Jerusalem in open defiance of the orders for his arrest by the Chief Rabbi had caught the admiration of the people. Someone in the crowd said, "Is this the man that the temple rabbis seek to kill? Did you hear how boldly he spoke and the rabbis didn't dare answer him? Can it be that the Chief Rabbi really knows that this man is the Messiah?"

Another voice said, "No, he cannot be the Messiah because he comes from Galilee." Some one else shouted, "Truly, this man *is* the Messiah!"

Another voice replied, "Can the Messiah come from Galilee? Doesn't the Scripture say that the Messiah must be descended from David and be born in Bethlehem where David was born?"

Ignoring these interruptions, Jesus continued, "If any man thirst, let him come unto me and drink, and he shall have everlasting life. Yet a little while longer shall I be with you and then I shall return to Him who sent me. You will search for me, but you will not find me; because where I go, you cannot follow."

Some one asked, "Where will he go, that we cannot follow him? Will he go to some foreign land?"

Rabbi Ahab, who had recovered his composure and his wits by now, decided to try a new line of attack, so he turned to Jesus and said, "If you really are the Messiah, tell us, when will the Kingdom of God become a reality upon this earth?"

Jesus answered, "You will not find the Kingdom of God by searching for it. Neither can any man say, 'Look, here it is,' or, 'See, there it is.' The Kingdom of God is within you!"

With these words, Jesus abruptly ended his sermon, wrapped his shepherd's cloak over his shoulders and walked toward a huddled group of men near the doorway. Within a few minutes, he was lost in the crowd. Meanwhile, the congregation again resumed its excited argument over the spiritual identity of Jesus.

While this animated discussion was occurring in the temple, Chief Rabbi Caiaphas was taking a midday rest in his private quarters. A servant entered his room and said, "Rabbi, I have come to tell you that the Galilean is in the temple arguing with Rabbi Ahab." The rabbi quickly rose from his couch and hurried into the meeting-room, where he saw Rabbi Ahab, Captain Shama and Nicodemus heatedly engaged in conversation.

Addressing them all, he bellowed, "Where is the Galilean?" As no one replied, he grasped Captain Shama's arm and shouted, "I said, where is the Galilean?"

In a very weak voice the captain replied, "He left, sir." The irate rabbi roared, "What? Didn't I tell you to arrest him?"

"Yes, rabbi," the captain apologetically replied. "But there never was a man who speaks like that Galilean does."

"What does it matter to you how that Galilean speaks?" the rabbi shouted. "He is deceitful, a law-breaker and a rebel. Can't you obey orders?"

While the captain stammeringly tried to answer, Nicodemus interrupted saying, "Rabbi, aren't you condemning this man before he has a chance to defend himself? You know our Mosaic law requires that every one be given a fair trial before he is condemned."

Chief Rabbi Caiaphas turned on Nicodemus and sarcastically said, "Are you another Galilean? Or has the Nazarene's persuasive tongue also seduced you into believing him? Search the Scriptures thoroughly and you will find that no prophet ever came out of Galilee."

With these words, the Chief Rabbi turned curtly on his heel and left the temple, dutifully followed by Rabbi Ahab. Captain Shama turned sheepishly toward Nicodemus and smilingly said, "Thank you sir, for interceding for me."

Quickly and silently, Jesus and his disciples walked through the winding streets of Jerusalem through the Fountain Gate and then out beyond the walled gate into the open country to their favorite hiding place in the Mount of Olives. After the disciples had made themselves as comfortable as they could on the ground around him, Jesus said, "And now I speak to you frankly. I know that some of you who have read the Scriptures carefully have been expecting that when my bodily existence shall end, that I shall go directly to heaven in power and glory and take all of you with me. However, I must tell you this; before that happens, the rabbis in Jerusalem will persecute me and condemn me to death and then I shall be crucified and buried. But I shall rise again from the dead three days after my crucifixion and ascend into heaven. Only then will I share the power and the glory of heaven with my Father."

Peter interrupted saying, "But we will not allow you to return to Jerusalem and be tortured and crucified. That shall never happen!"

Jesus quietly replied, "I know you mean well, Peter, but I have my Father's work to do and I must endure whatever persecution lies before me in order to do his work."

Peter said, "But you can do your Father's work without suffering the agonies of crucifixion. Why not just continue with your missionary work as you are now doing?"

Jesus answered, "I know that your intentions are of the best, Peter, and you tempt me with an easy way out of my duty to God. Sometimes, when I wake up in the middle of the night and find I cannot get to sleep, I wish I could follow your advice."

Peter replied, "But master, is it necessary to expose yourself any more than need be? You have just finished preaching in the temple in open defiance of the orders of the Chief Rabbi. Isn't it better to live and continue preaching than to have the Chief Rabbi kill you?"

Jesus answered, "Peter, you are not considering this matter from God's viewpoint, but from that of a man. However, I do appreciate your consideration for me."

Peter asked, "Then you are determined to return to Jerusalem?"

Jesus answered, "Yes, I shall return to the temple tomorrow and preach there again."

Peter bowed his head sadly and said, "Very well, we shall all go with you."

The following day, Jesus returned to the temple and was soon preaching again to a large and rapt congregation. While Jesus was in the midst of his sermon, Rabbi Ahab and several temple servants entered the building, pushing a dishevelled woman before them. The rabbi thrust the woman in front of Jesus and said in a scornful voice, "This woman is an adulteress. We caught her in the very act. According to the law of Moses, she should be stoned to death. But before we kill her, we want you to tell us whether or not you think it is right to kill her?"

This question was another of the typically forked questions with which the temple rabbis repeatedly tried to trap Jesus before the Jewish people. If he agreed with the strict wording of the Mosaic law, that the woman should be stoned to death, the rabbis would accuse him of being a heartless monster. But, if he said the woman should be spared from such cruel punishment, the rabbis would accuse him of advocating disregard for the Mosaic law.

Clearly understanding the trap that Ahab had set for him, Jesus remained silent and simply looked long and steadily at the rabbi and the temple servant. Then he knelt down on the dusty floor and with his finger wrote into the dust the name of the rabbi and the names of several of the men who were with him.

Unaware that Jesus had written his name on the dusty floor, Rabbi Ahab shouted, "Answer my question! Can't you talk? Do you or do you not agree with the Mosaic law that this woman should be stoned to death?"

Ignoring the angry rabbi, Jesus stood up, carefully noted the faces of the remaining accusers of the woman and then knelt down again and wrote their names into the dust.

Unaware that Jesus had written his name on the dusty floor, Rabbi Ahab angrily shouted, "Will you stop scribbling on the floor like a school boy and stand up and answer my question?"

From all outward appearances, Jesus acted as though he hadn't heard a word the rabbi said, and calmly studied the names written on the floor, carefully re-reading each name he had written there. Soon, various members of the congregation pushed their way through the circle of men gathered around Jesus, bent over his body and read the names of the men written on the floor. Before long, smothered smirks and ill-concealed laughter were heard throughout the congregation, as the names of each of the woman's accusers were loudly whispered from person to person.

When Rabbi Ahab and the temple servants heard their names being whispered in an audible undertone, they peered over Jesus' shoulder and saw with embarrassment that the names of each of them had been written there. While pointing his long, slender finger at the names written on the floor, Jesus now stood up, turned and faced Rabbi Ahab and said, "Now I will answer your question, rabbi. You who have accused this woman of adultery, now tell me which one of you is guiltless of this same sin? Let him who is without that sin, cast the first stone."

While Jesus was still speaking, Rabbi Ahab and the temple servants slunk ignominiously out of the temple, attempting to do so as inconspicuously as possible. As they went out the door, they could hear the scornful laughter of the members of the congregation reverberate throughout the temple. Jesus, who had remained quietly standing beside the woman during the shameful exit of the temple personnel, turned to the woman and said, "Woman, where are your accusers?"

She replied, "They have all gone."

Jesus asked, "Is there then, no one here who accuses you?"

She answered, "No one, Lord."

Jesus quietly said, "Then neither do I accuse you. Now go, and sin no more."

Chapter 14

The Roman Captain

Later on his way back to Capernaum, Jesus and his disciples were met by a group of the town's leading citizens headed by the mayor, who walked over to Jesus and said to him, "I hope you will excuse me for asking you to grant me a very special favor, but I know what an exceptional man you are and that fact gives me the courage to speak to you."

Jesus asked, "What is it?"

The mayor answered, "There is a Roman captain in our town named Catania, who has a servant that is desperately ill. This captain dearly loves that servant and has employed the best available physicians to cure him, but they have all failed. We know that you do not cure Gentiles and that you will have nothing at all to do with them, but this Gentile is an exceptional man who really loves our people. In fact, he has even built our synagogue for us. Therefore, I beg of you, please go see this captain's servant and cure him."

Jesus replied, "Very well. Let's go there."

As Jesus, the mayor and the large crowd following them

approached the home of Captain Catania, they were met by the captain who had seen them coming. His stern bronzed face was lined with sorrow and his demeanor was that of a man carrying a very heavy burden.

This was Jesus' first meeting with a Roman soldier and he wondered what an officer of the conquering army of Rome was like. The Roman captain spoke first, saying, "Master, I know the Mosaic law forbids a Jew from defiling himself by entering the house of a Gentile. So, I do not ask that you break your religious law by entering my house. However, I am a Roman captain and my soldiers and my servants obey my orders, whether or not I am present. I know that you are a man of God and therefore, your orders will be carried out, the same as mine are, whether or not you are present. Consequently, I only ask that you order my servant be cured and I know that your order will be carried out even though you do not see him."

While the captain was speaking, Jesus' keen eyes carefully scrutinized him to determine what manner of man he might be. When he realized the complete faith that this Gentile officer placed in him, his skeptical attitude quickly changed from one of curious aloofness to that of warmth and friendship.

Sympathetically he replied, "Go, Captain. Your faith in me has cured your servant."

The captain bowed his head and said, "Thank you very kindly."

After the captain left, Jesus turned and said to his disciples, "Not in all of Israel have I found a faith so great as this. In the Kingdom of Heaven there will be many of the people of Abraham, Israel and Jacob who will weep and mourn because they have scorned and rejected the word of God. Therefore, they will be cast into the outer darkness while many Gentiles will enter into the Kingdom of God. It shall

be said in that day many of those who were first, shall be last;
and many of those who were last, shall be first."

When Jesus returned to Peter's home in Capernaum he was
told that King Herod Antipas had imprisoned John the Baptist. That news saddened and made him more determined
than ever to fight for certain necessary reforms in the teaching
of Judaism.

Matt. 14 (3-12) Nu. 30 (1-2)
Mark 6 (14-29) De. 23 (21)
Luke 3 (19-20)

Chapter 15

John the Baptist Beheaded

Although Queen Herodias had been able to persuade her husband, King Herod Antipas, to imprison John the Baptist, she had been unable to persuade him to order the great evangelist executed, because at the time of his arrest his disciples and followers had demonstrated so violently that the king feared it might deteriorate into a riot that his soldiers could not control.

However, the Queen, who was extremely proud of the fact that she was the granddaughter of King Herod the Great for whom she had been named, was so furious because of the defamatory public tirades of John the Baptist in which he denounced her marriage to the king as adulterous and incestuous, that she had vowed that she would never rest until the evangelist was forever silenced.

The ancestry of both Queen Herodias and her husband is worth noting. Both were direct descendants of a Jew named

Antipater who had been a collaborator of the Romans when they conquered Judaea in 63 B. C. Antipater was a man of great wealth and influence in Palestine who served the Romans so well that Julius Caesar conferred Roman citizenship upon him and all his descendants in 47 B. C. In addition, he made Antipater governor of Judaea and his twenty-six-year-old son, Herod (73 B. C.- 4 B. C.), governor of Galilee.

As Herod demonstrated unusual ability to govern and develop the economic potentialities of the land, the Romans continuously increased his authority and his possessions, until he eventually became known as King Herod the Great. Among the imposing and magnificent buildings that he constructed was the completely rebuilt Jewish temple in Jerusalem.

Unfortunately, toward the end of his career, he became morose, suspicious and evil. Suffering from physical and mental disability he ordered his wife, Marianne, three of his sons and various relatives murdered. At the approximate time of the birth of Jesus, when the soothsayers told him that a newborn babe would succeed him, he ordered all newborn babes murdered.

After his death, his son, Herod Archelaus (22 B. C.-18 A. D.), became king of Judaea and Samaria and his son, Herod Antipas (21 B. C.-39 A. D.), became King of Galilee. This is the King Herod referred to in the New Testament to whom Pontius Pilate sent Jesus when he tried to avoid ordering his execution.

King Herod Antipas' first wife was an Arabian princess. While he was on one of his periodic trips to Rome, he met and fell in love with Herodias, who was the daughter of his dead brother, Aristobulus, and the wife of his younger brother, Herod Philip, which made her both his niece and his sister-in-law. In spite of unfavorable popular reaction to this love-match, King Herod Antipas wasted no time in divorcing his Arabian wife and marrying Herodias. Because of their unconventional marriage, King Herod Antipas and Queen Herodias earned the resentment of their Arab subjects and the contempt of their Jewish subjects.

When the Queen learned that her husband had cancelled the order for the execution of John the Baptist, she strode up to him and contemptuously said, "Who is the ruler of Galilee? You, or that mob outside that palace gate? Your father would have known how to treat that noisy rabble."

The king remained discreetly silent as he had quickly learned from bitter experience that his liquor-sodden brain was no match for the razor-sharp tongue of his young bride. He was as deeply irritated with the stinging insolent remarks of the great evangelist as was the queen, but he was sufficiently wise politically to know he could not afford to antagonize John the Baptist's deeply religious followers.

Queen Herodias had her own ideas about the fate of John the Baptist and none of her thoughts were concerned with the safety of her husband or his throne. She wanted revenge on John the Baptist for the scathing remarks he had made about her and she wanted that revenge without delay. With the approach of her husband's birthday, she saw her chance to obtain the revenge she so desperately wanted. She deliberately planned a huge banquet, to which she invited the most prominent persons from far and near. Knowing her husband's weakness for liquor and women, she ordered a sumptuous banquet with plenty of liquor and many beautiful dancing girls. While she busied herself with the orders for the oxen, lamb, sweetmeats, spices, wines, liquors, and dancing girls, she repeated over and over again to herself the Mosaic law that says:

"When thou shalt vow a vow unto the Lord, thy God, thou shalt not refuse to fulfill that vow."

All the queen's servants noted and wondered about the determined energy with which she planned and worked to make her husband's birthday party a huge success. Finally, all the preparations were completed and the great day commemorating the king's birthday arrived. The queen hovered in the background issuing last minute instructions to the servants in all the numerous details to make the royal banquet an outstanding success. To one servant she said, "Always stay at the king's side and keep his wine cup and his liquor cup constantly filled."

As usual at such banquets, there was far more drinking than there was eating. So great was the amount of meat, fruit, and the finest delectably tempting foods that the countryside could offer, that when the guests were all glutted with food, the tables were still overburdened with all kinds of tasty dishes.

During the lengthy banquet, the queen kept a watchful eye upon her sensuous husband. When she saw that he was surfeited with his favorite spiced meats and liquor, she ordered the dancing girls to begin their performance. To the accompaniment of the country's best musicians, the dancing girls twisted and twirled for the entertainment of the king and his guests. Quickly, they created an exciting tension of greater things to come. Following the queen's instructions, the dancers saved their most alluring glances and sensuous gestures for the king. Before long the king was so overcome with the gaiety and the excitement of the seductive dancing girls, that he shouted in drunken roar, "More! More! More!"

Queen Herodias watched the king scornfully through the narrow slits of her piercing eyes. When she thought that the king was at a proper stage of sensual excitement, she quickly rose from her place at the table and beckoned her daughter to follow her. The queen's daughter, Salome, was already noted throughout Galilee and Judaea for her beautiful, suggestive dancing in spite of the fact that she was still only fifteen years old. Within a few years, she was destined to become one of the world's most famous sirens. Only the queen's imperious supervision prevented her daughter from becoming the nation's most noted dancer at this early age. However, on this occasion of the celebration of her husband's birthday, the queen decided to give her daughter complete freedom to show her dancing ability and her sexually alluring body.

As soon as the two women had drawn the heavy drapes of the banquet room behind them the queen turned to her daughter and said, "Salome, I want you to dance tonight as you have never danced publicly before. Dance only for the drunken king. Dance the dance of the seven veils for him. Ignore everyone else in the room and concentrate your dancing upon him."

Salome wonderingly asked, "Why, Mother? You've never allowed me to perform the seven veils dance publicly before. Why do you ask me to dance it tonight before all these strange people?"

Between clenched teeth, the queen answered, "Never mind why. Just do as I tell you. I have a plan. Go and change quickly into your costume before the old fool drops off into a drunken stupor."

Salome answered, "All right, Mother. I'll do as you say, but I wish you would tell me what it's all about."

The queen replied, "I'll tell you about it later. Now hurry and change into your costume."

Before long, Salome was back in the darkened banquet room, clothed only in seven veils, slowly dancing and gyrating before the bulging eyes of the liquor-sodden king. His incestuous eyes feasted upon the youthful, swaying, sensuous body of his lovely step-daughter, while the stringed orchestra kept perfect time to the rhythmic motions of her suggestive body. Slowly and gracefully, Salome dropped one veil after another before the king's popping, bloodshot eyes. As each veil dropped, the veins and the arteries in the king's face and neck bulged larger and larger, until they seemed almost at the bursting point.

Finally, Salome slithered up close to the lustful face of the drunken king, dropped her last veil and ended the dance with one last mad whirl of sexual suggestiveness and dropped completely naked at his feet. Quickly, one of the queen's servants stepped forward and draped Salome's nude body with a heavy red cloak. Slowly and gracefully she rose, threw longing kisses at the king and tripped lightly from the room with her long black silken tresses streaming beckoningly behind her.

King Herod Antipas was now so completely beside himself from the intoxicating effects of the liquor and the sexual excitement of the dancing that he shouted, "Salome, come back! Dance for me just once more and I'll give you anything you want. Salome! Just dance for me once more!"

Behind the heavy drapes separating Queen Herodias and her daughter from the guests in the banquet room, the queen clutched her daughter tightly and snarled, "Let the drunken fool roar! Now is the time to get it!"

Salome innocently asked, "Get what, mother?"

Ignoring her daughter's question, the queen continued, "Yes, go out and dance for that stupid idiot just once more. But first, make him promise to give you anything you ask for."

Salome replied, "What more shall I ask for, mother? He has already promised me everything I want."

Queen Herodias sneered, "Everything *you* want! That's not enough! There is something *I* want, and that something is the head of John the Baptist!"

Salome said, "But, mother—"

The queen furiously interrupted saying, "Don't argue! I have stood for the insolence of that mad fanatic long enough. I have sworn by the souls of our ancestors that I shall revenge myself upon him, and now the time has come to even that score. Yes, Salome, go out and dance for that drunken fool!

Dance for him until his bulging eyes pop out of their sockets. But bring me back the head of that foul-mouthed John the Baptist!"

Salome looked at her mother in puzzled awe and fear; but when she saw the mad look in her mother's eyes, she remained discreetly silent and decided that it was best to obey her. So this immature girl covered herself again with the seven veils and her red cloak and re-entered the banquet room. Her appearance was greeted by a thunderous round of applause led by a loud clamor of the drunken king. Bowing gracefully to all the assembled guests, Salome tripped gayly over to the king, and once again became the desirably exciting, sensuous teen-age nymphet. Coming up close to her drunken step-father, she let her cloak drop back slightly to give him a close-up view of her firmly rounded breasts.

Winking suggestively, she said with an inviting laugh, "Father, do you still promise to give me anything that I want if I dance for you just once more?"

The king, who was now so groggy from his excessive drinking that he could scarcely sit up straight, shouted back, "I swear it, Salome! I swear it upon the soul of my father, King Herod the Great! I will give you anything you ask for—even half of my kingdom if you want it. Just dance for me once more and anything you ask for is yours."

Turning gayly to the king's illustrious guests, Salome laughingly said, "You children of Israel! Did you hear what my father swore to give me? He has sworn on the soul of his father, King Herod the Great, to give me anything that I ask for, if I dance for him just once more."

The king and all the guests clapped loudly as Salome gracefully curtsied before the king. Quickly a servant stepped forward and removed Salome's heavy red robe revealing her delicately pink nude body, covered only by the flimsy seven veils which simply emphasized the beautiful outlines of her rounded slender figure. Tripping lightly to the center of the room, she bowed gayly before the king and smilingly said to him, "And now, before I begin my last dance, father, I will tell you what I want. I want you to give me the head of John the Baptist!"

The words were barely out of her mouth before Salome was again twirling and shimmying before the king in her most sexually seductive manner, dropping the first of her seven veils. But this time, the king's head was twirling faster than Salome's nude body. Drunk as he was, he knew that he had been tricked by the queen and her sexually exciting daughter.

While Salome thrilled the assembled guests with her graceful dancing and her sensuous beauty, the liqour-sodden brain of the king tried to find a solution to the dreadful dilemma that confronted him.

Suddenly, he felt dreadfully alone in the overcrowded noisy room. The thumping music accompanied by the sound of stomping feet and the rhythmic beat of clapping hands struck a pitiless tattoo upon his muddled, intoxicated brain. He was now sufficiently sober to realize the dreadfulness of his position, without having the moral courage to face up to his problem. While he was still trying to find an answer to his twin-forked dilemma, the music stopped, the room became quiet and Salome was at his feet laughingly saying, "And now, father, give me what you promised me—the head of John the Baptist!"

The king gazed vacuously around the room and saw before him nothing but a sea of unfamiliar faces. He felt certain that never before had he seen so many strangers. He was trapped and everyone in the room knew it. If he ordered John the Baptist beheaded, he would endanger his weak hold upon his throne, because the devoted evangelists' disciples might riot and cause the Romans to dethrone him. And yet if he refused to keep his vow, he would be scorned by his relatives and guests as a man who broke the Mosaic law.

In that frightful moment of indecision, time stood still. Finally, the painful silence was broken by the cutting, sneering voice of the queen, who said, "Well, will the son of the famous King Herod the Great keep his solemn oath sworn on the soul of his father, or shall we be the witnesses to a broken kingly oath?"

Weakly, almost lifelessly, Herod turned to one of his guards and said, "Behead John the Baptist and bring his head to Salome."

Soon the grisly deed was done and the bloody head of the great evangelist with his eyes open wide was brought on a huge platter and presented to Salome. The young girl grimaced, shrank back from the repulsive sight and screamed, "Give it to my father!"

The king took one look at the wide-open defiant eyes and said in a sickly voice, "Give it to the queen."

Then sliding limply to the floor he vomited. Only the queen could stare at the bloody head of the great evangelist and mutter in grim satisfaction, "When thou shalt vow a vow unto the Lord, thy God, thou shalt not refuse to fulfill that vow. And now, you foul-mouthed bastard, you will never again insult me in your filthy sermons."

Matt. 11 (7-30)   Luke 7 (24-35)   Ps. 118 (22)
Matt. 21 (28-46)   Luke 10 (12-16)   Is. 42 (1-3)
Mark 12 (1-12)   Luke 20 (9-19)   Ma. 3 (1)

Chapter 16

Jesus Rebukes the Rabbis

The murder of John the Baptist removed an annoying irritant from the lives of the temple rabbis. The fact that he had been done to death by the unpopular King Herod Antipas made his end that much more pleasing to them. Now they could turn their full attention to that other bothersome preacher, Jesus of Galilee, and plot to do away with him by some similar method. Therefore, orders were issued to the temple spies and the temple agents to dog Jesus' every step and try to goad him into making some indiscreet remark that would get him into difficulties with any of the three authorities, Roman, Jewish or Herodian.

The news of the senseless butchery of John the Baptist quickly spread throughout Judaea and Galilee and Jesus received the news of his murder when he was preparing to leave Bethany to travel north into Samaria and Galilee. As he traveled north, he was in a black mood of anger and frustration. In all the years of their association with Jesus, the disciples had never seen him so angry. Tactfully, they left him completely alone.

At the end of the first day's journey north, Jesus and his disciples stopped in the town of Bethel in Judaea where there was a large group of Jesus' devoted followers. The following day, a huge crowd assembled to hear him preach. As usual, in the assembled crowd there was a considerable number of temple spies headed by Rabbi Ahab.

Throughout the crowd there was a feeling of tense expectation because everyone knew of the close family kinship and of the mutual spiritual relationship that existed between Jesus and his cousin.

Instead of preaching his usual sermon about the Kingdom of God to his large audience, Jesus directed his address directly to the group of temple rabbis before him. Obviously tense with emotion, he said, "John the Baptist came among you preaching the repentance of sins and the redemption of men's souls through baptism. He denied himself both food and wine so that he might dedicate himself both physically and spiritually to the work of God. And yet, you rejected him and said he was possessed of the devil. But let me tell you this: there has never been a greater man born than John the Baptist, because it was he whom the Scriptures predicted would be sent as a messenger to prepare the way before me.

"Now, I have come among you, also preaching the word of God as John the Baptist did, but without denying myself food and wine. And for this reason you call me a gluttonous wine-bibber and a friend of sinners and Gentiles; but I say to you there is no possibility of satisfying people who reject the gospel of God, no matter in what form it is presented to them. I have performed many mighty works of God in your cities, but in spite of that, you have not accepted me as God's messenger, nor have you repented of your sins. If I had performed these mighty works of God in the land of the

Samaritans, they would have repented of their sins long ago.

"Woe unto you, Judaeans! Woe unto you, Galileans! I tell you truthfully that on the day of judgment the punishment of the heathens and of the people of Sodom will be less than that of the Judaeans and the Galileans. You exalt yourselves to high heaven, but on the final day of judgment, instead of ascending into heaven, you shall be cast down into the depths of hell!"

Immediately the group of spies and agents of Chief Rabbi Caiaphas uttered piercing and shrieking sounds. Ignoring the noisy interruption, Jesus now addressed the crowd and said, "There was once a man who had two sons and he said to the elder one, 'Son, go to work in the vineyard today.'

"The son promptly replied, 'Yes, father, I will do as you say and go to work in the vineyard.' But as soon as his father left, he walked away and did no work in the vineyard.

"Then the father went to the younger son and said, 'Son, go and work in the vineyard today.'

"The younger son sullenly replied, 'No, I will not go to work in the vineyard.' Later, repenting of his disrespectful reply, the younger son did go and work in his father's vineyard."

Having seen the Rabbi Ahab as the leader of the hecklers, Jesus pointed an accusing finger at him and said, "Now, you tell me, which of those sons obeyed his father?"

Rabbi Ahab reluctantly replied, "The younger son."

Jesus answered, "Exactly so. That is why I say to you that the sinners and the prostitutes will enter heaven before you do. You accept God with your lips, but not with your hearts. John the Baptist came to you preaching the ways of right-eousness, but you rejected him. However, the sinners and the prostitutes did listen to him and repented and accepted him. And yet, even now that John the Baptist is dead, you have not repented and accepted him."

Rabbi Ahab glowered sullenly, but dared make no derogatory reply, because he knew that he would offend the crowd. As Rabbi Ahab remained silent, Jesus continued his sermon saying, "A landowner had a vineyard which he leased to several tenants. Later, he left the country and went to a foreign land. At harvest time, the land-owner sent his rent collector to those tenants to collect his rent. Instead of paying their rent they beat the rent collector and sent him away empty-handed. When the land owner learned what had happened to his rent collector, he sent two trusted employees to collect his rent. Once again the tenants beat up these two employees worse than they had the rent collector and sent them away empty-handed. This time, the land owner sent three of his burliest and toughest employees to collect his rent, but the tenants beat all three men so unmercifully that one of them died from his injuries.

"When the land owner learned how badly his tenants had treated all of his employees, he decided to send his only son to collect the rent. He said to himself, 'Surely my tenants will respect my son and pay me the rent they owe me.'

"But when the tenants saw the landowner's son approaching the vineyard, one of them said to the others, 'This young man who is coming toward us is the son of the landlord, and the sole heir to this vineyard. Let us kill him and then the vineyard will be ours.' As all the tenants nodded their heads in agreement, they silently waited for the son to approach them. When he did, they jumped on him and killed him."

Jesus paused for a second to let the meaning of his parable be clearly understood by all his listeners, then pointing an accusing finger at Rabbi Ahab, Jesus said, "Now you tell me, what punishment shall the landowner inflict upon those murderous tenants?"

Rabbi Ahab shifted uneasily from foot to foot, as he realized that this parable was aimed directly at the very heart of Judaism. He was sufficiently wise in religious parables to realize that the landlord was God; the vineyard was the Kingdom of God; and the tenant farmers were the temple rabbis; the dead employees were Jesus' disciples; and the landowner's son was Jesus himself. As Rabbi Ahab could make no adequate reply to Jesus' barbed question, he tried to act unconcerned as though the question had not been addressed to him.

When Jesus saw that Rabbi Ahab would not answer his question, he said, "Since Rabbi Ahab will not answer my question, I will answer it for him. The landowner will completely destroy those miserable tenants and then he will lease his vineyard to Gentiles who will pay him a reasonable rental for it."

Rabbi Ahab shouted, "That shall never be. We Jews have a covenant with God for our admission into heaven."

Jesus answered, "Then why have you rejected the messengers whom God has sent to you? Have you never read the Scriptures wherein it says that 'The very stone which the builders rejected has become the keystone of the arch'? That was the Lord's doing. Does it surprise you? I tell you that the kingdom of God shall be taken away from the Jews and given to those nations that produce the fruits of heaven."

Rabbi Ahab shouted angrily at Jesus, "That shall never happen." The temple rabbis now created a noisy din by shouting, hooting and whistling. When they had quieted down, Jesus said, "Have you never read the prophecy of Isaiah which says:

> " 'Behold my servant, whom I have chosen,
> My beloved, in whom my soul delights.
> I have put my spirit into him,
> He shall not fail, nor be discouraged
> Until truth and justice shall prevail
> And all nations shall be at peace.' "

Rabbi Ahab and his men angrily slunk out of the crowd to a meeting place where they could plot their next move. The following day, Rabbi Ahab sent a messenger to Chief Rabbi Caiaphas informing him that Jesus was now spreading a dangerous and revolutionary doctrine that the Kingdom of God was open to all persons who obeyed the will of God, regardless of whether such persons were Jews or Gentiles. By such unorthodox teaching, Jesus cut himself completely off from all amicable relations with the Jewish temple authorities, and thereafter he could only set foot in Jerusalem at his own peril. Henceforth, the Jewish temple authorities would never cease plotting to kill him.

Chapter 17

Supper with the Lawyers

Chief Rabbi Caiaphas had tried repeatedly to trap Jesus by various tricks but had failed on every occasion. Upon the insistence of his crafty old father-in-law, the Chief Rabbi agreed to try an indirect method of trapping Jesus. For this purpose, he chose a prominent business man of Capernaum named Simon and asked him to invite Jesus to supper and try to embroil him in some controversial subjects. Simon readily agreed.

When Jesus received the invitation to supper from Simon, he accepted it in spite of the fact that he knew that Simon was a close friend of the Chief Rabbi and therefore would be disposed to be unfriendly to him. Among the guests were several members of the Sadducees, a Jewish sect which did not believe in life after death. All these guests were elegantly clothed in their imposing religious garments that were richly embroidered with Biblical mottos.

While Jesus is usually portrayed as a well-groomed, spotlessly clean person, a more truthful picture of him would probably show that he was dressed in soiled clothing. It is difficult to picture him otherwise and be realistic; in a land where water was scarce and soap was unknown, a wanderer such as Jesus, who slept wherever he might at the end of a day's journey, could not possibly have kept himself immaculately clean.

From the description that the evangelists have given us of this supper, it is apparent that Jesus was not a welcome guest and he unquestionably knew it. When he sat down to supper he noticed that all the other guests sat as far apart from him as they possibly could, emphasizing his separateness from all the other guests present at that supper. From where he sat, Jesus could look through the door which Simon had left open in accordance with the custom of Palestine with its semitropical climate. After supper, Simon and his guests reclined in their seats and began a determined interrogation of Jesus.

The town's most prominant lawyer, a Sadducee, said to Jesus, "Master, Moses left us a commandment that if a man dies and leaves his wife childless, his brother must marry the widow and be the father of her children. Some time ago, there were seven brothers and the eldest one married, but died childless. In accordance with the Mosaic law, the second brother married his brother's widow, but he too died childless. In turn, each of the remaining brothers married the widow, but all of them died and left the widow childless, and finally she died. Now in the day of the resurrection that you so often speak about, when all the seven brothers and the widow shall rise again, whose wife shall the woman be, in view of the fact on earth she had been the wife of all seven brothers?"

Jesus slowly answered, "In this world, people marry and are given in marriage, but in the world to come, only those who are worthy of the kingdom of God shall ascend in to it.

Therefore, there is no assurance that husbands and wives will go in pairs from this earth into the kingdom of God. Even if they do, there will be no marriages in heaven because all persons will be similar and equal to the angels of heaven. Your mistaken idea of heaven is caused by the fact that you understand neither the Scriptures nor the power of God."

When Jesus finished speaking an uneasy silence prevailed over the entire room of assembled guests. After this stinging rebuke of the city's leading attorney, the remaining guests who had anticipated an enjoyable evening of belittling Jesus decided to remain discreetly silent. The prolonged silence that followed became embarrassingly painful as the guests shuffled uneasily in their frustration.

During this long pause, a woman known for her loose morals slipped through the open doorway and cast herself at the feet of Jesus. In her hands she carried a beautiful marble vase filled with a precious ointment. She wept so much that her tears wet Jesus' feet which she wiped with the long tresses of her dark hair. After thoroughly drying Jesus' feet, she kissed them and gently anointed them with the precious ointment.

While the woman was washing, kissing and anointing Jesus' feet, Simon stood up and sarcastically said to Jesus, "If you really were a prophet of God, as you claim to be, you would know that this woman is a sinner. Therefore, you would not even allow her to touch you, much less allow her to anoint you with a precious ointment."

Jesus quietly replied, "Simon, I would like to tell you a story."

Simon brusquely asked, "What is it?"

Jesus answered, "There was once a certain money-lender to whom two men owed money. One man owed this money-lender five silver pieces and the other man owed the money-lender five hundred silver pieces. After a period of time, both these debtors became bankrupt; but instead of punishing them for failure to pay their debt, the money-lender very generously decided to cancel the entire debt that both men owed him. Now tell me, Simon, which one of these two debtors would you say should be the most grateful to the money-lender?"

Simon cautiously replied, "Well, I suppose it should be the debtor who owed him the most money."

Jesus replied, "That's exactly right."

Rising from his seat and pointing his long slender finger at the woman at his feet, Jesus said, "Simon, do you see this woman of whom you speak so contemptuously?"

Simon belligerently answered, "Of course, I do."

Jesus continued, "When I entered your house, you did not have the decency to greet me courteously; but this woman has not ceased to kiss my feet since she first came into this room. After I entered your house, you gave me no water with which to bathe my feet; but this woman has bathed my feet with her tears and wiped them dry with the hair of her head. And when I sat down to supper, you did not anoint my head with oil but this woman has even anointed my feet with a precious ointment.

"Therefore, I say to you that this woman who has sinned greatly shall have her many sins forgiven, because her heart is full of repentance; but for you, in whose heart there is little love and no forgiveness, little will be forgiven."

Simon's flushed face displayed his bitter resentment at the lecture as he replied, "Who are you that you forgive this woman's sins so readily?"

Ignoring Simon's angry question, Jesus turned to the woman and said, "Go in peace. Your faith has saved you."

After the woman left Simon, who had begun the supper in gleeful anticipation of belittling Jesus and tricking him into making some compromising statement that would get him in trouble with the authorities, now completely lost his calm composure and shouted at Jesus, "Why do you break all our

Mosaic laws by refusing to observe even our most basic ones regarding cleanliness?"

Jesus scornfully replied, "You hypocrites are all alike. Unwashed hands do not defile a man, neither do food and drink because they are exterior material things which simply pass through a man's stomach and later are discharged as waste matter. There is nothing outside of a man that enters into him that can defile him. What defiles a man are those evil words that come out of his mouth and those sinful deeds that come from his heart. Therefore, a man can only be defiled by that which is within him and not by anything that is outside of him."

Although Simon attempted to interrupt him, Jesus continued, saying, "You religious fanatics place far greater importance upon the observance of rituals than you do upon the observance of God's commandments. You make monetary contributions into your temple treasury in the hope that these contributions will bring you eternal salvation, but you do not bring to God your love and your devotion. Would it not be far better for you if you had omitted the financial contributions to the temple treasury and brought to God your love and devotion?"

Simon glared angrily at Jesus, but he was so upset he could make no adequate reply. When it became apparent that Simon would not answer Jesus' question, Jesus said, "Doesn't your failure to answer my question prove that you are hypocrites, trying to appear outwardly pure and holy, while within, you are evil sinners?"

Another lawyer said to Jesus, "You do us an injustice by condemning us all as a group."

Jesus answered, "You all deserve to be condemned, because you have imposed grievous burdens upon the backs of our people, while you, yourselves, do not lift a single finger to ease those burdens. You have taken away the key of knowledge from the people and prevented them from entering God's storehouse of knowledge, while you yourselves will not enter that storehouse. Therefore, I say to you, 'Woe be unto you!' as it shall be to all religious hypocrites!"

By this time, Simon and all his assembled guests were so incensed at Jesus that they abandoned all diplomacy and tried to goad him into making some incriminating statement that would get him into difficulties with the Great Sanhedrin. However, Jesus, understanding their purpose, skillfully avoided the numerous traps set for him; and so the supper ended in bitter dispute and angry condemnations. After Jesus left, Simon and his distinguished guests plotted to trap Jesus on some future occasion.

Chapter 18

The Good Samaritan and Roman Tribute

It was a cold, cheerless day in Jerusalem and inside the great new temple the temperature was well below the comfort zone, so old Rabbi Annas was covered with a heavy robe as he entered Chief Rabbi Caiaphas's office. Briefly he greeted his gruff son-in-law and said, "Lawyer Ephraim is waiting in the anteroom to advise us on those procedures we must take to put an end to the subversion created by the Galilean."

"What do you have in mind, father?" Caiaphas dubiously asked.

Rabbi Annas replied, "I knew that we would need his services today before I came here, so I sent for him. If you will ring for your servant and have him bring in the lawyer, I am sure that he can be of great service to us."

Chief Rabbi Caiaphas knew from experience that the presence of Lawyer Ephraim in the temple meant that his father-in-law was intent upon carrying out another one of his sly schemes to harass Jesus. These indirect methods were repugnant to the quick-tempered mind of the Chief Rabbi, but he feared the power of his father-in-law as much as he respected that power. So, once again, Chief Rabbi Caiaphas knew that he must comply with the older man's wishes. Wearily, he rang for a messenger and ordered him to bring in Lawyer Ephraim.

Lawyer Ephraim was unquestionably Jerusalem's shrewdest and most highly respected lawyer. He and Rabbi Annas had been close friends for many, many years. After Lawyer Ephraim entered the Chief Rabbi's chambers and seated himself beside the older rabbi, Rabbi Annas said to him, "Lawyer Ephraim, you have no doubt heard of the ungodly pretensions of the Galilean upstart commonly known as Jesus of Nazareth. At one time, my son and I actually had hopes that he would help unite our people and lead them against the Roman invaders. Instead, he preaches a strange doctrine that perverts our people and thus divides them one against the other. He has even dared preach sacrilege and blasphemy right here in our own temple. Yet we dare not arrest him because he has too large a following among our people."

While the rabbi was speaking, Lawyer Ephraim's bland, impassive face nodded imperceptibly. It was a perfect mask for the active, fertile brain working feverishly beneath it. In Lawyer Ephraim's blank face, only his eyes seemed alive. They followed every movement of Rabbi Annas's face with searching intentness.

Rabbi Annas continued, "We need a really intelligent person to trap this Galilean and expose him to our people for the impostor that he is. So far, we have sent only fools to trap this rebel and he has exposed all of them for the idiots they are. We must put a stop to this man before he creates a really serious division among our people that will be beyond healing. Yet we must proceed with caution, while he has such a wide hold upon the minds of so many of our people; otherwise his arrest may create the very schism that we are trying to avoid."

Lawyer Ephraim quietly asked, "What is it that you wish me to do, rabbi?"

Rabbi Annas replied, "We want you to show up this Galilean publicly as a fraud, a law-breaker and an agent of the devil. He has broken enough Mosaic laws to justify his being stoned to death many times over; but his speech is so skillful and beguiling, that he has slipped out of every trap that has been set for him."

Lawyer Ephraim said, "In view of the Galilean's hold upon our people, wouldn't it be better to involve him in a dispute with the Romans?"

Rabbi Annas quickly replied, "By all means, but he never speaks about the Romans."

Lawyer Ephraim cautiously replied, "Maybe we can persuade him into doing so."

Chief Rabbi Caiaphas anxiously asked, "How?"

Lawyer Ephraim took a Roman coin out of his purse and looking at it carefully, replied, "There are ways."

Rabbi Annas looked searchingly at Lawyer Ephraim and said, "We trust in you implicitly, Lawyer Ephraim. If you can goad the Galilean into making some statements against Rome, that would relieve us of the responsibility of whatever punishment might befall him at the hands of the Romans."

Chief Rabbi Caiaphas eagerly added, "It would be the perfect case of killing two birds with one stone and two evil birds at that. It is time that the attention of our people was turned against the Romans instead of against us."

Rabbi Annas quietly added, "My son has stated the matter bluntly, but correctly."

Lawyer Ephraim nodded his head and said, "I understand."

Rabbi Annas said, "Good. I knew that you would think of

something to give this rebel his come-uppance. He has now gone to Bethany where he is preaching daily. Go there and engage him in whatever controversial subjects you think best. But whatever you say, I ask you to be very cautious and use your best judgment in dealing with this very dangerous man."

Rabbi Annas continued, "We cannot send an escort with you from the temple or from King Herod's palace, because these men might be recognized and incite the mob to riot. All we can do now is to send you out alone with our very best wishes."

Lawyer Ephraim quietly answered, "I won't need a military escort. I have learned to get along without one."

Rabbi Annas said, "Good. Now see how quickly you can bring this blasphemous Galilean to his proper punishment."

Lawyer Ephraim bade farewell to the two rabbis and hurried out of the temple, through Jerusalem to the Fountain Gate on the road to Bethany. It didn't take him long to locate Jesus, because he was preaching in the village square to a large and attentive audience. The lawyer melted unobtrusively into the crowd and soon had wormed his way to a place directly in front of Jesus. After listening quietly to Jesus' sermon, Lawyer Ephraim respectfully asked, "Master, which is the most important of all God's commandments?"

Jesus answered, "Thou shalt love the Lord, thy God, with all thy heart and with all thy mind and with all thy soul. This is the first and the most important of all the commandments."

Lawyer Ephraim respectfully said, "You have spoken the very truth, master, because there is only one God and to love Him with all one's heart and with all one's mind and with all one's soul is worth more than all the burnt offerings and gifts that anyone could offer on the altar of the temple."

Jesus looked at Lawyer Ephraim appreciatively and said, "You have spoken the very truth."

Lawyer Ephraim now began baiting his hook as he replied,

"Master, but what about the love of our neighbors, of which you preach so often?"

Jesus answered, "That is the second commandment and it is very similar to the first. This is it, 'Thou shalt love thy neighbor as thyself.' On these two commandments depend all the other commandments of God and all the teachings of the prophets."

With his hook firmly baited, Lawyer Ephraim now slyly asked, "But, master, who *is* my neighbor? Is it the Gentile who lives in the house next to mine? Or, is it the rabbi, who is the leader of my synagogue?"

By this question, Jesus knew that Lawyer Ephraim, who had sounded so friendly at first, was no ordinary innocent bystander, but an agent of the Chief Rabbi. Here was a trick question that, all Jews knew, required an answer that disclosed a person's belief in the basic roots of Judaism. It was a very challenging question.

Unless Jesus answered it very carefully, he was bound to antagonize a great number of persons in his audience. As a Jew, Jesus had been taught to believe that the God of Israel was the only true God and that all other gods were false. According to Jewish belief, the Jews were THE chosen people of the God of Israel and all other people were strangers to Him. Therefore, in using the word "neighbor" as meaning friend, Lawyer Ephraim was using the word in its traditional Mosaic sense; which meant that the only true friend one Jew could have was another Jew.

Consequently, Lawyer Ephraim's question, "Who is my neighbor?" was in effect, "Do you believe in the Mosaic commandment that says the Jews are God's chosen people and that God considers no other people equal to them?"

If Jesus had dared answer this question bluntly and said, "No, God has no chosen people; all good people everywhere of whatever nationality or race they may be are the children of God and therefore, all good people are one another's friends, neighbors and brothers," he probably would have been stoned to death on the spot.

So in order to prepare his audience for the answer he would make to the forked question, Jesus said, "Before I answer your question, let me tell you a story. A certain young Jew was traveling alone from Jerusalem to Jericho. On the way, he fell among thieves, who stole all his possessions, stripped him of all his clothing and beat him unmercifully, until he was more dead than alive. Later that day, another Jew who was traveling along that same road, saw the injured young man, but hurriedly continued on his way without even giving the injured young man a second glance. A short time later, a Jewish rabbi came by that same road and he also saw the injured young Jew, but he, too, only shrugged his shoulders, as he continued hurriedly on his way.

"Later in the afternoon, a Samaritan came by that way and when he saw the bleeding, naked Jew, he dressed his wounds, clothed him, set him on his donkey and took him to the nearest village. There, he took the injured youth to an inn, fed him and put him to bed. The next day, before leaving the inn, the Samaritan paid the inn-keeper for board and room, both for himself and for the young Jew, and then said to the inn-keeper, 'Take good care of that Jewish young man. If he needs something more, give it to him and if it costs more than what I have already paid you, I'll pay you the additional sum when I return.' "

Jesus paused for a moment to let the full impact of his story sink into the minds of his audience. Then, turning to Lawyer Ephraim, he quietly asked, "Now, you tell me which one of these three men who saw the injured young Jew, would you call his neighbor?"

Lawyer Ephraim very quietly replied, "The Samaritan."

Jesus answered, "Exactly. Now you go and behave as that Samaritan did."

Lawyer Ephraim dejectedly answered, "Yes, master."

But Lawyer Ephraim did not leave the audience. He now realized that he was up against a far tougher opponent than he had expected to meet when he first spoke to Jesus. However, he did not intend to return to Jerusalem and admit defeat until he tried to trap Jesus with the trick question he considered the best one that he had prepared. Therefore, he waited patiently until he felt that the crowd had forgotten the sting of Jesus' answer to his first question. At the next available pause in Jesus' sermon, Lawyer Ephraim said, "Master, we all know that what you teach us is the truth, because you only teach us to go in the ways of the Lord. We also know that you are a man of great integrity and accept favors from no man. Therefore, master, I'd like to ask you a question that puzzles a great many of us."

Having listened to one of Lawyer Ephraim's trick questions, Jesus was not impressed by the man's blatant flattery. Therefore, this time, Jesus bluntly replied, "You hypocrite, why do you keep trying to trick me with your forked questions?"

Lawyer Ephraim meekly replied, "I am not trying to trick you, master. I have only the highest respect for you, but several of my friends are puzzled regarding their relationship with the Romans; and they have asked me to ask you this question, 'Do you think it is right for us Jews to pay taxes to the Romans?' "

Here was another tough, tricky, forked question for a Jew to answer. If Jesus answered that the Jews should pay taxes to the Romans, the temple rabbis would accuse Jesus of being a disloyal Jew and a collaborator of the Romans. Whereas, if Jesus answered that the Jews should not pay taxes to the Romans, the temple rabbis would immediately report him to the Romans as a rebel who was inciting the Jews to revolt. Jesus again fully understood the implication of the forked question that Lawyer Ephraim asked him and the danger involved in making a straight-forward answer to the question. So, he cautiously replied, "Show me the money that is used to pay taxes to the Romans."

Lawyer Ephraim reached into his purse, drew out a Roman coin and handed it to Jesus. Jesus looked at the face on the coin and pointing to the image on it, asked, "Whose face is this?"

Lawyer Ephraim replied, "That is the face of the Roman emperor, Caesar."

Jesus turned the coin over and pointing to the inscription on the reverse side asked, "In what language is this coin inscribed?"

Lawyer Ephraim replied, "It is inscribed in Latin, the language of Rome."

Jesus returned the coin to Lawyer Ephraim and then looking squarely into his eyes, coldly said, "Then render unto Caesar the things that are Caesar's, and render unto God the things that are God's."

Matt. 12 (1-21)   Matt. 15 (1-20)
Mark 2 (23-28)   Mark 7 (1-23)
Mark 3 (1-6)   Ex. 20 (12)
Luke 6 (1-12)   Is. 29 (13)

Chapter 19

Defiling the Sabbath

Jesus was so distraught by the constant persecution he received from the temple rabbis that he felt compelled to get away from the land of the Jews for a while and rest in the land of the Gentiles along the quiet shores of the Mediterranean Sea. Upon arrival there, he spent almost two weeks walking along the water's edge feeling the soothing effect of the cool water trickling through his toes. Regretfully he reflected over the turn of events that had put him into open conflict with the Jewish temple authorities.

When Jesus began his missionary work he was a very religious Jew who scrupulously observed all the many Mosaic laws and rabbinical regulations. However, with the passage of time, a number of events occurred which radically changed his attitude toward strict conformance with religious Jewish ritual. His mode of living and his frequent travels from Judaea to Galilee with the non-Jewish nation, Samaria, in between made strict observance with the numerous Mosaic laws extremely difficult and often impossible, because they regulated so many inconsequential details of normal human existence. This failure on his part caused the temple rabbis to severely criticize him and later to persecute him. Jesus reacted to that persecution by rebelling against the Jewish authorities who were in charge of the religion he so dearly loved.

After enjoying his vacation along the shore of the Mediterranean, Jesus and his disciples returned to Galilee to continue with their work of preaching the gospel of God. In preparation for their return journey they took no food with them, expecting that as they traveled, they would find friends along the way who would feed and shelter them. This had always been their experience in the past on their many journeys across Galilee, and they had no reason to believe that they could not continue to rely upon the friendship and the cooperation of their people. Much to their dismay they learned when they entered Galilee that many persons who were formerly very friendly toward them now shut their doors against them. As a result they wandered further and further away from the road in search of food so their return to Capernaum was much longer and much more tiring than had been their journey from Galilee to Phoenicia.

The closer Jesus and his disciples came to Capernaum, the more difficult it became for them to obtain any food and on the last day of their week-long journey, they had nothing to eat at all. About five miles from Capernaum, they came to a wheat field and in their famished condition, they hurried into it to eat the dry kernels. It was a slow and unsatisfactory method of obtaining nourishment, because the dry kernels and the dust from the chaff parched their throats; but they were so hungry they even ate some of the chaff with the kernels of wheat.

As Jesus rubbed the head of a stem of wheat between his hands and blew away the chaff, he reflected sadly that this day was the Sabbath and that he and his disciples had not even had one good meal in three days. Even now, hungry as they all were, none of them could eat more than a handful of the dry kernels of wheat, because the more they ate, the drier and the thirstier they became.

Upon entering the wheat field, Jesus and his disciples were seen by a farmer who hurried into town and reported their arrival to Rabbi Ahab. He immediately hurried to the wheat field and when he saw Jesus, he angrily said to him, "Why do you and your disciples break our Mosaic law by gathering wheat on this Sabbath day?"

Jesus bluntly answered, "Do you know what David did when he was hungry on the Sabbath? He went into the synagogue and took and ate the holy bread, and not only did he eat that holy bread himself, but he also gave some of that bread to his men. Now you know it is not lawful for anyone to eat holy bread, except the rabbis, but David ate the holy bread and he ate it on the Sabbath day."

The rabbi shouted back, "That does not excuse you for wantonly breaking all the cherished traditions of our forefathers that distinguish us Jews from the Gentiles."

Jesus replied, "Then tell me, if you temple rabbis are so concerned with the observance of the Mosaic laws, why is it that you rabbis continually break the fifth commandment of God, which states, 'Honor thy father and thy mother'? The word, 'honor' is not just an empty word signifying conformance to ritualistic conventions. It means supporting one's parents; but you rabbis, for your own profit, have told the people they no longer need support their parents, if they will

give you the money they formerly gave their parents. You
hypocrites! Isaiah truly prophesied about you when he said,

> " 'These people honor me with their lips,
> But their hearts are far from me.
> In vain, do they worship me,
> Because their hearts are full of evil.' "

The rabbi glared angrily at Jesus, but made no reply as he
knew that Jesus had correctly quoted the scriptures. Jesus
then continued, "The Sabbath was made for man and not
man for the Sabbath. Therefore, the Son of Man is Lord of
the Sabbath."

This amazing statement so confounded the rabbi that he
remained speechless as Jesus and his disciples continued on
their way to Capernaum. The rabbi then hurried to the home
of the Chief Rabbi named Janum and quickly told him of all
the events that had transpired in the wheat field. Rabbi
Janum listened quietly and thoughtfully to the rabbi's account of his meeting with Jesus. Stroking his long black
beard, Rabbi Janum slowly replied, "I have lived in Capernaum for more than twenty years, almost since the first day
that I was consecrated as a rabbi. I know the families of the
disciples of this Jesus of Nazareth very well. They all come
from good Jewish families, but they are a simple people and
easily carried away by religious fanatics. Many of these men
were disciples of John the Baptist before they became disciples of this Jesus of Nazareth. I tell you these things because I
want to impress upon you the fact that whatever action we
take must be taken cautiously and deliberately, because these
men have a large popular following in this village."

Rabbi Ahab answered, "Rabbi, I already know all of these
things that you tell me about this Galilean, but it does not
alter the fact that he is perverting our people. I have just told
you how he openly broke the Sabbath today and defied me in

the presence of a large crowd. It is fine to say we must proceed with caution, but when do we act to stop this law-
breaker?"

Rabbi Janum replied, "I know the truth of what you say,
but remember the old saying which states that before you kill
a serpent with a long tail, you must first cut off the tail, because its power is concentrated in that tail."

Rabbi Ahab impatiently said, "Please come to the point,
rabbi; what do you have in mind?"

Rabbi Janum replied, "I know this man far better than
does our Chief Rabbi in Jerusalem who has done nothing to
date toward curbing this Jesus of Nazareth except to increase
his popularity with our people. If he continues along his present path, he will make a martyr out of the Galilean, just as
King Herod Antipas made a martyr out of John the Baptist."

With a considerable air of irritation, Rabbi Ahab replied,
"All right, all right, come to the point. What is your solution
to the problem?"

Apparently still deeply immersed in thought, Rabbi Janum
slowly replied, "This coming Sabbath the Galilean will surely
be preaching in the synagogue in his attempt to sway as many
persons as possible to become his followers. Therefore, when
you come to the synagogue on the Sabbath, bring with you
some helpless cripple. Tell him that Jesus of Nazareth will be
there curing all those who come to him. In the meantime I'll
be in the synagogue waiting for you."

As the full meaning of Rabbi Janum's words became clear
to Rabbi Ahab, his face took on a cunning smile and he
looked at Rabbi Janum appreciatively for the first time. Smiling slyly, he answered, "I promise you that on the Sabbath I
will be at the synagogue with just the man you want."

The following week Jesus again went to the synagogue to
pray and preach. By this time the argument between Jesus
and Rabbi Ahab had been told and re-told so many times
that to all the townspeople, it was a well-known tale from

which not a single word, gesture, or intonation of the voice of either Jesus or Rabbi Ahab had been omitted. Therefore, on this particular day, the synagogue was full to over-flowing as the people expected another clash between Jesus and the rabbi. They were not to be disappointed. To add to the drama of the day, the rabbi arrived early and occupied a seat in the front of the rostrum that Jesus would use if he were going to preach.

When Jesus walked up to the rostrum, he could feel the eyes of the entire congregation centered upon him, particularly those of Rabbi Ahab. Before he could begin his sermon, a man with a withered hand walked up to him and said in a voice filled with deep emotion, "Master, please cure me. All my life I have begged and hungered because I could not do a man's work, and I want to work the way other men do. Please cure me, master."

Before Jesus could answer, Rabbi Ahab jumped to his feet and shouted, "Tell us, Jesus of Nazareth, is it lawful to heal on the Sabbath?"

Looking directly into the hate-filled eyes of the temple rabbi, Jesus said, "Before I answer you, tell me, is it better to do good or to do evil on the Sabbath?"

Rabbi Ahab angrily answered, "I asked you a question first. Answer my question: Is it lawful to heal on the Sabbath?"

"I will answer your question," Jesus replied, "but before I do, let me ask this congregation a question." Then turning toward the audience Jesus asked, "Which of you who own a sheep that accidentally fell into a well on the Sabbath would refuse to reach into that well and rescue that sheep? And if you would save the life of one of your sheep on the Sabbath, would you let a man drown who had fallen into that well because it was the Sabbath? Is not the life of a man far more important than the life of a sheep?"

As no one answered, Jesus turned to the rabbi and said,

"Don't you rabbis break the Sabbath by the work that you do on that day? And don't the Scriptures hold you blameless for that work? Now, rabbi, I will answer your question. Yes, it is lawful to heal on the Sabbath!"

Turning to the crippled man, Jesus defiantly said, "Come here! Stretch forth your hand!"

As soon as the man stretched forth his hand, Jesus touched it and it was immediately restored to its full growth and strength.

Ahab angrily shouted, "Law-breaker! Rebel! Blasphemer!"

Determinedly, Jesus replied, "Before you stands the Son of Man, who is greater than any rabbi you have in your great new temple in Jerusalem!"

In rage and frustration, the rabbi hissed angrily and rushed out of the synagogue. The hot-headed agents of Chief Rabbi Caiaphas gathered around him and urged him to follow Jesus and stone him to death. But from many members of the congregation came muttered voices of defiance. Soon the rabbi and his agents found themselves surrounded by a group of angry townspeople, who gave them no room to move. Rabbi Ahab decided that it would be far more prudent to bide his time and wait for a more opportune occasion to kill Jesus.

Twice recently, Jesus had openly defied the authority of the Chief Rabbi of Jerusalem. Knowing the danger that he faced, Jesus decided that it was best to go into hiding and keep out of the way of Chief Rabbi Caiaphas' agents. So once again, Jesus disappeared from public view and went into one of his favorite hiding places in the wilderness.

Matt. 12 (38-45)   Mark 8 (10-21)   Luke 11 (29-30)
Matt. 16 (1-12)   Mark 10 (2-12)   Luke 12 (1-12)
Matt. 19 (1-12)   Luke 12 (54-57)

Chapter 20

Divorce

After being publicly rebuked by Jesus in Capernaum, Rabbi Ahab returned to Jerusalem to make a full personal report to Rabbi Annas and Chief Rabbi Caiaphas of his encounter with Jesus. The Chief Rabbi was at the home of his father-in-law, Rabbi Annas, when Rabbi Ahab arrived. Both Rabbi Annas and the Chief Rabbi listened attentively to Rabbi Ahab's report of Jesus' activities in Capernaum. The reaction of the two older rabbis to their agent's report was diametrically opposite. Old Rabbi Annas' face remained calm and placid, and as immovable as a mask; while the Chief Rabbi's face glowered and reddened and his beard twitched nervously as he strained to control his inner desire for immediate action.

As soon as Rabbi Ahab had stopped speaking, the Chief Rabbi ordered him to take a detachment of men from the temple guard, proceed to Capernaum and kill Jesus. Only the intervention of his calm father-in-law persuaded the younger rabbi to cancel this order. Patiently and quietly Rabbi Annas spoke to his stubborn son-in-law until the Chief Rabbi had quieted down to the point where the older rabbi could reason with him.

Then Rabbi Annas spoke in the typically measured tones he used when he was concerned regarding matters of grave importance to Judaism's survival, saying, "Son, please listen patiently to me, your old father, who loves you as his own son. Always remember that fruit must not be eaten before it is ripened; otherwise, when it is eaten it will create internal bodily discomfort. The fruit of which this rebel Galilean is made, is rapidly nearing the plucking stage. Each time this rebel speaks, he becomes bolder. Soon the time will come when this fruit will be fully ripened and it will fall at our feet like an over-ripened plum."

Chief Rabbi Caiaphas' dark face was flushed with anger and his black eyes were so blood-shot that they appeared red rather then black. His breathing was heavy and labored as though he had been through an exhausting physical effort. Obviously, only the tremendous respect he had for his aged father-in-law kept him under control.

Slowly, he turned his face toward Rabbi Annas and said in an obviously restrained voice, "Father, these many months, I have faithfully followed your advice. Yet with each passing day this rebel becomes bolder and bolder. First, he publicly broke our ancient traditions, then he publicly ridiculed our rabbinical regulations. Next, he broke our Mosaic laws; then he wrote his own set of religious laws; and now, he likens himself to God! How much more abuse must we take from this Galilean before we take some positive action against him?"

Rabbi Annas gently placed his hand upon his son-in-law's head as he replied in a very low voice, "I know, my son, I know. I am as anxious to silence this son of the devil as you are. You may not think so, but maybe I am even more anxious than you to put an end to this rebellious blasphemer. I have devoted my entire life to the cause of Judaism and all my fathers before me have done the same. Now, I am old and I have no son of my own to carry on with my work and so I place my entire trust in you to protect our faith. We must not fail; and we must be patient, because the time has not yet come when we can crush this new enemy of our nation. Be patient, my son; be patient, just a little while longer. The time will soon be here when we can finally crush this rebel."

Chief Rabbi Caiaphas said with an air of exaggerated resignation, "Very well, father. What shall we do, then?"

Rabbi Annas softly replied, "Let us instruct Rabbi Ahab to return to Capernaum immediately and continue to engage the Galilean in controversial subjects. The Galilean has already antagonized many of our people and many of them have stopped following him. That means that our present policy is producing results."

Chief Rabbi Caiaphas heaved a deep sigh and said, "Yes, father, yes, father. Only let it be soon; let not the day of vengeance be delayed too long, dear God, or else I shall kill this Galilean myself."

Rabbi Annas stroked his son-in-law's head sympathetically but made no reply. Slowly Rabbi Caiaphas rose, bade his father-in-law and Rabbi Ahab good-by and left the house. The two older rabbis remained in the study of Rabbi Annas for hours discussing every detail of the various ways of trapping Jesus. It was almost midnight before Rabbi Ahab said goodnight and left.

The following morning Rabbi Ahab left for Capernaum where he consulted with the local rabbi regarding the action they would take against Jesus. As they anticipated, on the following Sabbath Jesus walked up to the podium of the synagogue to address the congregation. But, before he could start his sermon, a voice from a darkened corner of the building interrupted saying, "Is it lawful for a man to divorce his wife for any reason?"

Jesus had spoken on this subject on several previous occasions, and he knew that divorce was the cherished privilege of well-to-do Jewish husbands, who justified their selection of new young wives in their old age by Mosaic regulations. Jesus also knew that Jewish women and orthodox Jewish men were firmly opposed to divorce, particularly in those cases where the divorces were obtained for purely sexual reasons. Therefore, he knew that whatever reply he made to the question of divorce, was sure to antagonize some persons in the congregation.

Understanding the forked nature of the question, Jesus decided to answer it indirectly. So he replied, "Haven't you read in the Scriptures that when God made this world, he also made all the creatures in it male and female? And for this reason, a man must leave his father and his mother and be joined to his wife. That man and that woman, who are joined in matrimony, then become one flesh. Therefore, they are no longer two separate individuals, but one body. And I say to you, what God has joined together, let no man put asunder."

Rabbi Ahab, who had asked this question from the shadow of the synagogue, now walked out to the center of the building and said, "Then tell us, why did Moses allow a man to divorce his wife by simply writing her a bill of divorce?"

Jesus answered, "Moses allowed himself to be persuaded that divorce was permissible only because some evil-hearted persons such as you are demanded it. But in the beginning of the world, divorces were not allowed. Therefore, I say to you that whoever divorces his wife for any cause, except adultery, and then marries again, commits adultery himself. And he who marries a divorced woman also commits adultery."

A rich merchant of Galilee stood up and said to Jesus, "A commandment such as yours is too harsh to bear. When a man gets old and his wife no longer attracts him, he needs a fresh young face in his household to brighten him up. If all men were to be bound by your commandment, it would be better if we didn't marry at all."

Jesus answered, "It is not everybody who can live up to God's commandments. There are some who are incapable of marriage from birth, or because of some physical reason, or perhaps because of some mental reservations. However, I do say this, that for those who are capable of accepting this commandment, there will be great happiness in lifetime marriage. Therefore, to those persons, I say, accept this commandment."

When Rabbi Ahab saw that he was making no progress with his argument on divorce, he shifted his attack and said, "You constantly quote God to use as your source of authority, but you have never given us any proof that you have the right to speak with the authority of God. In addition, you frequently speak of the coming of Judgment Day, but you make no specific prediction when that day will come. Give us some definite proof that you are a prophet of God and give us a clear statement of the date when the Day of Judgment shall come."

Jesus looked critically at Rabbi Ahab and said, "In the evening, if the sky is red, you say, 'Tomorrow, we will have fair weather,' while in the morning, if there are clouds in the west, you say, 'Today, we shall have rain.'

"Tell me, why is it that you hypocrites can read the formations of the clouds in the sky so well and yet you cannot understand the commandments of God? You are one of those sinners who ask God's messengers to prove their identity to you. And yet, because of your sinfulness, you also ask that you be warned of the coming of Judgment Day in the hope that you may come to God with a last-minute plea of repentance for your sins. But I say to you that no proof of the identity of God's messengers will be given to you and neither will you receive any warning of the coming of Judgment Day."

In obvious irritation, Rabbi Ahab abruptly left the synagogue and Jesus and his disciples left shortly afterward and headed for the lake shore, where their boat was anchored. During the trip across the lake, no one spoke, as it was apparent to the disciples that Jesus was in a depressed mood.

Engrossed as Jesus was in the spiritual problems of the world, it never occurred to him that his disciples had left Capernaum so hastily that they had taken no food with them for their journey into the foreign land of Jordan. Once ashore, Jesus turned to his disciples and said, "Beware of the food of the self-righteous Jews."

The disciples misunderstood his meaning and thought that Jesus was giving them a subtle rebuke, because they had forgotten to take any food with them from Galilee into Jordan. When Jesus heard their mumbling, he turned to Peter and asked, "What is everyone mumbling about?"

Peter answered, "Judas and several of the disciples said that you were scolding them because we forgot to bring some food with us."

Impatiently Jesus replied, "I was not speaking of food to eat when I spoke of the food of the Pharisees. I was referring to their hypocritical actions."

"Oh," Peter apologetically answered.

Chapter 21

Jesus Loses Many of His Disciples

It is remarkable that from the beginning of Jesus' missionary work to the date of his execution about thirty months later his initial twelve disciples stayed with him throughout his entire missionary life, uncomplainingly accepting the hardships and the abuse heaped upon them by the temple rabbis, with one single exception. However, other disciples did join the initial twelve disciples, but they only followed Jesus intermittently. At one time there might have been as many as seventy disciples and the following is the story of the desertion of these temporary disciples when the opposition from the temple rabbis became severe.

Several months prior to Jesus' crucifixion he was preaching along the northwestern shore of Lake Tiberias during the time that his life was constantly in danger; and yet he felt that the amount of the progress he had made among the people was far short of his missionary goal. He realized that while he was faced with mortal enemies in the pay of Chief Rabbi

Caiaphas, there were hidden enemies which were far more dangerous than his physical ones. These enemies are the human frailties of mankind—indifference, selfishness and ignorance.

After he and his disciples arrived at Tiberias, Jesus preached constantly in all the communities near the lake shore. During these sermons, he noted a marked lack of attention from his audience and observed that some persons simply crowded around the baskets of food that his disciples distributed to the expectant public.

Deeply irritated with this lack of attention, Jesus cut short his series of sermons and re-crossed Lake Tiberias and returned to Capernaum, where he felt at ease to rest and pray. Following his usual custom, he went to the synagogue to pray and preach. However, instead of finding the usual friendly reception in his adopted community, he was approached by several men led by a burly agent of Chief Rabbi Caiaphas, named Akkub.

Quickly recognizing Akkub as one of those persons who had gorged himself with the disciples' food at Tiberias, Jesus viewed him skeptically. Akkub assumed an air of humble friendliness as he said, "Master, we didn't see you leave Tiberias. If we had, we would have arrived here much sooner. When did you get here?"

As Jesus realized that Akkub's superficial friendliness concealed animosity, he bluntly replied, "Never mind asking when or how I got here. You did not follow me here because you are interested in the work that I am doing. You only followed me here because you want to fill your belly with the food we distribute at our meetings. Don't work so hard to obtain food that quickly decays; instead, seek food that gives mankind everlasting life."

Akkub answered, "What must I do to obtain this food of everlasting life?"

"Do the work of God," Jesus answered.

"And what is the work of God?" asked Akkub.

Jesus answered, "The work of God is to understand his message and to believe in him whom God has sent to you with that message."

Akkub looked slyly at Jesus and with a cunning smile asked, "Can you prove to us that you really have been sent to us by God so that we can safely put our trust in you? For example, can you perform some miracle for us such as Moses performed for our forefathers when he gave them heavenly bread to eat?"

Jesus answered, "It was not Moses who gave your fathers that bread; but it was my Father who gave your fathers that bread. What is more, that bread was not bread from heaven, but bread from this earth. Besides, those who ate that bread are now all dead; whereas, the bread from heaven is God's bread, which gives mankind everlasting life."

Akkub replied, "Oh, master, give us some of this wonderful heavenly bread so that we may all have everlasting life."

Jesus said, "I am the bread of life that has come down to you from heaven, and the bread that I give is my own flesh."

Akkub sarcastically answered, "How can you give us your own flesh to eat?"

Jesus replied, "Truly, I say to you that unless you do eat of my flesh and drink of my blood, you will have no life in you. Whoever eats of my flesh and drinks of my blood will have everlasting life; and he who does so shall dwell in me and I in him. On Judgment Day I will raise those persons up into heaven."

Akkub clapped his hands over his ears and screwed up his face into a frightful frown to indicate his repugnance and disbelief in Jesus's statement. Walking disgustedly away, he turned to the crowd and said, "This fellow is mad. He says that he came down to us from heaven. If that is so, why is it that his parents are those common people, Joseph and Mary, who live in Nazareth?"

From the crowd there came a rumble of agreement to Akkub's accusation. Realizing the opposition that was apparent in the public's attitude toward him, Jesus quietly said, "Don't grumble among yourselves, but read the Scriptures. It is written there that every one shall be taught about God and everyone, therefore, who has learned about God shall come to me. Truthfully, I say to you that he who believes in me shall have everlasting life."

From among the crowd came angry mutterings of dissent and disapproval. By this time, Akkub had reached the door where he turned and shouted back, "Don't pay any attention to that crazy blasphemer, or you too will suffer the same punishment from God that he does."

Slowly the entire congregation, including many of Jesus's disillusioned followers, filed out of the synagogue, leaving behind only Jesus and his twelve closest disciples. After the departure of the large crowd, Jesus and his twelve disciples were a pathetically small and disconsolate group in an otherwise empty temple. As Jesus watched the last person in the crowd leave the synagogue, he could hear his twelve disciples uneasily arguing among themselves. Turning to them he asked, "Have I also offended you? Will you, my closest disciples, also desert me?"

After a long silent pause, Peter slowly said, "Lord, to whom shall we turn? You represent everything in this world to which we can cling. For us, you are the way of eternal life. We are sure that you are the Messiah and the Son of the Living God and therefore, we shall always remain your loyal disciples."

Jesus very quietly replied, "Thank you, Peter."

The die was now cast. Up until this time, Jesus had referred to himself as God's messenger in public only vaguely, generally saying he was the Son of Man. Henceforth, he would refer to himself as the Son of God and these words would later be flung back at him and constitute his death warrant. If

Jesus had said that the power of the Holy Spirit had filled him with the spirit of any one of the former great Jewish prophets, most Jews would probably have accepted his announcement as an obvious statement of fact and the temple rabbis would have had a very difficult time in arousing the public against him.

But when Jesus said that he was the Messiah, the Son of God, he likened himself to God and made himself equal to Him. To the orthodox Jew, Jesus' claim to divinity constituted extreme blasphemy and as such it could neither be accepted, nor tolerated. Thereafter, the final fate of Jesus was as foreordained and implacable as the hand of time. The only questions now remaining regarding his death are the time, the place and the method of his execution. Jesus, himself, accepts the inevitability of his own death, and even the place—Jerusalem—with the resignation of a fatalist.

Chapter 22

The Pool of Bethesda

In the spring of the year about 30 A.D. when Jesus was thirty-four years old, he and his disciples arrived in Bethany to visit Lazarus and his sisters about a week before the beginning of the seven or eight day festival of the Passover (Pesach). This holiday celebrates the most important event in the history of Judaism because it commemorates the date when the Jews were freed from their bondage to the Egyptians. In addition, this holiday commemorates the passing over of the homes of the Jews by the angel of death, while killing the first-born males of the Egyptians, and thus this holiday was named the Pass-over. To remind the Jews celebrating this holiday of the extreme hardships suffered by their ancestors during this journey, all religious Jews have been required to eat only unleavened bread during this week-long holiday.

Jesus and his disciples entered Jerusalem through the Lion's Gate and then turned north toward the Pool of Bethesda. This pool was known to all Jews because of the numerous miraculous cures that had taken place there. According to an oft-repeated legend, an angel of the Lord had flown over the pool many years ago and rippled the surface of the water with the movement of his wings. A short time later, a crippled person entered the pool and was immediately cured of his infirmity. Thereafter, whenever the wind rippled the surface of the water, the first person who entered the pool was immediately cured of whatever ailment he might have.

Around this pool there were a series of columns supporting five arches, which provided refreshingly cool shade from the hot tropical sun. Ever since that first day when the angel of the Lord had flown across the pool of Bethesda, thousands of sick and crippled persons had huddled under the shade of these arches anxiously watching the surface of the pool for the first sign of movement of the water, hoping that they might be the first person to enter the pool after its surface was rippled and thus be cured of their particular infirmity. Some persons scanned the sky like seasoned sailors hoping to anticipate the coming of a slight breeze from the formation of the clouds and the coloring of the sky. Naturally, at the first indication of a breeze, there was a mad rush by everyone to get into the pool first—everyone that is, except a man named Heber.

Heber was the most pathetic person lying in the shade of the arches, because he was paralyzed from his hips to his toes and therefore could only watch helplessly whenever the wind rippled the waters of the pool and watch all the persons around him scramble madly to be first to enter the pool.

While Jesus and his disciples were walking past this pool, a light breeze rippled its surface and they saw the mad rush of sick and crippled persons to get into the pool first, with the exception of Heber, who remained lying on his cot. Jesus walked over to him and asked, "Why didn't you rush to the pool?"

"I can't," the man replied. "I'm paralyzed from my hips to my toes."

"Then why do you remain here?" asked Jesus.

"I enjoying seeing others cured. It makes me feel better," Heber replied.

"How long have you lain here?" asked Jesus.

"I've been here thirty-eight years. When I first came, I tried repeatedly to get into the pool first by lying in the sun right at the water's edge, hour after hour. And although I prayed hard that the water would stir while I lay there, it never did. I got so badly burnt by the sun so many times that I finally decided I would never try it again. Now I am reconciled to the will of God, so I just lie here and rejoice that others can get into the pool and be cured."

Jesus asked, "Wouldn't you like to be cured?"

Turning his sorrowful tearful eyes up to Jesus, he replied, "Of course I would; but there is no hope for me."

"What is your name?" Jesus asked.

"Heber," the man replied.

Jesus answered, "Heber, the Lord has heard your prayers and now he has answered them. Rise up. Take up your cot and walk home."

Finding himself immediately cured, Heber rose, took up his cot and thanked Jesus profusely for his miraculous cure. Jesus said to him, "Just one thing, Heber, I must ask you not to tell any of the rabbis or any of the temple soldiers that I cured you."

Heber bowed low and gratefully said, "Yes, master, yes, master. I promise you that I will not tell anyone that you cured me." Then he hurried down the street toward his home with his cot on his back, anxious to see and rejoice with his family and friends his miraculous cure. As he was approaching home, he was stopped by two temple guards who gruffly asked him, "Why do you break the Sabbath by carrying your cot?"

He replied, "The man who cured me said, 'Take up your cot and walk home,' and that is what I am doing."

The guards asked him "Who was it that told you to take up your cot and walk home?"

Heber answered, "I don't know. He was a stranger that I never saw before. He probably was just a visiting pilgrim. After he cured me, he disappeared into the crowd."

One of the guards turned to the other and said, "It sounds to me like the doings of that rebel Galilean. Let's take this fellow to the guard house; the captain may want to question him."

The guards pushed Heber between them and took him to the temple guard house where they informed Captain Shama of their meeting with him. Captain Shama repeatedly questioned Heber about the whereabouts of the man that cured him, but could get no specific information out of him.

In anger and frustration, Captain Shama struck Heber several stinging blows across the face and shouted, "Now get out and search everywhere for the person who cured you. I will have one of my men following you wherever you go and if you try to give him the slip, I'll find you and before I'm through with you, you'll be a cripple again. Only this time no miracle man will ever be able to put your crooked bones back together again."

Poor, frightened Heber meekly replied, "Yes, sir; yes, sir."

Heber left the temple grounds with a guard following closely behind him as he started out on his search for Jesus. Although he searched everywhere through the streets of Jerusalem, he could not find Jesus. Tired and weary, he slowly retraced his steps toward the guard house to tell Captain Shama that Jesus was nowhere to be found. However, instead of going directly to the guardhouse, he first went into the temple to rest and pray that Captain Shama would not beat him again.

As soon as Heber's eyes grew accustomed to the semi-darkness of the temple, he turned and was startled to see that he was looking directly into the bright, shining eyes of Jesus. This unexpected meeting with Jesus so unnerved him that he stammered, "Er—er—greetings, master."

Noting his guilty behavior, Jesus asked, "Why are you here?"

Heber lamely replied, "I have come to pray, master, that I may be forgiven of my sins."

Jesus answered, "Your sins have already been forgiven. You are now cured. Go and sin no more, lest some worse evil befall you."

Out of the corner of his eye, Heber could see the temple guard watching his every movement and carefully listening to his conversation with Jesus. So he mumbled, "Yes, master; yes, master."

As he got up, Heber could feel his heart thumping fearfully. He knew he was caught in an evil trap. Either he would be forced to betray Jesus; or else he would get unmercifully beaten again by the temple guards. When he arose and left, the temple guard followed closely behind him and led him into the guard house. Captain Shama asked him, "Did you find the Galilean?"

Heber meekly replied, "N-n-no, Captain."

The words were scarcely out of his mouth before the temple guard struck him a resounding blow across the face, causing the blood to flow freely from his nose and mouth. The guard shouted at him, "Then who was that man you spoke to in the temple?"

Before Heber could answer, the guard took Heber's wrist and gave it a quick twist that brought his arm up sharply behind his back. Heber's face was wreathed in anguish as the guard twisted his arm further and further. Captain Shama put his face next to Heber's and snarled, "Now tell us the truth or we'll twist that skinny arm of yours right out of its socket."

The guard twisted his arm again, and Heber felt certain that he would faint before he could utter another word. With his face wreathed in pain, Heber slowly said, "It was Jesus of Nazareth that I met in the temple. It was he who cured me."

Captain Shama asked, "How is he dressed?"

Heber answered, "He is dressed like a shepherd."

Turning to the guard, the captain said, "Let him go. Come into the temple with me and point out the man he spoke to."

Inside the temple, the two men walked past the congregation, until they heard the voice of Jesus preaching to an attentive audience in the south wing. Motioning toward Jesus, the guard said, "There he is."

As soon as Jesus paused momentarily, the captain said, "We found a man a few minutes ago carrying a cot who says that you told him to take it up and walk. By what right do you urge our people to break this holy day? And by what right do you break this holy day yourself by working on the Sabbath?"

Jesus answered, "My Father works on holy days and if it is proper for him to work on those days, it is also proper for me to do so."

Suspiciously, the captain asked, "Who is your father?"

Jesus quietly answered, "God is my Father."

Captain Shama angrily replied, "How dare you relate yourself to God?"

Jesus answered, "Because I am the Son of God."

Not daring to continue this controversy publicly, before a crowd obviously sympathetic to Jesus, Captain Shama compressed his lips and angrily strode out of the temple.

Chapter 23

Hanukkah

Hanukkah is a Jewish semi-holiday beginning at sundown on the 25th day of the Hebrew month of Kislev and lasting eight days. It usually comes in December and is called the Feast of Dedication because it commemorates the rededication of the Jewish temple after it was defiled by the King of Syria, who captured Jerusalem during a war between Syria and Judaea. In 165 B.C. the Jewish general, Judah Maccabee recaptured Jerusalem and drove the Syrians out of Judaea. According to legend, when the Jews recaptured their temple, there was only sufficient undefiled oil to light the Holy Lamp for one day. However, after the Holy Lamp was lit, it remained lighted for eight days. Thereafter the distinguishing characteristic of the Feast of Hanukkah became the lighting of one additional candle at sundown on an eight-branched candelabra on each day of the holiday, until all eight candles were lit. For this reason the Feast of Hanukkah is also called the Festival of Lights.

Chief Rabbi Caiaphas had instructed his people that Jesus

was the enemy of Judaea and therefore no Jew should give him any aid upon penalty of being excommunicated from the temple. As a result, the hostility of the people became so great that Jesus and his disciples separated and went to their respective homes. However, Jesus decided to go on to Capernaum and stay with Peter, rather than risk returning to his own home in Nazareth where only a cold reception awaited him.

Wherever he went in Judaea or Galilee, Jesus could feel the bitter hostility of Chief Rabbi Caiaphas. Therefore, while staying at Peter's home, he remained quietly out of sight in order that Peter and his family might avoid being excommunicated by the Chief Rabbi. The combination of inactivity and hiding made time pass very slowly; however, the months did roll by and the time finally came in the latter part of December when Hanukkah would be celebrated.

Tradition and rabbinical regulations required all Jews to celebrate the Feast of Hanukkah in Jerusalem, so Jesus, Peter and Andrew left Capernaum for Jerusalem well in advance of the beginning of the festival. Enroute, they were joined by the remaining twelve disciples.

As Jesus and his disciples arrived at the outskirts of Jerusalem prior to the beginning of the festival, they took the precaution of remaining in hiding in order to avoid being arrested. The location they chose for their hiding place was just outside the city wall, in the garden of Gethsemane on the Mount of Olives. This garden was an ideal hiding place, because they could easily see anyone approaching the garden without being seen themselves. In addition, it had the very important advantage of being within easy walking distance to Jerusalem.

On the first Sabbath day of the Hanukkah festival, Jesus and his disciples boldly set out for Jerusalem, secure in their belief that Jesus was safe from arrest, because the Mosaic laws forbid practically all human activity during the Jewish

Holy Days. On their way to the temple, Jesus and his disciples passed through a very poor section of Jerusalem where they met a blind beggar named Jared.

When Jared heard Jesus and his disciples approaching, he advanced toward them with his cane in one hand beating a sharp tattoo against the cobbled stones of the street, and with a cup in his other hand, seeking coins from passers-by. As he walked forward, Jared piteously begged, "Please, kind sirs, give help to the blind."

Jesus said, "We have no money to give to you. We, ourselves, are just poor missionaries of God, but tell me, would you like to be cured of your blindness?"

Jared vehemently replied, "Of course I would, but that is impossible. I have been blind since birth. Say, who are you?"

Jesus answered, "I am Jesus of Nazareth."

Jared quickly fell to his knees, stretched out both his arms toward Jesus and sobbingly said, "Blessed master, please cure me."

Jesus knelt down, spat on the ground, made a mud pack of clay and applied it to Jared's eyes and said to him, "Now go and wash out this clay mud pack from your eyes in the pool of Siloam."

As soon as Jared was beyond the point of hearing, Andrew turned to Jesus and said, "Master, who was it that sinned that caused this man to become blind? Was it he that sinned, or was it his parents?"

Jesus replied, "Neither. Certainly this man, who was born blind, could not have sinned prior to his birth. Neither are his parents to blame for a fact of life which was beyond their control. The truth is that there are many events that occur in this world which are beyond the understanding of mankind. God performs his work in many ways which are too mysterious for men to understand."

When Jared arrived at the pool of Siloam, he hurriedly washed out the clay mud pack from his eyes and suddenly found that he could see. During the days that followed, Jared's neighbors scrutinized him closely, debating whether or not he was the blind beggar whom they had known from birth. Only a few days previously, Jared had been blind and known throughout the neighborhood by the peculiar tip-tip-tip sound of his gnarled cane striking against the cobbled stones as he walked down the street. Now he walked about as freely as any normal person. It was beyond the understanding of Jared's simple, puzzled neighbors and one of them said, "Isn't this man, Jared, the beggar who was born blind?"

Some one else replied, "He certainly looks like Jared, but it cannot be he; because I saw him the day he was born and I know that he was born blind and that he has been blind ever since."

Finally one curious neighbor went up to Jared and asked, "Are you Jared, the one who was born blind?"

Jared answered, "Of course I am."

The inquisitive neighbor replied, "Then how is it that you can see?"

Jared answered, "That man who is called Jesus of Nazareth, made a mud pack of clay, applied it to my eyes and then said to me, 'Go to the pool of Siloam and wash out this mud pack from your eyes.' I did exactly what he told me to do and after I washed out the clay mud pack, I found that I could see. That is all there is to it."

The inquisitive neighbor said, "Where is this man who restored your sight?"

Jared replied, "I don't know."

All of this sounded very suspicious to Jared's skeptical neighbors, particularly in view of the repeated warnings they had received from their rabbi that they must have nothing to do with Jesus or anyone associated with him. So, Jared's neighbors debated and argued the matter over and finally decided that the only safe thing to do was to take Jared to the temple and let the Chief Rabbi decide what should be done with him. As Jared was being led off by a group of his neighbors, a friend ran to the house of his parents and told them what had happened. Both parents immediately hurried out of the house and followed the large crowd that had formed around Jared. When the crowd arrived at the temple gates, they told the guards they wished to see the Chief Rabbi. Overhearing the conversation, Captain Shama walked over and listened impatiently to the conflicting and confusing stories of how Jared's sight had been restored. Turning toward Jared, the incredulous captain asked, "How was your sight restored?"

Patiently and quietly, Jared told the captain of his meeting with Jesus, the application of the mud pack to his eyes, how he had washed out the clay mud pack in the Pool of Siloam, and as soon as he did, he found that he could see. After he had finished his story, there was a prolonged silence. Normally, the captain would have ordered Jared and the whole crowd out of the temple grounds as a pack of fools, but the repeated mention of the name of Jesus caused him to pause and act cautiously. Finally, he said, "Come into the Court of Solomon and tell your story to the Chief Rabbi."

When the captain explained the situation to the Chief Rabbi, he immediately came out of the temple, walked over to Jared and asked, "How was your sight restored?"

By this time, Jared had told the story of the restoration of his sight so many times that he had become impatient with the constant request to repeat his story. However, since it was the Chief Rabbi who now asked him this question, Jared concealed his irritation and said, "The man called Jesus of Nazareth put a mud pack of clay over my eyes and then he told me to go to the Pool of Siloam and there wash it out. I did exactly what he told me to do and as soon as I had washed out the mud pack, I could see immediately."

Chief Rabbi Caiaphas' eyes narrowed dubiously as he said, "When did this happen?"

Jared answered, "Several days ago, on the Sabbath."

Chief Rabbi Caiaphas triumphantly replied, "Well, then, that proves that this Galilean is not a man of God, because no good man works on the Sabbath."

Jared incredulously asked, "But how can a sinner perform such miracles?"

Ignoring this embarrassing question, the Chief Rabbi asked, "What do you think of this Galilean?"

Jared quietly answered in a voice filled with deep emotion, "I think that he is a man of God and a prophet."

Having been frustrated in his every attempt to discredit this story of the power of Jesus, Caiaphas angrily shouted, "Where are your parents?"

From out of the crowd, Jared's father came forward and timidly said, "Here we are."

Pointing to Jared, the Chief Rabbi roared, "Is this man your son?"

Jared's father quietly answered, "Yes, rabbi, he is."

Glowering suspiciously at Jared's father, Chief Rabbi Caiaphas asked, "Was he born blind?"

Jared's father answered, "Yes, rabbi. He was."

In a voice dripping with skepticism, the Chief Rabbi asked, "Then how is it that he now can see?"

Jared's father remained silent as his brain throbbed with fear and the excitement of all the possible consequences that might be inflicted upon him if he made the wrong answer. Trying to find a neutral ground by pleading ignorance, he evasively replied, "Rabbi, how it is or why it is that my son now can see, I don't know. All that my wife and I know is that this is our son, Jared, who was born blind, and now he can see. By what means his sight was restored is beyond our understanding."

Chief Rabbi Caiaphas' temper, which flared out of control easily, now got the best of him as he roared at Jared's father, "Tell me the whole truth!"

Jared's father meekly replied, "Rabbi, I have told you all I know. If you want to know any more about my son, ask him. He is of age. He can speak for himself."

Calming down somewhat, the Chief Rabbi turned to Jared and said, "Praise God for restoring your sight and not this Jesus of Nazareth; because we all know that he is a sinner."

Stubbornly, Jared answered, "Whether or not Jesus of Nazareth is a sinner, I don't know. But one thing I do know is that whereas formerly I was blind, now I can see."

The Chief Rabbi's brow was furrowed with deep wrinkles as he puzzled over the testimony of the two men before him. He could not admit defeat before the large group of assembled townspeople, nor could he publicly admit to the supernatural powers of Jesus. In desperation and frustration he again asked Jared the same question that Jared had repeatedly answered before, saying, "Exactly what did this Galilean do to you? How *did* he restore your sight?"

Jared replied with considerable irritation, "I have already told you what Jesus of Nazareth did to me. What is the good of my telling you the story all over again when you don't believe anything I say?"

Chief Rabbi Caiaphas' anger now burst forth in a torrential fury, as he shouted at Jared, "You miserable man, you are another one of this rebellious impostor's collaborators, but we rabbis are the disciples of Moses, and we know that God spoke to Moses; but as for this Galilean, we don't even know where he comes from."

Jared's voice was filled with bitter sarcasm as he answered, "Jesus of Nazareth performed a miracle by restoring my sight, and yet you say you don't even know where he comes from. If he were not a man of God, he could do nothing good, because we know that God does not answer the prayers of sinners. Since the world began, no man could make the blind see unless he was a man of God."

The rabbi's dark face was red with impassioned anger as he

stood up and shouted, "Get out of here! You are a sinner and you were born in sin. How dare you try to teach me, the Chief Rabbi of Jerusalem, in the ways of God? Get out, you are excommunicated, and never again return to this temple."

Matt. 12 (22-37)   John 8 (12-59)
Mark 3 (22-30)   John 10 (1-42)
Luke 11 (14-26)   Ps. 82 (6)
Luke 13 (30)

Chapter 24

The Rabbis Try to Kill Jesus

The news of the expulsion of Jared from the temple continued to be the main topic of conversation throughout
Jerusalem. In a community so completely immersed in religion as Jerusalem, expulsion from the temple was in many
ways more serious than any physical disability. Therefore,
animated discussion groups gathered all over the city heatedly debating the effect of Jared's expulsion. Naturally, the
companion topic and one of even greater importance was
Jesus' open defiance of the Jewish religious authorities.

A lesser person than Jesus would have sought safety outside of Judaea as quickly as possible until the resentment that
he had created among the powerful rabbinical authorities
had subsided. Instead, Jesus was back in the court of Solomon on the following day, preaching in his customary place.
In the crowd gathered around Jesus, there was an unusually

heavy sprinkling of temple personnel under the supervision of Rabbi Ahab with orders to keep Jesus under close surveillance. None of the temple personnel made any attempt to interfere with his preaching, or to arrest him as that would only inflame the public and probably create an uncontrollable riot.

As Jesus spoke, Rabbi Ahab kept his eyes fixed intently upon him like a bird of prey, waiting for the exact right moment to pounce upon its victim. During his sermon, Jesus said, "I am the good shepherd and I know my sheep and my sheep know me. My sheep know my voice and they listen to me and they follow me. I also have other sheep, who are Gentiles, and they also listen to my voice and follow me. Some day, I shall bring all my sheep together into one fold, and then they will all worship God together.

"I shall lay down my life for my sheep, when they are threatened by evil forces. A hired man would run away when the lives of his master's sheep are threatened, because he does not truly love his sheep. But I love my sheep and when wolves threaten them I shall not run. That is why God loves me, because He knows that I will cherish and protect my sheep regardless of any dangers that may be involved. No man shall take my life from me; but when need be, I will lay down my life, willingly. I have the power to lay down my life and I have the power to take it up again; and that power I have received from God, my Father."

Having listened impatiently to Jesus' words, Rabbi Ahab turned to the crowd and indignantly said, "This man is mad! Why do you stand here and listen to him? I tell you he is full of the devil. Now, keep moving and go and pray for forgiveness for listening to this son of the devil."

Jesus calmly replied, "There is no devil in me. The truth is, that I live in accordance with God's wishes, and I always do those things that please Him."

Rabbi Ahab sneered, "You always sing your own praises, but your record is a false one."

Jesus answered, "It is written in the Scriptures that the exact testimony of two men shall be accepted as being true. My testimony is true, because it is supported by me and by my Father."

The burly rabbi snarled, "Where *is* your Father?"

Jesus replied, "There is no point in my telling you where my Father is; because you would not recognize Him, even if you saw Him, any more than you recognize me. If you had known who I was, you would have known who my Father is. As it is, you know neither me nor my Father."

Between clenched teeth, Rabbi Ahab answered, "Exactly who *are* you? You keep hinting and suggesting that you are the Messiah. If you are the Messiah, why don't you say so openly, instead of leaving us in doubt about your claims to divinity?"

Jesus quietly answered, "I have already told you who I am, but you don't believe me. The deeds that I perform in my Father's name bear witness to my words. But you do not believe anything that I say or do. The fact is, you do not even trust your own eyes to tell you the truth of those things you see me do. However, my disciples hear my voice and I give them eternal life. They shall never perish and no one will ever take them away from me and my Father because my Father and I are one."

In an uncontrollable rage, Rabbi Ahab and the temple servants took up stones to throw at Jesus as they shouted, "Kill him! Kill him! Kill the blasphemer!"

Jesus quietly stood his ground and calmly said, "With my Father's help, I have performed many good deeds among you. For which of these deeds do you stone me?"

Rabbi Ahab shouted, "We do not stone you for any good deeds that you may have done, but we will stone you for speaking blasphemy. You are only a man and yet, you make yourself equal to God."

Jesus answered, "Don't the Scriptures say that one of our prophets told our people, 'You are gods.' If he was right in calling our people gods, who had received the word of God, then why do you say I speak blasphemy, because I say I am the Son of God when He has chosen me to do His work? If I don't do the work of God, don't believe in me; but if I do the work of God, believe in those works even though you do not believe in me. Then you will know that the Father is in me and I in Him."

While Jesus was speaking, a man who was both blind and dumb approached him and mutely begged to be healed. Jesus turned towards him and prayed to God that the man might be cured of his infirmities. The man was immediately cured and thanked Jesus profusely for his miraculous cure. Some one in the congregation shouted, "This man who has performed this miraculous cure before our very own eyes and also cured the blind Jared a few days ago, must surely be the son of David and the Messiah whom we seek."

Rabbi Ahab angrily advanced toward Jesus and jerking his thumb insolently at him, said, "This Galilean is no son of God! This fellow is a son of the devil, which is proven by the fact that he has power over the evil spirits."

Jesus turned toward the angry, black-bearded rabbi and quietly said, "Every house and every city and every nation that is divided against itself must fall. If the devil fights against himself by destroying evil, why then does evil still exist?"

As the rabbi made no reply, Jesus said, "You have children who are rabbis and they also cast out evil. Now if I cast out evil by the power of the devil, by whose power do your children cast out evil?"

Finding it impossible to answer this embarrassing question, the rabbi remained discreetly silent; so Jesus continued, "Evil can only be destroyed by the power of God. Therefore, rabbi, your own children who destroy evil will some day judge you and condemn you."

Turning to the congregation, Jesus said, "I cast out evil through the power of God. Therefore, when I cast out the evil spirit of the devil, you must know that the Kingdom of God has come among you. I am the light of the world and he who walks with me shall not walk in darkness, but shall have the eternal light of heaven. Soon, I shall leave you and where I go, you cannot follow."

Rabbi Ahab sneered, "Where are you going, Galilean, that no one can follow you? Don't tell us that you are going to commit suicide?"

Jesus looked at Rabbi Ahab contemptuously and replied, "You are from hell and I am from heaven. Therefore, you can never understand me."

Turning once again to the congregation, Jesus said, "If you will live in accordance with my instructions, you shall know the truth and the truth shall make you free."

The rabbi, who was now desperate because of his repeated failure to discredit Jesus, shouted at him, "What do you mean by saying that we shall be *made* free? We are the children of Abraham and we have never been slaves to any man."

Jesus replied, "I know that you are descended from Abraham, but you have tried to kill me because you are evil. Whoever is evil is the son of the devil. I am the truth and I do those things that are in keeping with my Father, while you do those things that are in keeping with *your* father."

Rabbi Ahab shouted, "Abraham was my father."

Jesus answered, "If Abraham was your father, you would perform the good deeds that he did. Instead, you are now trying to kill me because I speak the truth."

The rabbi angrily answered, "When you state that I am not a son of Abraham, you are saying that I was born in sin and that I am a bastard."

Jesus quietly replied, "You are the son of the devil and perform his evil, lustful deeds. The devil is a lying murderer and has never been anything else since the beginning of time."

The enraged rabbi shouted at Jesus, "I said at the beginning that you are in league with the devil. Now I say that you are also a blasphemer and a Gentile!"

A man in the congregation spoke up and said, "He doesn't sound like a Gentile or a man possessed of the devil to me. Before our very own eyes he has just cured a man who was both blind and dumb, and several days ago he cured Jared, the man who was born blind. Can a man who is possessed by the devil cure the blind and the dumb?"

As Rabbi Ahab remained silent, Jesus quietly said, "There is no devil in me. I live in accordance with my Father's wishes. If a man will live in accordance with the instructions that my Father gave to me, he will never die."

Rabbi Ahab sarcastically said, "Now I know that you are possessed by the devil. Our father, Abraham, is dead and all the prophets are dead and yet you say that if a man lives in accordance with your instructions he will live forever. Are you greater then than our father, Abraham, and all the other prophets who are now all dead? Who do you think you are?"

Jesus replied, "If I glorified myself, my glory would amount to nothing, but it is my Father who glorified me. You say that my Father is your God, but as I said before, you have never known my Father. If I refused to acknowledge my Father, I would be as much of a liar as you are. But I do acknowledge my Father and I am faithful to his commandments. With regard to Abraham, whom you call your father, let me tell you this; he was happy to know me and to see me coming to save the world."

Rabbi Ahab shouted derisively, "You aren't yet forty years old and yet you say that you saw our father, Abraham?"

Jesus quietly answered, "Before Abraham was born, I

lived! Have you never read the Scriptures wherein it says that the stone the builders rejected shall become the most important one of the building. Therefore, those Gentile nations from the north and the south and the east and the west who abideth by the will of God shall sit down with Abraham, Isaac, and Jacob in the kingdom of heaven, while the children of the kingdom shall be cast out. Verily I say unto you that the tax collectors and the prostitutes shall go into heaven before you do, fulfilling that ancient prophecy that the first shall be last and the last shall be first."

In an uncontrollable burst of fury, Rabbi Ahab and the temple servants took up stones and other loose objects and threw them at Jesus. They would have undoubtedly killed him on the spot if the crowd had not quickly formed around Jesus to protect him. Soon he was lost in the milling throng, and Jesus quickly fled outside the temple walls and then hastened past the city gates before he slackened his pace. Then, he turned and said, "Oh, you generation of vipers! What evil deeds you do perform!"

In fear of pursuit, Jesus continued travelling steadily northward until he reached the wilderness adjacent to the Jordan River where his cousin John the Baptist had fled so often before him. Jesus had left Jerusalem so quickly that he had been unable to contact any of his disciples in Jerusalem. So, Jesus remained alone in the wilderness, pondering what steps to take next to further his godly mission upon earth.

Matt. 5 (13-16)   Mark 4 (21)   Luke 12 (22-32)
Matt. 6 (1-8)   Luke 8 (16-17)   Luke 14 (34-35)
Matt. 6 (16-34)   Luke 11 (33-36)   Luke 16 (13-15)

Chapter 25

Sermon on the Mount I

In the spring of the year 29 A.D., Jesus was alone in the wilderness frequented by John the Baptist, deeply immersed over a fateful decision—should he or should he not continue with his mission of teaching the gospel of God to his people? If he continued his preaching, the Jewish rabbis would certainly kill him. On the other hand, he could return to his home in Nazareth and live out the remainder of his normal life unnoticed, as a carpenter in Galilee.

What should he do? He looked at the empty wilderness about him and then at the limitless sky above him, as though somewhere outside of himself he might find the answer to his problem. But neither the land nor the sky had the answer to the question that troubled him. He knew he could only find the answer within himself and he did. He decided to continue preaching.

Walking quickly now, he crossed a mount that gave him a

clear vision over the surrounding area, and he paused there briefly, as though he might be addressing a vast audience. Casting aside all doubts, he decided this would be the place where he would proclaim a new religious doctrine—which the world would name Christianity and would call the sermon that he gave there the Sermon on the Mount.

Returning to Capernaum he told Peter of his intention to proclaim his new doctrine to all the people of Palestine. Peter alerted the disciples and they soon informed the people of Judaea, Samaria, Galilee and Syria that Jesus planned to give the most important sermon of his life, so that on the appointed day vast throngs from all parts of Palestine came prepared to hear Jesus preach.

The Sermon on the Mount was a very long one, and it probably lasted about three days. It was divided into three parts: One part was devoted to one's own ethical behavior; another part was devoted to one's behavior toward others; and the final part was devoted to a revision of the basic Mosaic laws.

The first day's sermon was probably the shortest because it began late in the day. Jesus began slowly, saying:

"You are the salt of the earth, but if salt loses its quality of saltiness, who can restore that quality to it? No one. Thereafter the salt is worthless and men will throw it away into the street where it will be trampled under foot by men and beast alike. So shall it to be with you, if you lose your faith in God.

"Your eye is the lamp of your body. Therefore, when your eye is clear, your whole body is full of light. But when your eye is evil, then your whole body is full of darkness. Therefore, be careful that the light that shines within you be that of kindness and goodness; and always beware that the forces of darkness and evil do not extinguish that light.

"Remember that if you are to find the pathway to God, you must stop worrying about material possessions. Money, land, sheep, and goats are the material things which the devil uses to entice the weak and the greedy to become his slaves. It is true that certain material things are essential to living, but most evil in men's lives arises from man's accumulation of unnecessary things, which are frequently harmful as well as being unessential.

"Therefore, don't lay up treasures for yourselves upon earth where rust and moths will destroy them and where thieves can break in and steal them. Instead, store up treasures for yourselves in heaven where neither rust nor moths will destroy them and no thief can break in and steal them. Always remember that where your treasure is, there also is where your heart will be. So, don't worry about tomorrow because tomorrow will take care of itself, sufficient unto the day is the evil thereof.

"Let me ask you this—is there any one of you who can add a fraction of an inch to your height by any thought or action of your own? Think for a moment of the lilies of the field. They make no plans of their own and they do no work and yet Solomon in all his glory was never dressed as beautifully as one of these. If God takes such good care of the lilies of the field, will He not take much better care of you who are His children?

"No man can serve two masters. If he is loyal to one, he must of necessity be disloyal to the other. Therefore, no man can serve both God and the devil. So make your choice and stay with it and don't try to serve God on the Sabbath and the devil on weekdays. This means that right principles must never be sacrificed for some material benefit. Otherwise, we shall reject God and serve the devil.

"Remember that while I instruct you to seek the Kingdom of Heaven by performing deeds of goodness and mercy, you must never be ostentatious about your righteous actions. When you perform your deeds of righteousness, don't have someone sound a trumpet before you the way the hypocrites do.

"Gifts to charity should be made without your right hand knowing what your left hand is doing. Perform your good deeds secretly and your heavenly Father, who sees everything, will reward you publicly. Likewise when you fast, don't imitate the hypocrites who put on a sorry face and disfigure themselves in order to excite the pity of others. When you fast, wash your face and anoint your head, so it won't appear to others that you are fasting.

"Finally, when you pray, don't pray the way the hypocrites do, who love to pray standing in the front of the synagogue or posing on a street corner. When you pray, go into your bedroom, shut the door and pray to God, earnestly and privately. And above all, avoid using foolish repetitions, the way heathens do, who think that God will listen to them because they monotonously repeat the same prayer over and over again."

As soon as Jesus stopped speaking a richly dressed rabbi sneeringly said, "Do you expect us to believe all that nonsense?"

Jesus quietly replied, "Evidently you are one of those temple rabbis who worship money and power; and what you worship is an abomination in the eyes of God."

Then turning to his audience, Jesus said, "Tomorrow morning, we will meet here again two hours after sunrise. Good night and God bless you."

Matt. 5 (1-12)   Mark 4 (24)   Luke 6 (37-49)
Matt. 6 (24)   Mark 11 (24-26)   Luke 11 (9-13)
Matt. 7 (1-29)   Luke 6 (20-26)   Luke 13 (24-30)

Chapter 26

Sermon on the Mount II

When the crowd gathered on the following morning to hear Jesus continue his sermon, the day was hot and humid. The crowd was smaller than on the previous day, because many of the curiosity-seekers had left, and some others, who were tired of standing in the hot sun for many long hours, decided that the spiritual reward of listening to Jesus was not worth the physical strain. But, although the crowd was smaller, it was also a more alert group and they listened with greater attention, as they knew Jesus was preaching a new revolutionary religious doctrine.

Jesus advanced to the edge of the abrupt mound and after saying a short prayer, said:

"Most of you, I know, are good people; but do not let that goodness lead you into criticizing others. If you do criticize others, be prepared to be criticized in return. Instead of criticizing the weaknesses and the sins of others, I recommend that you forgive the trespasses of others; and in return, you will find that God has forgiven you your trespasses. Give and you shall receive a full measure, running over, of the same treatment that you have given to others.

"I know there are many among you who pride yourselves upon your kind behavior toward your children; and yet, those same persons often doubt and fear the treatment they will receive from God. If your children should ask you for bread, would any of you give them a stone? And if your children should ask you for fish, would any of you give them a serpent? If your actions to your children are those of goodness and kindness, why do any of you doubt the goodness and kindness of God to those of you who are His children?

"Remember, that the gate that leads to a good life is narrow and the pathway to it is restricted. Therefore, there are few who find this narrow gate and that restricted roadway. But the gate that leads to self-destruction is wide and the road that leads to it is unlimited. Therefore, there are many who go through that broad, evil gate and take the pathway to destruction. So I warn you that if you want to go through the narrow gate that leads to heaven, take the restricted pathway.

"Men do not harvest figs and grapes from thorns and thistles. Every good tree brings forth good fruit, while a corrupt tree brings forth evil fruit. Just as you recognize a rotten tree by the bad fruit it bears, so will you know the false prophets by their evil deeds. Therefore, I say to you by their fruits you shall know them.

"Let me warn you to beware of the false prophets who come to you dressed in sheep's clothing; while within, they are like ravenous wolves who will devour you. These false prophets hide their evil intentions behind an exterior cloak of beguiling smiles and flattering compliments.

"Just as I say to you beware of the false prophets, so do I say to you, avoid the hypocrite who can see a speck in his brother's eye, while his own eyes are full of dirt. Shall we not say to that hypocrite, 'First remove the large amount of dirt that is in your own eyes, before you try to remove the speck that is in your brother's eye'?

"This is the message I bring to you from God, my Father; seek Him and you shall find Him; ask Him for goodness and mercy and you shall receive them; knock at the gate of heaven and it shall be opened up unto you; because he who seeks shall find; and he who asks, shall receive; and to him who knocks, it shall be opened. Therefore, I say to you that when you pray to your heavenly Father for whatever you need, believe that you have already received those things that you have prayed for, and you shall find that you will have received them. However, always remember this, that if in your prayers, you desire that others shall do certain things for you, you must do likewise for others.

"There will come a day when I am in my Father's house when many hypocrites will say to me, 'Lord, Lord, please let us into Heaven. Didn't we preach in your name, and didn't we cure the sick in your name, and didn't we do many other wonderful things in your name?'

"In that day, I will act as though I had never seen those persons before. Then I will say to them, 'Get away from me, you evil people.' Upon that day of judgment, many of the children of Israel will be weeping and wailing, when they see Abraham, Isaac and Jacob and all the prophets sitting in the Kingdom of God; while they, themselves, will be left out. Meanwhile, many Gentiles from all parts of the world will come and sit down in the Kingdom of God; because many of those who were first, shall be last, and many of those who were last, shall be first.

"Therefore, those who hear my words and reject them, shall be compared to the foolish man, who built his house upon the sand. Then when the rains came and the waters rose and the winds blew upon that house, it fell, and great was the fall thereof. However, those who hear my words and accept them, will be like the wise man who built his house upon a rock. Then when the rains came and the waters rose and the winds blew and beat upon that house, that house did not fall because its foundations were solidly built into that rock."

Jesus was now visibly tired. He looked hopefully up at the sky as though he might draw some strength from it. Slowly, he took a drink of water from his leather flask and carefully wiped his lips. Raising both his arms and closing his eyes, he ended his sermon with this prayer:

> "Blessed are the poor in spirit,
> For theirs is the Kingdom of Heaven.
> Blessed are they who mourn,
> For they shall be comforted.
> Blessed are the meek,
> For they shall inherit the earth.
> Blessed are those who seek righteousness,
> Because they shall find righteousness.
> Blessed are the merciful,
> For they shall receive mercy.
> Blessed are the pure in heart,
> For they shall find God.
> Blessed are the peacemakers,
> For they are the children of God.
> Blessed are those who are persecuted,
> For the sake of righteousness,
> For theirs is the Kingdom of Heaven.
> Blessed are those who are persecuted for my sake,
> Because they shall go to Heaven."

As Jesus descended from the mount, the huge throng quickly surged around him. Peter and the other disciples immediately surrounded Jesus, trying to keep the milling crowd from crushing him; but it was a superhuman task that no small band of men could adequately perform. Many persons firmly believed that the supernatural powers of Jesus were so great that by simply touching him or even his garments that they would be immediately cured of whatever illness or infirmities they had.

In the milling crowd seeking to reach Jesus was a woman who had been hemorrhaging for twelve years. She had spent her entire life savings to obtain help from numerous physicians, but none of them had been able to cure her. In fact, her illness had become steadily worse, so that she knew that unless she was cured quickly, she would soon die.

When she heard of the miraculous healing powers of Jesus, she determined that she must see him. On the first day of the Sermon on the Mount, she found herself too far away from the natural platform that Jesus used during his sermon to reach him when the sermon ended. On the following day, she placed herself early at the foot of the mount where Jesus must pass when he descended from his elevated platform.

Upon the conclusion of the second day's sermon, she waited determinedly for Jesus to pass by her, filled with the strength that only desperation can give to the weak. Setting her feet firmly into a slight depression in the ground, she braced herself against the tremendous pressure of the crowd that passed by her and pressed her withered body low against the ground. Soon she could tell from the excited buzzing of the crowd that Jesus was approaching. For a moment as Jesus walked next to her, she was almost swept off her feet, then thrusting her hand out quickly between the legs of two of the leading disciples, she firmly grasped the hem of Jesus' garment. Her hemorrhaging ceased immediately and she could feel within her body that she was healed of her disease.

At that moment, Jesus felt his strength being suddenly sapped away and he cried out, "Who touched me?"

Peter turned to him and said, "Lord, do you see this tremendous crowd of people who are all trying desperately to touch you, and then do you still ask, 'Who touched me?'"

Jesus made no reply, but looked around with a troubled puzzled look. The cured woman now stood up between Peter and Jesus and in a trembling voice said, "Master, forgive me. It was I who touched you. I have had a hemorrhage for the past twelve years, but no doctor could cure me. I knew that if I could just touch your garment that I would be cured of my ailment. And now that I have touched you, I am cured. Forgive me. I meant to do you no harm."

Jesus answered, "You have done me no harm. Thank God for the cure of your ailment."

Matt. 5 (17-48)   Mark 9 (43-50)   Luke 16 (16-18) Deu. 24 (1)
Matt. 6 (9-15)   Mark 10 (11-12)   Luke 17 (11-19) Nu. 30 (1-2)
Matt. 8 (11-12)   Luke 6 (27-36)   Ex. 20 (13-14)   Lev. 24 (17-20)
Matt. 21 (31)   Luke 11 (1-4)   Ex. 21 (22-25)   Lev. 19 (18)
Matt. 21 (43-46)   Luke 13 (25-30)   Deu. 19 (21)

Chapter 27

Sermon on the Mount III

The third day of the Sermon on the Mount began with a
freshening breeze from the west. The crowd had thinned ap-
preciably. Most of those with physical ailments had left when
they found that Jesus was confining his efforts to preaching
instead of performing miraculous cures. Practically all persons with children had left because they had exhausted their
meager food supplies and because the effort of watching their
irrepressible children and listening to Jesus' sermon had become too great. There now remained mostly a hard core of
confirmed disciples and followers of Jesus, plus the usual
spies of Chief Rabbi Caiaphas who were under orders to remain and spy upon Jesus constantly.

As Jesus and his disciples walked toward the Mount, he
was approached by ten lepers, nine of whom were Jews and

the tenth was a Samaritan. When they saw Jesus approaching in the midst of his disciples, they shouted in unison, "Jesus, Master, have mercy upon us and cure us."

Jesus stopped, turned toward them, and said, "Go to your synagogue and pray before the rabbi that you will be healed."

As the ten lepers turned to go, they found they had been miraculously cured. The Samaritan quickly turned, ran after Jesus, fell down at his feet and in a loud voice, glorified God and thanked Jesus for his miraculous cure.

Jesus said to him, "Stand up and go on your way. Your faith has restored your health."

Turning to Peter, Jesus said, "Were there not ten lepers who were healed? Where are the other nine? Are there none among the nine Jewish lepers with enough gratitude to praise God? Is there only gratitude in this one Samaritan?"

Peter made no reply and Jesus continued walking thoughtfully ahead. He now faced his greatest crisis. For two days he had lectured his people on improving their ethical behavior. Now he must discuss the revision of the basic Mosaic laws which he knew would place him in direct conflict with the religious authorities of Judaism. Slowly he walked up to the mount, motioned to the audience for silence, and opened his sermon with a prayer. When he had finished his prayer, he said,

"There are those who say that I have come to destroy the laws of Moses and the laws of the prophets. But I say to you, I have not come to destroy the laws of Moses, or those of the prophets; in fact, I have come to amplify those laws. The laws of Moses and the laws of the prophets prevailed until the day of the death of John the Baptist. Since that day the good news of the coming of the Kingdom of God has been proclaimed and all men seek to enter that Kingdom. However, I warn you that you will never set foot in the Kingdom of Heaven unless your good deeds exceed those of the self-righteous hypocrites in Jerusalem."

It was a warm day and Jesus stopped to take a drink of water from the leather flask strapped to his shoulder. Wiping his mouth and the beads of perspiration from his face he continued: "Moses gave you a commandment that says, 'Thou shalt not kill.' But I say to you that whoever is angry with his brother shall be in danger of the fires of hell. Therefore, if you bring an offering to the altar of God and there remember that your brother has some grievance against you, leave your gift at the altar and go back and find your brother. First, become reconciled with him and then return to the altar and make your gift to God. In general, remember this, that it is far better to agree with an adversary quickly before a minor disagreement becomes a major dispute.

"Another one of the laws of Moses states, 'Thou shalt not commit adultery.' But I say to you that whoever looks upon a woman lustfully has already committed adultery with her in his heart. Therefore, if your eye causes you to sin, pluck it out and throw it away; because it is better for you to lose one part of your body than to have your entire body destroyed in the fires of hell.

"Another Mosaic law states that whoever divorces his wife must do so by giving her a written certificate of divorce. But I say to you, that whoever divorces his wife, except for the reason of adultery, causes her to become an adulteress, and therefore is an accessory to the sin that she commits. Furthermore, whoever marries that divorced woman, also commits adultery."

Once again, Jesus paused briefly to take a drink of water from his leather flask, wipe his brow and rest his vocal chords. He was beginning to get very tired from addressing so large a crowd in the burning sunshine in his weakened condition over so long a period. However, now he planned to attack an old Jewish commandment that had resulted in the murder of his cousin, John the Baptist; so with renewed vigor and determination, Jesus said:

"Another of the ancient laws of Moses states that if you swear to God to perform some deed, that you must perform that deed, regardless of the consequences; but I say to you that you must not swear at all, either by heaven, because it is God's throne, or by this earth, because it is God's footstool. And above all, don't swear by your head, because you cannot change a single hair in it. Therefore, whenever you do make a statement, let it be a simple positive or negative statement. Anything more than this is unnecessary and comes from a heart that is evil.

"In the ancient Scriptures, it also states that if a man harms his neighbor, that he shall be punished in like manner—an eye for an eye, and a tooth for a tooth; but I say to you, don't resist the man who attacks you. If someone does strike you on one cheek, turn your face and let him strike the other cheek also. Likewise, if a man sues you in court for your coat, give it to him and, in addition, give him your overcoat as well."

Again, Jesus paused briefly as the strain of the long sermon began to tire him visibly. Then he concluded his sermon by saying:

"And lastly, it is also written in our ancient Scriptures that you shall love your neighbor and hate your enemy. But I say this to you, love your enemies; bless those who curse you; do good to those who hate you, and pray for those who persecute you.

"If you love only those who love you, what reward do you deserve for that love? Do not sinners also love those who love them? And if you exchange greetings only with those of your own kind, are you doing anything more than what the pagans do? Therefore, be kind and just to both Jew and Gentile as God, your Father, is kind and just to you. If you live in accordance with these precepts, you may be truly called the children of God. Always remember, that God lets the sun shine both upon the good and the bad and He lets the rain fall both upon the just and the unjust."

Jesus was now very tired. He had been preaching a revolutionary doctrine for three days in the broiling sun, with little to eat and with very little rest. His drawn, haggard face showed the effect of the deep emotion within him. The crowd remained quiet and tense, waiting for him to continue. Very slowly, he said,

"And now before we leave, let us all join together in this prayer to God—

"Our Father, Who art in heaven.
Hallowed be Thy name,
Thy Kingdom come;
Thy will be done on earth,
As it is in Heaven.
Give us this day our daily bread
And forgive us our trespasses,
As we forgive those
Who trespass against us,
And lead us not into temptation,
But deliver us from evil,
For Thine is the Kingdom and the power
And the glory, forever and ever, Amen."

So ended the world's greatest sermon. The world would never again be the same. Wherever men might be, regardless of their faith or beliefs, the Sermon on the Mount would have its lasting effect upon all of them. Thus, Jesus made his final break with Judaism and laid the moral foundation for all those religions and all those persons who call themselves Christian.

Jesus had now reached that stage in his life when the people of the world are no longer simply divided into Jews and Gentiles, with the Jews admitted into the Kingdom of God because they are Jews, and the Gentiles sent to the devil because they are Gentiles. At this stage he divided people on

the basis of their performance and not upon their ancestry—
the good people belong to the kingdom of God, the evil people belong to the devil. However, he always leaves the door
open for the sinners to repent and enter into the gates of
heaven with the good people. This is a basic belief of Christianity and it is the reason why it is the world's greatest
religion.

It is also the reason why the temple rabbis were determined
to kill him. According to the rabbis, they possessed the keys
to the gates of heaven and they placed a high price of admission to any Jew who wished to enter those gates. Therefore,
they had no intention of allowing Jesus to destroy their mo-
nopoly on a happy life in heaven by teaching that any good
person, Jew or Gentile, could enter heaven by simply living a
good life.

Matt. 20 (18-19)   Luke 18 (31-34)
Matt. 23 (1-36)   Luke 20 (45-47)
Mark 10 (32-34)   John 11 (1-16)
Mark 12 (38-40)   John 12 (23-50)

Chapter 28

The Passover

Jesus spent the remaining months of his last winter on earth resting quietly and living alone along the banks of the Jordan River. Occasionally, he was joined for short periods of time by Peter, Andrew, John and James, who secretly brought him supplies to supplement the meager food that he could find in the wilderness. Each time Jesus and Peter met they discussed their plans to attend the Passover, which was the next important Jewish festival to be celebrated in Jerusalem in the early part of the spring. Peter tried his best to dissuade Jesus from making plans to go to Jerusalem even though he would presumably be safe from arrest during the religious festival of the Passover; but Jesus was adamant.

The Passover is the most important of all the Jewish religious holy days because it commemorates the real and practical birth of Judaism. In folklore, the birth of Judaism pre-dates the original Passover by many centuries; but this folklore is mostly mythology. This holy day commemorates the Jewish exodus from Egypt, during which the Jews suffered tremendous hardships on their journey around the deserts and the mountains of the Sinai peninsula. During this seven or eight day holiday, only unleavened food such as matzoths could be eaten. It also commemorates the passing over of the Jewish homes by the angel of death who killed the first-born of all Egyptian families and thus it acquired the name Pass-over.

As the time drew near for the beginning of the Passover, there was tremendous speculation among the Jews regarding the probable arrival of Jesus in Jerusalem during this festival because strict orders against collaborating with him had increased in their severity. Therefore the intensity of the public speculation regarding the possible arrival of Jesus increased with the approach of the beginning of this festival. Few there were who predicted that Jesus would dare show up in Jerusalem; and none there were who offered to welcome him if he did arrive.

Early in the spring of the year 30 A.D., when Jesus was a little over thirty-four years old, he set out for Jerusalem with Peter, Andrew, James and John. This was to be his last journey on earth. The five men started out on their journey about three weeks prior to the beginning of the Passover, so that they could travel in easy stages and avoid the mass pilgrimage that would take place during the week prior to the beginning of the Passover.

On their way to Jerusalem, they were joined by the remaining seven disciples. It was not a happy group, because there was in the minds of all of them an air of foreboding doom. For the first time during the ministry of Jesus, his disciples took the precaution of arming themselves. All the disciples carried clubs or staves, except for Peter and another disciple, who armed themselves with swords. The closer they got to

Jerusalem, the more obvious it became that the people were aloof and fearful. It was apparent that the increased severity of the punishment threatened by the Chief Rabbi upon all Jews who helped or followed Jesus, had had its effect. Everywhere, there were signs requiring all Jews to notify the authorities of the whereabouts of Jesus upon penalty of excommunication from the temple and the local synagogues.

Wearily and despondently, Jesus and his disciples arrived in Bethel, situated about twelve miles north of Jerusalem. Never before had Jesus' disciples felt so footsore, tired and hungry. Their dirty, ragged clothing hung limply on their gaunt bodies, and their skimpy clothing was just barely sufficient to conceal their nakedness. Worse than their physical strain, was the low ebb of their morale. Since they were welcome in no home in Bethel, Jesus and his disciples spent the night in a ravine, close to a running stream of water, where they were out of sight of casual passersby.

The following morning, a handful of courageous villagers came out to see Jesus. Although the villagers had done their best to conceal their movement from town, their departure from the village had not gone unnoticed by the local rabbis and the temple spies. Knowing that several of these villagers were followers of Jesus, Rabbi Ahab and his men followed them to the ravine where Jesus and his disciples had camped for the night.

They heard one of the villagers ask, "Master, do you think that we should obey the evil men who now control the temple in Jerusalem?"

Jesus replied, "The temple rabbis now occupy the seat of Moses. Therefore, follow their instructions, but do not imitate their actions because they are hypocrites who do not practice what they preach. While they place grievously heavy burdens upon the backs of our people, they, themselves, do not lift a single finger to ease those burdens.

"All they want to do is parade before the public in their

expensive clerical garments, and live like kings from the contributions they collect from our people. The temple rabbis love to occupy the most prominent seats in the synagogues and in other public places and be greeted reverently with the flattering title of 'Honorable Rabbi,' but truly their behavior is nothing more than an ostentatious display of hypocrisy."

While Jesus was speaking, Rabbi Ahab and his men silently moved in among the villagers. The rabbi's face was tense with hatred as he shouted at Jesus, "You are a religious impostor and you have no right to speak of our temple rabbis in these slanderous terms. They have devoted their entire lives to Judaism and to the maintenance of the cherished traditions of our Mosaic laws; while you spend your time perverting our people, undermining our ancient traditions and breaking our Mosaic laws. You are a rebel and a traitor!"

Rabbi Ahab's belligerence kindled within Jesus a righteous wrath which he had never shown before. It may have been that Jesus was overwrought from fatigue, hunger, and constant persecution. In any case, Jesus' reply to the angry rabbi was a bitter denunciation of all rabbinical life. Jesus turned toward Rabbi Ahab, eyed him quietly and then indignantly said, "Woe be unto you, hypocritical rabbis! You are like the whited sepulchers, whose exterior surfaces are clean and beautiful, but whose interior surfaces are decayed and putrid.

"You present yourselves to our people as their spiritual and national leaders, while in fact, you lead them to spiritual and national disaster. Therefore, God must send prophets to our people to cleanse out the corruption you temple rabbis have created.

"You murderous rabbis have discouraged and tormented those prophets, and now God has sent you another prophet whom you will crucify and kill. For this reason, all the righteous wrath of the prophets whose blood has been shed upon this earth, shall fall upon your heads and destroy you!"

Rabbi Ahab made a feeble attempt to stop Jesus' bitter

denunciation of the temple rabbis by shouting at him, "That is not true," but Jesus interrupted him saying, "You hypocrites! You shut men out from heaven; while you, yourselves, cannot enter into it. You steal homes from the widows and then you make a pious pretense of saying a long prayer to cover up your theft.

"Woe be unto you stupid hypocrites! You are so concerned about the gifts that are made to you that you have forgotten the more important matters concerning God. The things that are important to Him are good deeds, mercy and faith. These are the things that should have received your primary attention; but, instead of attending to those matters that are important to God, you temple rabbis have wasted your lives on ritualistic formalities; and thus, you justify the truth of the ancient proverb which says, 'Blind guides strain at a gnat and swallow a camel.' "

Once again, Rabbi Ahab made a futile attempt to stop Jesus' explosive denunciation of the temple rabbis, but Jesus continued with increased determination, saying, "You tell our people that if a man swears by the altar without placing a gift there for you, that his oath is not binding; but if he leaves a gift of gold for you upon that altar, then his oath is binding. You blind fools! Which is greater, the altar in the temple, or your fee of gold that rests upon that altar?

"You hypocrites! You cross land and sea to make a single convert and after you have made that convert, he becomes twice as great a child of hell as you are.

"Woe be unto you hypocrites! You are the children of the murderers of the prophets! Woe be unto you, serpents! You generation of vipers! You shall not escape the damnation of hell!"

This last bitter tirade so unnerved Rabbi Ahab that he slunk away from the crowd, followed by his dejected agents. When Jesus stopped speaking, he felt completely exhausted and sat down among the rocks. His disciples huddled quietly and protectively around him while the villagers said goodbye to Peter and to the other disciples and returned to Bethel.

When Jesus appeared sufficiently rested, Peter said to him, "Master, since you know that the rabbis will surely kill you if you go on to Jerusalem, why not return to Galilee, or even to Samaria, where you know you will be safe from attack from the temple rabbis?"

Jesus quietly answered, "Peter, I say this to you, that unless a grain of wheat is dropped into the ground and dies, it remains just another grain of wheat. But if it dies and germinates, it will bring forth a bountiful harvest. So, must I die in order that I may do my Father's work and save mankind."

Peter slowly said, "But, master, wouldn't it be better for you to live a while longer so that you can perform more of God's work?"

Jesus answered, "Truthfully, Peter, I will admit to you that my soul is sorely troubled, because I know that I shall be betrayed, scourged and crucified. But even though my soul is troubled, what can I say? 'Father, save me'?

"Remember, this is my purpose in life, to save mankind; and I shall carry out that purpose, even though I shall die for it."

Peter sat down next to Jesus, shaking his large, shaggy head disconsolately. Peter was a man of action and not given to deep philosophical thought. When Jesus spoke to him of facing death in calm terms of resignation, as though his execution was part of an implacable fate, Peter felt frustrated.

As Peter and Jesus sat quietly beside each other, a weary traveler came up the ravine and said to Jesus, "Master, I have been searching everywhere for you this past week in every village between here and Bethany. Your friends Martha and Mary Magdalen have sent me to find you and give you this message. Their brother, Lazarus, is dangerously ill and near death. They want you to come immediately and save him."

Peter replied, "If Lazarus was near death a week ago, when

you left Bethany, what makes you think he is still alive?"

The messenger replied, "I don't know that he is still alive; but Martha and Mary Magdalen were positive that no matter what the circumstances were, the master would come and help them, as soon as he knew they needed him."

Peter growled, "Do you realize what risk my master takes in going to Bethany, on the outskirts of Jerusalem, before the Passover even begins? It will be dangerous enough for him to go there on the first day of the Passover, but to go there before the Passover even begins is just plain suicide."

The messenger replied, "I realize the danger to your master in going to Bethany at this time, but I am only a messenger and I have delivered my message. What reply shall I make to Martha and Mary Magdalen?"

Peter answered, "Tell them that—"

Jesus interrupted and said, "Peter, this is a decision that I must make." Turning to the messenger, he said, "Tell Martha and Mary Magdalen that I will come immediately."

Peter's face was a picture of resigned frustration. The messenger thanked Jesus and left. Peter turned to Jesus and said, "The temple rabbis stoned you the last time you went to Jerusalem. Is there any point in your going there a second time to be stoned? The next time they will surely kill you."

Jesus answered, "In every man's life there are twelve hours of daylight and twelve hours of darkness. If a man walks in the daylight, he will not stumble. But, if he walks at night, he will surely stumble; because there is no light within him to see where he is going. God has given me the light to see where I am going and I must use that light for the glory of God, during the hours of daylight that are left to me."

When Jesus spoke like that, the meaning of his words were not clear to Peter or to the other disciples. After a brief pause, Jesus tried to lighten the gloom among his disciples by explaining to them the reason for his trip to Bethany, saying,

"Our friend, Lazarus, is only asleep, and I must go there to waken him."

Peter replied, "Lord, if he is only sleeping, he is just resting and will soon waken again, Therefore, there is no need for you to go to Bethany and risk your life just to waken him."

Jesus looked intently at Peter and said, "Actually, Peter, Lazarus *is* dead in the ordinary sense of the word. That is why I must go to Bethany and restore him to life."

Peter and the other disciples looked at each other questioningly and apprehensively. Finally, Thomas broke the long, painful silence by saying, "Well, if it is the master's intention to go to Bethany at the risk of his life, let us say no more about it, because we shall all go there with him. And if the master gets killed, we shall all die with him."

Jesus looked at the bowed heads and dejected faces of his disciples and quietly said, "Thank you, Thomas. Now let us get a good night's sleep so that when we go on to Bethany tomorrow, we shall all be refreshed."

Matt. 26 (3-5)　　　　John 11 (17-54)
Mark 14 (1-2)　　　　John 12 (10-11)
Luke 22 (1-2)

Chapter 29

The Resurrection of Lazarus

Well before noon on the following day when Jesus and his disciples were approaching Bethany, they saw a group of people waving at them from the outskirts of the village. From out of the group, Martha came running down the road to embrace and greet Jesus. She had been crying so uncontrollably and she had run so fast, that she was unable to speak. Finally, through her tears, she said, "Lord, if only you had come sooner, my brother would not have died."

Jesus asked, "When did your brother die?"

She answered, "Four days ago."

Jesus said, "Your brother will rise again."

Martha sorrowfully replied, "Yes. I know that he will rise again on the day of resurrection."

Jesus looked at her intently and said, "Martha, look at me."

She turned toward Jesus, looked at him and answered, "Yes, master."

Jesus said, "Martha, *I am the resurrection.* He who believes in me, will never die. Even he, who is dead and believes in me, shall live again. Do you believe in me, Martha?"

She answered, "Yes, Lord, of course I do."

But she was now so close to tears that she bowed her head, covered it with her shawl, and ran back home. When she arrived there, she told her sister of her encounter with Jesus and all the things he had said to her. Mary decided that she wanted to speak to Jesus herself so, accompanied by her sister, she ran down the road to meet him. She repeated Martha's words, and said, "Lord, if only you had been here sooner, my brother would not have died."

Mary wept disconsolately and Jesus tried his best to console her. When her heavy sobbing stopped, Jesus said to her, "Where have you laid Lazarus?"

She answered, "Come with me and I will show you the cave where we buried him."

She led Jesus to a rocky area at the edge of the village, where the townspeople had created a cemetery by digging caves out of the rocks and covered the openings with huge rock slabs. Mary led Jesus to one of the caves and said, "This is the place."

The sight of the cave started Mary and her sister crying loudly all over again, and Jesus was so moved by their tears that he wept with them. A large crowd had followed them to the cemetery, and there were many expressions of sympathy for the two sorrowing sisters. From out of the crowd someone said, "Could not this man, who has opened the eyes of the blind and of those who are strangers to him, have saved the life of Lazarus, his dearest friend?"

Meanwhile, Jesus walked up to the large stone blocking the entrance to the tomb of Lazarus and said to Peter and the other disciples, "Roll back this stone."

Martha walked over to Jesus and said, "Don't do that.

Lazarus has been dead for four days and by this time, his body will be badly decayed and stinking."

Jesus turned to Martha, looked at her sorrowfully and said, "Didn't I tell you that if you would have faith in me that you would see the glory of God?"

"Yes, Lord, but"—and Martha's voice dissolved into tears.

While the disciples struggled to roll back the huge stone, Jesus knelt and prayed. Then he walked to the entrance of the opened tomb and shouted, "Lazarus, come out!"

From within the cave came muffled sounds and then a slow measured step, and within a few minutes Lazarus strode out, still partially bound in his linen burial clothes. His face, which had been wrapped in a linen shawl, was ashen gray, but it was only partially visible because only a portion of the shawl had fallen away from the upper portion of his face. Turning to the two sisters, Jesus said, "Unwrap him and take him home."

Mary and Martha fell to their knees at Jesus' feet and gratefully said, "Praise be to the power and glory of God!"

Throughout the crowd there were gasps of awe and excitement. A powerfully strong resonant voice was heard above the sounds of the crowd, saying, "Now we know that this man is truly the Messiah. No man could have raised Lazarus from the dead unless he had the power of God within him."

From the crowd came hushed awed voices of assent saying, "Amen! Amen!"

Again the powerful voice from out of the crowd spoke, saying, "Let us take Jesus of Nazareth into Jerusalem and crown him King of the Jews."

Another voice shouted, "Yes, let us place him in the seat of David!"

Scattered throughout the crowd, watching these proceedings with beady, searching eyes were the spies of the Chief Rabbi. Slowly, they withdrew from the crowd, and then hastened down the road to Jerusalem to report all they had seen and heard to the Chief Rabbi.

Chief Rabbi Caiaphas listened so attentively to the report of his spies that for once he remained motionless and silent until they had completed their story. Then he jumped up from his seat and summoned the captain of the guard to dispatch messengers to the other seventy members of the Great Sanhedrin for an emergency meeting in the temple.

After all the seventy members of the Great Sanhedrin arrived at the temple, the meeting opened with Rabbi Annas seated, as usual, beside his son-in-law. A casual observer, taking a glance at the old man, might have thought he was sleeping. His head was bent low over his chest so that his long, white silken beard glistened brightly against the dark background of his clerical robes. Chief Rabbi Caiaphas opened the meeting with a detailed discussion of the many occasions upon which Jesus had broken the Sabbath, scoffed at the Mosaic laws and ridiculed the rabbis. The Chief Rabbi told them in detail how, acting upon the advice of Rabbi Annas, he had shown the utmost tolerance toward the carpenter from Galilee.

"However," he continued, "increased tolerance of the man has only resulted in greater and greater boldness on the man's part, until very recently, he has even advocated the rewriting of the Mosaic laws. As though this has not been enough, he has recently called himself the Messiah and the Son of God. In order to convince the gullible public of his heavenly powers, he has now resorted to the lowest tricks of the charlatan."

Pausing to take a drink, he continued, "Just now I received a report from Bethany that this impostor made a false burial of one of his accomplices and then four days later before a large crowd claimed to have brought this man back to life again."

From all parts of the room came an angry roar, "Kill the rebel! Kill him! Kill the rebel!"

Chief Rabbi Caiaphas held up his hands in a gesture asking for silence. Then he said, "Wait, wait! I haven't yet told you all. Now, he claims that he is the King of the Jews and his followers claim that they will crown him King of Israel right here in this temple and put him into power in our place."

Again, from all parts of the room came the repeated angry shouts of "Kill the rebel! Kill him! Kill him! Kill him!"

The uproar from all parts of the room became a bedlam as various members of the Great Sanhedrin tried to outshout their fellow members. When the noise had reached an intolerable din, quiet little old Rabbi Annas slowly rose to his feet and stood motionless at the rostrum next to his son-in-law. The two men spoke to each other in low undertones until the members of the Great Sanhedrin had shouted themselves hoarse. Then the gentle old rabbi raised his hands, requesting silence from the angry rabbis.

In a very low voice, the old rabbi slowly said, "Members of the Great Sanhedrin, you have made a very wise decision and I agree with that decision wholeheartedly. This Galilean rebel must be killed and killed quickly. However, while we are killing this one rebel we must proceed with the greatest caution lest we destroy the very institution that we are trying so desperately to preserve. To begin with, let us understand our enemy before we deal with him. Like John the Baptist, this Galilean has a very large public following that is very devoted to him. We must not make the same mistake that King Herod did by killing this rebel ourselves."

A council member asked, "Who else will kill this rebel for us? You have continually advised procrastination toward this man and as a result, matters have gone from bad to worse. If he is allowed to go on freely any longer, we will have another civil war in Judaea."

Rabbi Annas quietly replied, "I am not suggesting that we allow this Galilean to continue his rebellious activities; all that I am suggesting is that we have someone else put an end to him. Please hear me out."

The impatient council member flounced angrily back into his seat and Rabbi Annas continued, "Let me repeat again that I agree with you—all of you—that it is better that this one man should die, rather than to have our entire nation perish. However, let us here remember that each attempt that has been made upon this man's life in the past has been thwarted by our own people."

Chief Rabbi Caiaphas walked over to Rabbi Annas and said, "Father, we all honor and respect you, but what do you propose that we *do*? All that you continually say to us is, 'Go slow, proceed with caution, don't be hasty.' We have done all of these things. Now, tell us what we should *do*?"

As usual, when others around him became angry and impulsive, Rabbi Annas became more deliberate. Very quietly, he said, "One thing we must *not* do is kill the Galilean ourselves. We must have the Romans do that."

Nicodemus stood up and said, "But the Galilean has committed no crime against Rome. The charges that we here bring up against him will have no influence upon the Roman governor. This Galilean is rebelling against us and our Mosaic and rabbinical laws—not against Roman laws."

Pausing for what seemed to be an interminably long period, Rabbi Annas patiently replied, "Unfortunately, the statements made by our esteemed council member are entirely true. The Galilean is rebelling against our laws and not against Roman laws. And we, the members of this great council, can make this admission here freely and frankly among ourselves.

"Therefore, it is our duty to find reasons why the Romans should execute this rebel. There are many charges that we can bring against him to prove that he is a rebel against Rome.

We can charge him with refusing to pay taxes to Rome, inciting our people to rebel against Rome, and illegally declaring himself King of Judaea.

"Whether or not any of these charges against the Galilean are true or not, is immaterial. In fact, it is not even important that we prove the charges to be true to the satisfaction of the Roman governor. The only important thing is for the Roman governor to carry out our death verdict."

Nicodemus asked, "How can you do that against the power of Rome?"

Rabbi Annas quietly replied, "Always remember that we have a very powerful weapon at our command against the Romans and that weapon is the threat of mob violence. As you all know, I have been to Rome on several occasions to negotiate with the Romans on problems confronting our nation. On each occasion, I won my arguments with the Romans by subtly suggesting that if they insisted upon forcing certain unpleasant decisions upon us, our people would riot. I know the strength and the weaknesses of Rome. Her troops are scattered thinly over thousands of miles in many hostile nations. Their troops in Judaea are particularly weak, because not only are they hundreds of miles away from Rome, but in addition, those hundreds of miles are over an unpredictable sea. Furthermore, those troops are not even Romans; they are Syrians.

"Therefore, I know that Governor Pilate's basic orders from Rome are to maintain peace and order in Judaea at all costs, because Rome has no troops to spare if Governor Pilate needs reinforcements. Do I need to say any more?"

For several minutes there was a stunned silence in the council chambers while the members of the Great Sanhedrin pondered over the clever, sly scheme that Rabbi Annas proposed. Then, as the cunning plan of the old rabbi was clearly understood by one member after another, the room echoed and re-echoed with an answering roar of approval. Above the jubilant shouting of the members of the Great Sanhedrin there was wild handclapping and applause. Here was a scheme worthy of the brain of the revered old rabbi. Quietly and unobtrusively, Rabbi Annas sat down and once again seemed to retire within himself.

Smiling broadly, the Chief Rabbi walked over to the rostrum in an obviously self-assured manner and said, "There is much that we younger men could learn from our esteemed father. He has clearly put the necessary plan before us to eliminate the rebellious Galilean and it is now our job to carry out his plan successfully. We are going to need some troops from King Herod's palace to arrest the man at night and then we will need the help of all the council members to provide the necessary mob in front of the governor's palace when the Roman govenor condemns the Galilean to death. All council members should remain close to their homes during this trying period so that we may have all of you available for whatever services may be required on very short notice."

A council member stood up and said, "Chief Rabbi, your plans and those of Rabbi Annas are excellent insofar as they concern the Galilean, but what about his collaborator, who feigned death and now tells our people that he has been restored to life by that rebellious impostor?"

Chief Rabbi Caiaphas confidently answered, "We know him very well. His name is Lazarus and he lives in Bethany with his two sisters and one or both are women of doubtful character. He has given aid and shelter to the Galilean on many occasions in the past. However, he is a man of no importance and we can kill him ourselves whenever we wish without raising any public disturbance. As a matter of fact, it would be far better for us to have him stay alive until he admits that his so-called death and resurrection are false. Then at the proper time we can have him stoned to death as he deserves."

The council member replied, "Thank you, rabbi. I just

wanted to make sure that when we kill the rebel that we also kill his partner."

"I assure you that we will," Caiaphas replied. Then turning to the council members he said, "I wish to repeat again, stay close to your homes until you receive further orders. This meeting is over."

Matt. 21 (1-11)   Mark 12 (41-44)   Luke 19 (28-40)
Matt. 25 (1-46)   Mark 13 (9-37)   Luke 21 (1-4)
Matt. 26 (6-13)   Mark 14 (3-9)   John 12 (1-22)
Mark 10 (32-34)   Luke 12 (35-48)   Zec. 9 (9)
Mark 11 (1-11)   Luke 13 (31-33)   Ps. 118 (26)

Chapter 30

The First Palm Sunday

On the Sabbath, a week before the beginning of the Passover, the village of Bethany was ablaze with excitement. The heated discussions pertaining to the resurrection of Lazarus and Jesus' open defiance of the Chief Rabbi had raised the public's anticipation of future dramatic events to fever pitch. The reasons behind this public excitement were easy to understand. Bethany was not only the scene of the miraculous resurrection of Lazarus, but Lazarus himself was a local citizen of Bethany. Therefore, the entire village shared in the spotlight of publicity and attention that were being bestowed upon Lazarus.

Night and day, the village was crowded with curiosity-seekers who wanted to see and touch the miracle man who had been raised from the dead; but more importantly, the people wanted to see and touch Jesus, the man who had resurrected Lazarus. In the popular excitement that naturally followed this supernatural event, there was a great deal of heady talk of forcibly making Jesus King of the Jews. In contrast to this daring suggestion, Jesus' disciples, and Peter in particular, advised Jesus to proceed with caution. The disciples could not quickly forget that only a week before they had all been hunted men.

Jesus calmly considered the advice that he received from his aggressively minded friends in contrast to that which he received from his conservatively minded disciples. He had much to think about. On the one hand, there was the soul-stirring suggestion that he march boldly and openly into Jerusalem in the name of the Lord, proclaiming the coming of the Kingdom of God; and on the other hand, there was Peter's cautious, conservative advice to make progress slowly and avoid an open confrontation with the powerful temple rabbis.

Jesus was faced with a very difficult problem. Had the time come when he should openly challenge the temple rabbis, and thereby risk all his life's work as a missionary; or should he follow Peter's prudent advice and continue his hide-and-preach game and only enter Jerusalem during the holy days? As he paced up and down the road with his white robe flowing behind him, he was the picture of the dedicated man of God, seeking communion with him. Everyone who saw him stopped and gazed in admiration at the stirring figure of a man inspired with a faith that was beyond all human understanding.

Suddenly, he stopped and Peter, who had been struggling to keep up with him, bumped into him. Still puffing from his efforts, Peter said, "Excuse me, master, I didn't expect you to stop so quickly."

"That's all right, Peter." Jesus answered, "I've finally solved it."

"What have you solved?" Peter cautiously asked.

Jesus replied, "My problem."

Peter slowly asked, "What is it?"

Jesus answered, "There is a passage in Zechariah, Peter, which goes like this:

> " 'Rejoice, O daughter of Zion,
> Your godly king comes unto you!
> Humble and riding on a donkey
> Bringing you peace and salvation.' "

When Jesus stopped speaking, there was a faraway look in his eyes and Peter asked with an air of apprehension, "Does that mean, master, that you will openly challenge the temple rabbis in Jerusalem?"

Very slowly, but with great determination, Jesus answered, "Yes, Peter, it does. At the Festival of Hanukkah, and again at the Feast of the Tabernacles, we entered Jerusalem like thieves in the night. This time, we shall enter Jerusalem openly and triumphantly in accordance with the prophecies of Zechariah and Isaiah."

Peter dubiously said, "Master, that is very dangerous, extremely dangerous. However, if that is your decision, we shall go with you. I suppose if we wait until the Sabbath, the first day of the Passover, we might avoid being arrested."

Jesus replied, "No, Peter. We are not going to wait until the Sabbath to go into Jerusalem. We are going there tomorrow."

Peter now vigorously protested, "Tomorrow? But, master, for us to go into Jerusalem in broad daylight is just asking for trouble. It is not even a holy day; the agents of the Chief Rabbi will certainly arrest you and kill you. In fact, they may kill all of us."

Slowly Jesus answered, "No, Peter. They will not kill me nor any of us in broad daylight, even though it is not a holy day. For their purpose, the rabbis need the enveloping cloak of darkness in which to perform their evil deeds. What the temple rabbis expect us to do and want us to do, is to come into Jerusalem in the middle of the night when they can arrest us and kill us like criminals. What the rabbis least expect us to do is to face them boldly in broad daylight before the Passover even begins."

Peter said, "Master, I will follow you wherever you go, but I hate to see you take this one bold step and lose all that you have accomplished among our people by one foolish move."

Jesus replied, "Peter, it is time we showed ourselves openly to our people so that they can protect us from our enemies. Only then can we all worship God freely without fear of punishment. If we can arouse enough of our people to the need for a change, we may be able in the future to preach openly instead of continuing to slink into our holy city in the middle of the night like criminals."

Peter protested, "But Lord, the people are powerless against the might of the temple rabbis."

Jesus answered, "That is true, Peter, as long as our people are leaderless. Without a leader, the people are just a mob that can be dominated by the organized forces of the temple rabbis. Therefore, it is up to us to give our people the spiritual leadership they need to oppose the evil forces of the rabbis."

Peter frowned and said, "Maybe you are right, but why don't we wait a little while longer until we have obtained more public support to oppose the Chief Rabbi with more power?"

Jesus replied, "The public has already shown its willingness to support us; but if we continue to hide in the shadows, they can have no faith in our leadership. Right now, the agents of the Chief Rabbi will be searching for us in every rat hole and darkened alley in Jerusalem. What they don't expect us to do is to come into Jerusalem in broad daylight, marching in a band, followed by a group of faithful disciples."

Peter remained silent for awhile and then said, "Lord, if that is your will, it is my will also. Maybe it will work. In fact,

I must admit that I can think of no better alternative, unless we remain hidden forever like ground moles."

Jesus said, "Good. I am glad you agree with me, Peter. Now in order to fulfill the prophecy of Zechariah, we must have a donkey."

Peter asked, "Where will we find a donkey?"

Jesus answered, "Send two of the disciples down the road to Jericho. At the first crossroad they come to, they will see a house with a young donkey tied to a post in front of it. Tell them to take that young donkey and bring it here."

In astonishment, Peter said, "But what shall the disciples say if the owner of the donkey objects?"

Jesus answered, "Tell them to tell that owner that the Lord has need of that young donkey."

Dubiously, Peter replied, "Yes, master."

Peter followed Jesus' instructions and sent two of the disciples down the road to Jericho to bring back the donkey Jesus had spoken about. Just as Jesus had predicted, the two disciples found the house at the first crossroad with a young donkey tied in front of it. After they had untied him and were leading him away, the householder came out and said to them, "Why are you taking away my donkey?"

The disciples answered, "The Lord needs him."

The householder calmly replied, "Very well."

The disciples led the donkey back in to Bethany where a tremendous crowd had gathered in front of the house of Lazarus. The news that Jesus planned to ride the donkey into Jerusalem in accordance with the prophecy of Zechariah in defiance of the temple rabbis quickly spread throughout the village and created intense excitement as everyone realized the danger that Jesus faced in openly marching into Jerusalem before the Passover even began.

Soon, all the villagers were lending a helping hand to get the brave little band of men started on their momentous journey. Lazarus, Mary Magdalen and Martha made an impromptu saddle out of an old blanket and some wornout clothing. Some persons brought the disciples fruit, others brought them flowers; but mostly, they brought their cheering, encouraging spirits and expressions of best wishes for a successful journey. From all the preparations that were being made and the hubbub that was created, a stranger might have thought that Jesus and his disciples were departing on a long and distant journey through some unknown foreign land, instead of traveling a few miles over a well-known and familiar road. However, that short journey became the most fateful trip in the history of the world.

When this pathetic little band of men finally started moving out toward Jerusalem, they were followed by the cheers of the men and the hopeful tears of the women. First one and then another of the villagers ran after Jesus and his disciples, until very soon the entire road was clogged with villagers wishing them good luck. As Jesus and his disciples marched slowly down the road, they sang one hymn after another, filling the air with the sound of their stirring voices.

By the time they were going through the walls of Jerusalem at the Fountain Gate, they sang,

> "Behold ye the Lord and praise him,
> Lift up your heads and bless him;
> For the Kingdom of Heaven is nigh,
> When the righteous shall be rewarded,
> And the heavy-laden shall be rested,
> While the wicked shall be punished.
> So, behold the Lord and praise Him,
> Because the Kingdom of Heaven is nigh."

Quickly recognizing the boldness and the bravery of Jesus' open defiance of the temple rabbis, the people reacted spontaneously. They cheered, waved, and applauded in a mighty gesture of tumultuous welcome for these determined men whose only weapon was their faith in God. As Jesus moved down the winding streets, astride his young donkey, flowers, palm branches and even clothing were laid before him in such profusion that his young donkey walked on a thick matting of foliage and flowers.

Soon, from out of the crowd came shouts of:

"Praise be to God!
Blessed is he who comes
In the name of the Lord.
Blessed be the Kingdom
Of our father, David!
Praise be to God!"

The enthusiasm of the crowd was contagious. It increased from minute to minute so that by the time Jesus reached the temple grounds, it expressed itself in a mighty, continuous roar. As Jesus entered the temple gates, young and old shouted,

"Praise God for this Son of David!
Praise God for Jesus,
The Prophet of Galilee!
Praise God for the Messiah!"

When Jesus entered the Court of Solomon, he was met by a group of extremely angry temple rabbis headed by the Chief Rabbi himself. They were furious with rage. The Chief Rabbi shouted at Jesus. "Do you hear what that mob outside is shouting?"

Jesus calmly replied, "I do."

In a burst of fury, the Chief Rabbi rushed at Jesus, clutched his outer garment and shouted, "Then rebuke them for uttering those damned blasphemies, particularly the young children who don't know what they are saying."

Jesus quietly answered, "Haven't you heard that out of the mouths of babes comes the real truth?"

Matt. 21 (12-13) Mark 11 (15-19) Luke 13 (31-33) John 2 (13-25)
Matt. 21 (23-27) Mark 11 (27-33) Luke 19 (41-48) John 12 (42-44)
Matt. 24 (1-28) Mark 13 (1-33) Luke 21 (5-38)

Chapter 31

Jesus Drives the Merchants from the Temple

Several days later Jesus and his disciples were met by two men whose faces were partially hidden behind their enveloping cloaks. As they came closer, the two men threw back their cloaks and one of them said, "I am Nicodemus, a member of the Great Sanhedrin."

Startled out of his reverie, Jesus replied, "Yes, I recognize you."

Pointing to his companion, Nicodemus said, "This is my friend, Joseph of Arimathea, who also feels as sympathetic towards you as I do."

Turning to Joseph, Jesus said, "I am glad to know you, Joseph."

Nicodemus added, "Joseph is also a member of the Great Sanhedrin, and it may surprise you to know, master, that you have more friends in that council than you realize. But still, I must confess, that we who sympathize with you are only a small minority in the Great Sanhedrin."

Jesus replied, "Even having one friend in the Great Sanhedrin is one more than I expected. So, I am very happy to know that there are a few of you who do feel friendly towards me."

Nicodemus' face now turned grave as he said, "Master, I must warn you to leave Judaea as quickly as possible. Your life is in grave danger. The temple grounds are full of soldiers from King Herod's palace, and the temple guards have been greatly increased. Therefore, you may expect to be arrested at any time after dark, and this time, they definitely intend to kill you. Their only concern now is to avoid a riotous clash that will create a public disturbance and so invite interference from the Roman authorities."

Jesus remained silent for a few minutes while he gazed steadily toward Jerusalem six miles away. With his eyes still fixed upon the horizon, Jesus replied, "What would you have me do? Run like a rabbit before the forces of evil? Ahead of me I can see my Father's house, beckoning to me as a light on the shore welcomes the homecoming sailor. There is much work to be done in my Father's house and my Father has entrusted me to do that work. Shall I shirk the work that my father has given me to do?"

Peter interrupted saying, "Master, there is much to be considered in what Nicodemus tells us. We have already accomplished far more among our people than we originally thought possible. If you and all the rest of us get killed in Jerusalem, what good will it do? Isn't it better that we continue to live so that we can come back another day and continue with our work?"

Jesus looked at Peter and smilingly said, "Get behind me, Satan; but I must confess that I wish I could follow your advice."

Nicodemus said, "Then your mind is made up to re-enter Jerusalem?"

Jesus answered, "Yes, it is. I appreciate your coming here and I realize the risk that you and your friend took in doing so. Nevertheless, I must do my Father's work and not just do those things that I would like to do."

Joseph said, "We are sorry, master, to see you expose yourself to this grave danger and yet we can understand how you feel about it, and we honor you for it. We wish you well. There are a number of us in the Great Sanhedrin who believe in you and would like to help you, but at present, we are powerless to do so. For us to disclose our belief in you would only result in our ruination without changing in any way the inevitable result. However, I do promise you that if the occasion arises when we can be of help to you, we will do so."

Jesus simply replied, "Thank you, Joseph."

Nicodemus and Joseph said goodbye to Jesus and Peter, and again wrapping themselves carefully in their long enveloping cloaks, returned to Jerusalem.

Jesus told Peter to call the disciples together, and when they were all assembled, Jesus informed them that they would all proceed immediately to Jerusalem where he intended to preach again in the temple. As the disciples moved slowly down the road toward Jerusalem, they were a subdued and a serious-looking group of men. Gone now was the excitement of the great adventures that lay ahead. Few persons turned to look after them or follow them as they marched through the city gates into Jerusalem and turned toward the temple grounds. No one sang. The spirit of gaiety was all gone. There was only serious, dangerous confrontation that lay ahead for them with the temple rabbis.

As they approached the walls of the temple that shone brilliantly in the sunshine, James stood in awe before its gleaming walls and said to Jesus, "Look, master, see the brilliant stones that have been used in the construction of this wall. Aren't these buildings beautiful?"

Jesus answered, "Yes, James, these buildings are beautiful, but their beauty is only skin-deep. Before long, they will all come tumbling down until there is not one stone resting upon another."

Andrew asked, "Master, when will these things happen?"

Jesus answered, "No one knows the exact hour and the exact day when these things will happen, but there will be forewarnings for those who understand the signs and the acts of God. But before that day comes, you will be persecuted and delivered up to the rabbis in the synagogue, because you are my disciples.

"When that day comes, don't be afraid of answering your persecutors because at that time I shall fill your mouths with wisdom. Some of you will be killed and all of you will be hated because of me. Yet not a single hair of your heads will perish; because of your faith in God, your souls will be saved."

While Jesus was speaking, Rabbi Ahab came up behind him and listened to him talk. As soon as Jesus stopped speaking, the rabbi turned to him and said, "Your imagination runs away with you."

Jesus replied, "To prove my faith in God and God's power in me, I say to you that if you destroy this temple, I will rebuild it in three days."

Rabbi Ahab laughed contemptuously as he replied, "It took us forty-six years to build this temple, using thousands of men to perform the work of construction, but you say that you can rebuild it all by yourself in three days. Bah!"

Rabbi Ahab walked disgustedly away, making gyratory motions with his hands indicating he considered Jesus crazy. Ignoring the contemptuous rabbi, Jesus and his disciples crossed the Court of Solomon to the entrance of the new temple. When they tried to enter, they found the entrance

blocked by merchants who were selling a wide variety of livestock, doves and temple money.

The livestock offered for sale were various birds and animals specified by the Mosaic law as those acceptable to
Jehovah as sacrifices in atonement for sins committed by repentant sinners. If a sinner was very poor, he was allowed to
offer a pair of doves as a suitable sacrifice; but if a sinner was
well-to-do, he was expected to offer lambs, goats or even oxen
as a sacrifice to Jehovah.

According to Mosaic law, all animals offered for sacrifice
had to be taken into the temple alive and killed at the altar.
Therefore, the livestock merchants kept their animals in temporary stalls or cages on the steps of the temple in anticipation of their immediate use as sacrificial animals. As the
animals were killed soon after they were bought, the merchants made no provision for feeding or watering them. Consequently, the animals set up a continuous howling din of
bleating, bellowing and screeching for food and water. With
the passage of time, the smell of animal refuse pervaded the
entire atmosphere, so that the entrance to the temple more
closely resembled a livestock yard rather than a place of
worship.

To add to the commercial aspect of the scene, one end of
the temple steps was set aside for the money-changers. Each
money-changer had his own table, which was covered with
temple money and foreign money from many nations. These
money-changers were needed during the Passover, because
the rabbis refused to allow anyone to contribute foreign
money to the temple, since they claimed it would defile the
temple. As many of the Jewish pilgrims came from foreign
lands, the only money they had was foreign money. Therefore, those foreign pilgrims wishing to make a monetary gift
to the temple were compelled to exchange their foreign
money for temple money. In making these exchanges, the
money-changers made a handsome profit.

Since the available space on the temple steps was strictly limited, and as each merchant took all the space that his competitors would allow him, each pilgrim who entered the temple had to fight his way through a narrow gauntlet of shouting, rapacious merchants, while he threaded his way carefully around smelly, dirty cages filled with bellowing, screeching animals. It was a major feat of physical and mental endurance to struggle through this repulsive obstacle course.

Jesus watched this disgusting scene for a few minutes and then walked quickly to a corner of the temple steps where he found a long piece of heavy rope. Skillfully, he cut off a dozen pieces of rope about two feet long and tied hard round knots into each end. Next, he tied a long piece of the rope around the middle of the short knotted piece over and over again until he had fashioned a suitable handle for the knotted rope.

Taking this improvised whip, he lashed furiously at the merchant nearest to him until the man fled in panic. Methodically, he whipped each merchant in turn, allowing each one only sufficient time to take his livestock with him. After he had driven off the last of the livestock merchants, Jesus turned his attention upon the money-changers and lashed at them more viciously than he had the livestock merchants. While lashing angrily at the money-changers, he overturned their tables scattering their money in all directions. When the last of the money-changers had been driven away, Jesus shouted after them, "My Father's house is a house of prayer, but you have made it into a den for thieves."

During this noisy commotion, Chief Rabbi Caiaphas had been in his private chambers, just beyond the temple steps. When he heard the angry shouts of the merchants and the frightened bellowing of the animals, the Chief Rabbi rushed outdoors to determine the cause of the unusual tumult. He arrived just in time to see Jesus driving off the last of the money-changers. He strode angrily over to Jesus and shouted at him, "By what right do you drive away these merchants? Don't you realize they are the principal source of financial revenue for the temple?"

Jesus scornfully said, "These merchants support your temple from the money they have gouged from the pilgrims. Apparently you love the money you get from the merchants and the money-changers more than you do the loyalty of our pilgrims to God."

Chief Rabbi Caiaphas sneered, "If the existence of this temple depended upon you and your Galilean pilgrims, there wouldn't be any temple. Your Galilean pilgrims spend the entire day in our temple, praying and worshipping, but they leave only the smallest of temple contributions. You forget that it takes hundreds of rabbis and workers to run this huge temple."

Jesus scornfully answered, "It is evident that you love the money that you get from the livestock merchants and the money-changers; and your love of money is an abomination in the eyes of God. Although you claim you serve God, actually you serve the devil, and no man can serve two masters because if he is loyal to one, he will be disloyal to the other."

Chief Rabbi Caiaphas advanced menacingly toward Jesus and shouted at him, "Enough of your saintly sermons! I asked you a question. Answer it! By what authority do you drive these money-changers away from this temple?"

Jesus calmly replied, "First, let me ask you a question and after you have answered my question I will tell by what authority I do the things I do. My question is this, 'Was John the Baptist baptized by man or by God?' "

The Chief Rabbi's angry, snarling face slowly changed from one of indignant rage to one of puzzled bafflement. He had sent out many men to trick Jesus with forked questions and they had all failed. He felt sure that all of them were idiots and that if he had encountered Jesus he could have succeeded in tricking him. Now he was on the spot himself with the eyes and the ears of all Jerusalem focused upon him. He knew that by nightfall all Jerusalem would be buzzing with the news of his encounter with Jesus. How would he measure up?

The question that Jesus asked Chief Rabbi Caiaphas was a very important one to the Jews. In this question, we see again the Jewish belief in the intervention of God in man's affairs. In this particular instance, the intervention consisted of infusing the spirit of one of the ancient prophets into a human being. In effect, Jesus' question to the Chief Rabbi was, Do you consider that John the Baptist was an ordinary man; or do you believe that John the Baptist was a prophet infused with the spirit of God?

What could the Chief Rabbi say? He knew that many of the people of Judaea and Galilee believed that John the Baptist had been infused with the spirit of God; and therefore was one of God's prophets. So, if he answered that he believed that John the Baptist had been baptized by man, he would offend many of his people. Yet, if he answered that he believed John the Baptist had been baptized by God, he was certain that Jesus' next question to him would be, then why didn't you accept John the Baptist as one of God's prophets when he was alive?

The Chief Rabbi's big red face suddenly seemed to droop and his angry blazing eyes became lackluster. His big, bulky body sagged on its heavy, bony structure. His brain was in a whirl, but it spun uselessly. What answer could he make to Jesus before the sharply critical audience before him?

The Chief Rabbi was in a sweat. Never before had he felt so alone in his own temple, and never before had the eyes of the people in his own congregation appeared so hostile to him. Time hung still for the Chief Rabbi, as his overworked brain stopped working entirely. Finally, he answered in a weak, faraway voice, "I don't know the answer to your question."

Jesus coldly replied, "That's not true. The truth is, that you don't dare answer my question, and therefore, I won't answer your question."

Turning his back upon the Chief Rabbi, Jesus left the temple, leaving the Chief Rabbi and his agents standing helplessly in the midst of the wreckage of the merchants' stalls and the money-changers' tables. In a fit of anger, the Chief Rabbi struck one of the temple guards a resounding blow, because he thought the man was looking at him in an insulting manner. Chief Rabbi Caiaphas now turned and dashed into the temple and entered his private chambers, unaware of the fact that his father-in-law was following closely behind him. In the privacy of his room, the Chief Rabbi slumped wearily into a chair. When he looked up, he saw the calm eyes of Rabbi Annas looking patiently down at him. Weakly, the Chief Rabbi said, "What shall we do now?"

Rabbi Annas quietly answered, "That rebellious Galilean must be arrested as quickly as possible. Do you have any information yet regarding his hiding place?"

The Chief Rabbi disconsolately answered, "None."

Rabbi Annas replied, "Then you must quickly offer a very large reward for information leading to his arrest at nighttime. We have no time to lose. That rebel must be caught, tried and executed in the next few days before the Passover begins. Once the Passover begins, it will be too late."

The Chief Rabbi asked, "How big a reward shall I offer?"

Rabbi Annas answered, "It must be a very large reward—large enough to get us immediate action. I would say thirty pieces of silver should get us the necessary action that we need."

Chief Rabbi Caiaphas suddenly bolted upright and incredulously asked, "Thirty pieces of silver? That's enough money for a king's ransom. That rebel Galilean isn't worth thirty shekels."

Rabbi Annas determinedly replied, "He certainly is worth

thirty silver pieces to us. He has already cost us far more than that in the wreckage he created on the temple steps, to say nothing of the loss of prestige we have suffered in the eyes of the public. Thirty pieces of silver will be a small price to pay to get rid of that rebel."

Chief Rabbi Caiaphas wearily got up from his seat and slowly said, "Very well. I will let it be known through our informants that we will pay a reward of thirty pieces of silver for information leading to the arrest of this rebel, but I still think it's outrageous to waste all that temple money on that small bit of skin and bones when we could have him killed for thirty shekels."

Matt. 26 (1-5) Mark 14 (1-2) Luke 22 (1-6)
Matt. 26 (14-18 Mark 14 (10-15) John 11 (55-57)

Chapter 32

Judas and Chief Rabbi Caiaphas

Jerusalem was in violent turmoil. The Feast of the Passover, which was normally one of the happiest festivals in the
capital of Judaea, had become the occasion for a nerve-
wracking battle between two determined, conflicting forces.
On the one hand, there were the powerful temple rabbis who
insisted that Judaism required the strictest observance of all
the Mosaic laws and all the rabbinical regulations; while on
the other hand, there was Jesus who preached that the laws of
God were far more important than the Mosaic laws and the
rabbinical regulations. It was already evident that these two
conflicting forces were creating a serious split among the Jewish people. This was the one event that the wily old Rabbi
Annas had repeatedly warned his hot-headed son-in-law
against and the one event that he had tried so hard to
prevent.

There was no use denying any longer that the Jews were
rapidly aligning themselves into two opposing and conflicting

camps—those who supported the temple rabbis and those who believed in Jesus. The main outward difference between these two opposing groups was that those who supported the temple rabbis were the upper-class, well-to-do Jews; while those who believed in Jesus were the poor, exploited Jews. The well-to-do Jews could well afford to be outspoken in their support of the temple rabbis; while the poor, exploited Jews had to express their belief in Jesus surreptitiously and secretly.

However, the spontaneous reception that Jesus had received in Jerusalem left no doubt in the minds of the temple rabbis where the sympathies of many of the Jews rested. The events of the previous day when Jesus had single-handedly driven the livestock merchants and the money-changers from the steps of the temple confirmed what the temple rabbis already knew—Jesus had the solid support of the average Jew. For years the Jews of Jerusalem and of the surrounding countryside had been exploited during the celebration of their religious holy days by the merchants and the money-changers of Jerusalem with the open connivance of the temple rabbis. Average religious Jews had been repelled by the commercialization of their most cherished religious festivals, but they had not dared express their resentment of this commercialization because of their fear of the temple rabbis. Now Jesus had given voice to this dissatisfaction and he had received outspoken public acclaim.

So, Jerusalem buzzed with excitement. What would Jesus do next? The big question now was—would Jesus dare celebrate the Passover in Jerusalem? And if he did, would he celebrate the Passover openly or would he do so secretly? The answer must come soon, because on sundown of the following day, the Passover would begin.

That morning Peter and Jesus were quietly walking down the road in Bethany between the houses of Lazarus and Simon, and Peter, knowing the problems that Jesus faced, walked quietly beside him, waiting for him to speak. Finally, Jesus said, "Peter, I have made up my mind where we shall celebrate the Passover."

Peter anxiously asked, "Where have you decided, master?"

Jesus answered, "We shall celebrate the Passover in Jerusalem."

Peter protested, "But, master—"

Jesus interrupted. "I know what you are going to say, Peter, and this time I will say I agree with you."

Peter asked in obvious surprise, "But I thought you said that we would celebrate the Passover in Jerusalem."

Jesus answered, "Yes, I did, Peter; but we will not celebrate the Passover in Jerusalem tomorrow night on the first day of the Passover, but tonight—one day before the Passover begins. The fact that we celebrate the Passover one day early is not important to God. The important thing is that we celebrate the Passover in Jerusalem and still remain alive to continue preaching the word of God to the people of Judaea. They are now beginning to listen to our message."

Peter's bronzed, weather-beaten face changed immediately from one of apprehension to one of laughter and gaiety. Fervently, he said, "Praise be to God!" Then as he thought of the chagrin the rabbis would feel when they learned that Jesus had escaped them again, he smilingly said, "How I would like to see the face of Chief Rabbi Caiaphas when he learns that you escaped him again by celebrating the Passover in Jerusalem one day early."

Peter then broke out in a gale of laughter that quickly brought all the disciples running toward him to find out what all the merriment was about. When Peter told them of Jesus' plan to celebrate the Passover in Jerusalem one day early, they all rocked with laughter as they mimicked the Chief Rabbi looking for Jesus on the night of the Passover. Still smiling broadly, Peter turned to Jesus and said, "Where in Jerusalem shall we celebrate the Passover?"

Jesus answered, "I have arranged with Nicodemus that we shall celebrate it at his home. Peter, you and John go there this noon and prepare our Passover supper."

Peter asked, "But where is the home of Nicodemus?"

The disciple Judas spoke up and said, "I know where it is. It is a large two-story house surrounded by a beautiful garden enclosing a fountain, between the Fountain Gate and the Forum."

Jesus said, "That is right. But you will have no trouble finding it, Peter, because after you pass through the Fountain Gate, a man carrying a vase full of water will meet you at the fountain. You can easily pick him out because all the others carrying water will be women. Follow that man and go into the same house that he does. When you meet the master of the house, just say, 'The Master sent us. Where is the guest chamber where he will celebrate the Passover with his disciples?'

"He will lead you to a large room upstairs where you will find all the utensils you need and a fireplace prepared where you can cook our Passover supper. Judas will bring you the Passover lamb, the bread, the wine and all the other items necessary for our supper. The rest of us will drop in one or two at a time so as not to attract attention to our meeting there."

Peter answered, "Splendid, splendid. This shall be the happiest Passover of my life."

Then he burst into another gale of laughter as he thought of Jesus' sly scheme to outwit the Chief Rabbi. The other disciples crowded around Peter and joined in with him in laughing, back-slapping and merry-making. When the laughter had subsided, Peter turned to Judas and smilingly said, "Now you miserable Judaean, get us a tender lamb for this Passover. Open up those moneybags of yours and let some of the moths out. The last lamb you bought us had horns on it and it was tougher than any goat I ever ate. This is to be a happy Passover and we want to celebrate it with something more than just skin and bones."

John added to Peter's ribbing by saying, "Yes, and this time bring us some wine made of grapes. That last wine you brought us tasted like pickled brine."

Judas's dark face flushed angrily as he replied, "Please remember that our money supply is a lot smaller than that of the Chief Rabbi. If you want all the things that you are asking for, you should be eating your Passover supper with him."

John said, "You are supposed to be a shrewd bargainer, but if you paid more than ten shekels for that last goat you brought us, you were cheated."

Judas replied, "Remember we are here during the Passover. The city is crowded with pilgrims from all parts of Judaea, Samaria, Galilee and many foreign lands. The merchants take advantage of the situation by charging outrageous prices for everything. Please also remember that we are not in Galilee."

Jesus interrupted the argument by saying, "Judas, we all know that you are spending our limited funds to the best advantage of all of us. Peter and John are just being carried away with the spirit of the occasion. Just go into the market place in Jerusalem and do the best that you can."

Peter added, "And be sure to bring the lamb or the goat, or whatever else it is that you bring early so we can cook it long enough to tenderize the meat."

Judas was now so angry at the teasing he had received that he was unable to answer. He walked abruptly away, grinding his teeth in bitter resentment knowing that he was not popular with his fellow disciples. The teasing itself was innocent enough, but it had become almost a daily affair. One day it would be a sly suggestion that he was appropriating their joint funds for his personal use; another day it would be a remark that he was not collecting sufficient funds from those who had promised to make contributions to Jesus. But worst of all were the sly digs that he was the only Judaean in the group and spoke Aramaic with a Hebrew accent. Hebrew and Aramaic were similar enough so that the disciples understood Judas whenever he used Hebraic phrases, but if the disciples were in a joking mood, they pretended that Hebrew was just another foreign language, and they could not understand a word he said. Sometimes he wished that he had never taken on the job of being keeper of their joint funds and purchasing agent for their common needs.

His job placed him in constant contact with the commercial world and denied him the contact with the spiritual world of Jesus. As he walked down the road toward Jerusalem, he reflected bitterly that it was easy enough for Jesus and the other disciples to preach continually about the spiritual world, but it was his job to provide the necessities of life from the material world that made it possible for the others to eat and preach about the spiritual world.

The further Judas walked, the more bitter he became. One bitter thought led to another bitter thought, until the bitterness within him became a raging fire. At the time he had not thought too much about it, but now he reflected how Jesus himself had rebuked him at the feast in Simon's house when he had protested the foolish waste of the precious ointment which Mary Magdalen had poured over Jesus' head and feet. If the disciples wanted a good supper for the Passover, why hadn't they protested then, as he had? Think of all the fine food that could have been bought with the price of the precious ointment.

Judas continued walking silently toward Jerusalem when the thought occurred to him that he didn't really belong with Jesus and his disciples at all. By the time he arrived at the Fountain Gate, he was in a black sullen mood of resentment and anger against Jesus and all his disciples. Dispiritedly, he headed for the market place and trudged from one stall to another, bitterly arguing with the food merchants over the exorbitant prices they charged for all the items needed for their supper. Suddenly he felt a sharp tug at his elbow. Turning around, he saw a sharp face accentuated by bright, piercing eyes almost hidden beneath a dirty, heavy shawl. The stranger said, "Follow me!"

When they arrived at a quiet corner away from the market place, the stranger turned to Judas and abruptly asked, "Aren't you one of the Galilean's disciples?"

Judas indignantly replied, "Of course not! What are you talking about? I am a Judaean and I live in Bethany with my father. Jesus of Nazareth and all his followers are Galileans."

The stranger coldly replied, "Even so, I think you are one of the Galilean's disciples."

Judas answered with increased indignation, "I have already told you that I am a Judaean and that I am not a disciple of the Galilean. What do you want anyway?"

The stranger slyly replied, "Nothing. It's too bad that you are not a disciple of the Galilean, because if you were, you could earn thirty pieces of silver."

Judas gulped hard and quickly, asked, "How?"

The stranger coldly replied, "Since you are not a disciple of the Galilean, it doesn't matter."

Judas apologetically replied, "No, I am not a disciple of the Galilean, but I was curious how any one could earn such a huge sum of money."

The stranger sharply answered, "Well, if you happened to be one of the Galilean's disciples and led us to his hiding place tonight, you would earn thirty pieces of silver."

Judas whistled softly saying, "All of that money just to lead you to the hiding place of the Galilean?"

"Yes," the man replied, looking quizzically and expectantly at Judas.

Judas slowly said, "How would anybody know that you would keep your word?"

The stranger quickly answered, "Go to the temple immediately and see the Chief Rabbi. He will confirm everything I have said."

Judas replied, "I didn't say that I knew the Galilean's hiding place. I was just asking a question."

The stranger moved quickly away and Judas returned dazedly to the market place. Mechanically, he fingered food and mumbled prices with the argumentative merchants, but his mind did not hear their voices, nor did his eyes see the food he handled. All he could think of was the thirty pieces of silver—thirty shining pieces of silver! He had never seen a silver piece in all his life, let alone possess one.

As he turned from one stall to another, he accidentally knocked down one of the supporting props, spilling part of the merchandise to the ground. The angry merchant shouted, "Watch out what you're doing, you stupid country lout! You come here mumbling like an idiot and then walk away half asleep without buying anything."

While the merchant continued shouting angry reproaches at him, Judas walked dazedly away, hearing neither the merchant's voice nor the discordant noises of the market place. Although his ears heard nothing, his beady eyes shone brightly picturing the many treasures the thirty pieces of silver would buy for him.

He had forgotten all about Jesus and the disciples by now. They could look out for themselves. In fact, they had never appreciated him anyway. From now on, he was going to look out for just himself. Subconsciously, his pace quickened until he was almost in a trot which quickly brought him before the huge gates of the new temple.

Suddenly they seemed very huge and overwhelming and he, by contrast, seemed very small and insignificant. He loitered hesitatingly before the gate, until one of the temple guards noticed him and yelled, "Keep moving, you filthy countryman! This gate is reserved for the rabbis."

Judas meekly replied, "I want to see Chief Rabbi Caiaphas."

The temple guard sneered to another guard inside the gate and said, "Look at the filthy, country bumpkin who wants to see the Chief Rabbi."

The other guard laughed and said, "Ha! Ha! Maybe he wants to offer himself as a sacrifice at the altar."

The first temple guard sneered, "What? That goat? Don't you know that skinny goats like that have to be sacrificed in pairs?"

The two guards laughed uproariously. When their laughter had subsided, Judas said, "I have something very important to tell the Chief Rabbi about Jesus of Nazareth."

The temple guards instantly changed their bantering manner to one of grave concern as one of them asked, "Do you know that blasphemer?"

Judas quietly replied, "I have nothing to say to you. Take me to the Chief Rabbi."

Quickly and almost fearfully, one of the guards led Judas to Captain Shama, the captain of the temple guards. As soon as Captain Shama understood the nature of Judas' mission, he quickly led him across the Court of Solomon into the private chambers of the temple where Chief Rabbi Caiaphas was reclining half-asleep on a couch. "Honorable Rabbi," the captain said, "this man says he has something very important to tell you about the Galilean."

The Chief Rabbi bolted upright as he carefully scrutinized Judas. Abruptly he said, "Do you know the Galilean?"

Judas nodded and mumbled, "I do."

The Chief Rabbi's eyes narrowed into two thin slits as he asked skeptically, "Who are you?"

Judas's voice dropped a notch lower as he replied, "I am Judas Iscariot, one of the twelve disciples of the Galilean."

The Chief Rabbi's eyes traveled over the dirty crumpled

figure before him like a torchlight searching into the pitch-black darkness. Then he barked, "Then why are you here?"

Judas answered, "To get the reward that you have offered for information leading to the arrest of Jesus of Nazareth."

Chief Rabbi Caiaphas shouted, "You're a liar. Your speech betrays you. You are a Judaean, and not a Galilean. Captain, take this man away."

Captain Shama stepped forward and firmly took Judas by the shoulder as Judas protestingly said, "Wait! I can prove what I say."

The Chief Rabbi snarled, "Go ahead."

Judas said, "It is true that I am a Judaean, while all the other disciples are Galileans, but I still am one of the disciples of Jesus of Nazareth. Ask me anything you want to know about him and I will answer you."

The Chief Rabbi asked, "Where was the Galilean last night?"

Judas answered, "At the home of Simon in Bethany."

Again the Chief Rabbi asked, "Where was he the night before?"

Judas answered, "At the home of Lazarus in Bethany."

The Chief Rabbi slowly asked, "Where will he be tonight?"

Judas replied, "Do I get my reward?"

Chief Rabbi Caiaphas snapped back, "Of course you will get your reward if you lead us to the Galilean's hiding place. Now where will we find him tonight?"

Judas slowly asked, "Do I get thirty pieces of silver as my reward?"

Chief Rabbi Caiaphas shouted, "Thirty pieces of silver? Are you crazy? Why, that's a fortune. We'll give you five pieces of silver."

Judas firmly replied, "I was promised thirty pieces of silver."

The Chief Rabbi breezily said, "Some crazy idiot must

have promised you that. We never offered any such huge sum; but I am in a hurry to get this thing over with so I'll give you ten pieces of silver."

Judas looked at the Chief Rabbi and without another word started walking toward the door. When Chief Rabbi Caiaphas saw that Judas was determined to leave, he shouted at him, "Wait! Wait! You robber! I'll give you twenty pieces of silver and not a shekel more."

Judas turned around, looked squarely in the face of the Chief Rabbi and determinedly replied, "You will pay me thirty pieces of silver and not a shekel less!"

Disgustedly Chief Rabbi Caiaphas said, "I said before that you were a robber and now in addition, I say that you are a Gentile! All right, I'll give you thirty pieces of silver. Now, let's get down to business. Where will the Galilean be to-night?"

Judas answered, "In Jerusalem."

The Chief Rabbi's black eyes were now fixed so intently upon Judas that he felt the rabbi's eyes could burn holes right through him. The rabbi's body was tense with excitement as he leaned forward, grasped Judas with both his sweaty hands and said, "Why will the Galilean be in Jerusalem tonight? The Passover does not start until sundown tomorrow."

Judas slowly answered, "Jesus believes that you will not expect him in Jerusalem tonight, and therefore he can cele-brate the Passover in Jerusalem tonight and leave the city before you have an opportunity to arrest him."

The Chief Rabbi suddenly relaxed as he drew away from Judas and said, "The scoundrel! He breaks the Sabbath, eats with sinners, overturns the laws of Moses, leads our people astray and now he dares celebrate the Passover in Jerusalem even before the beginning of the Holy Days. But that is typi-cal of that blaspheming rebel."

The Chief Rabbi now became strangely quiet as he pondered over the steps he must take to capture his quarry. Slowly a faint smile swept over his face as he said, more to himself that to Judas, "Maybe this time the sly fox has outfoxed himself. So he is going to celebrate the Passover in Jerusalem one day early. Well, well, well, that will be just perfect."

Then turning to Judas, he said, "You shall have your thirty pieces of silver—thirty nice, shiny pieces of new silver. Now tell me where in Jerusalem will the Galilean be tonight?"

Judas slowly answered, "Have your thirty pieces of silver ready for me and after you pay me, I will lead you to him."

The Chief Rabbi impatiently replied, "I told you I will pay you the thirty pieces of silver. Don't be so distrustful. Be here tonight one hour after sundown."

Judas answered, "Yes, Rabbi."

But instead of leaving the room, Judas paused hesitatingly. The Chief Rabbi turned and asked, "Now what is it?"

Judas slowly said, "Chief Rabbi Caiaphas, you must promise me one thing."

The Chief Rabbi looked contemptuously at the dirty ragged figure before him that fate had unexpectedly made his collaborator, and who now asked him, the Chief Rabbi, to make him a promise. Skeptically, the Chief Rabbi asked, "What is it?"

Judas meekly said, "You must promise me that you will not kill Jesus of Nazareth. Whatever else Jesus may be, he is a good man and he does not deserve to die."

The Chief Rabbi's face flushed with anger as he replied, "You know that our rabbinical laws forbid us to kill anyone."

Judas answered, "Yes I know that. But I also know that your agents have already made several attempts to kill him and, therefore, I want you to promise me that you will not kill my master."

The Chief Rabbi shouted back, "All right, I promise you

that we will not kill your master. But you know as well as I do
that there is no need for me to make such a promise. Now go,
and be here promptly tonight one hour after sundown."

Judas bowed low and meekly replied, "Yes, Rabbi."

Matt. 12 (14)   Luke 6 (11)
Matt. 26 (3-5)   John 11 (47-53)
Mark 3 (6)

Chapter 33

The Great Sanhedrin

As soon as Judas walked out the door, the Chief Rabbi turned quickly to Captain Shama and said, "Send two guards to follow that man wherever he goes. He is a disciple of the rebel Galilean. If he enters a house, have one man remain there and have the other report back to me immediately. When that guard comes back, send him in to see me as soon as he arrives. Now, quick—don't lose that follower of the blasphemer."

Captain Shama bowed low and said, "Yes, Rabbi."

Having accomplished this much, the Chief Rabbi sat down, puzzled as to what to do next. He dared not admit even to himself that he had botched every attempt he had made to trick, trap or kill Jesus. How he wished that he had his father-in-law's cool, calculating brain. He needed him desperately right now, but there was nothing that he hated worse than turning to his father-in-law for help and advice. He could feel the cool contempt that the older man held for him, even though Rabbi Annas was always the quintessence of politeness and even deferred important religious matters to his judgment. However, nothing so unnerved the Chief Rabbi as having the older rabbi refer important rabbinical matters to him, when he knew that the older man had a far better knowledge of proper religious procedure than he did.

The Chief Rabbi struck his knee in frustration. He was a huge, sullen, moody man of only mediocre intelligence, chosen for his office solely because he was the son-in-law of the former Chief Rabbi Annas. The two men were in direct contrast to each other physically and mentally. Rabbi Annas, a deeply religious teacher, was highly revered for his detailed knowledge of the Torah. All the members of the Great Sanhedrin greatly admired the wise old rabbi and deeply regretted that his failing health required that he resign his post which virtually forced the council to accept his impetuous son-in-law as his replacement. There were times when Rabbi Caiaphas wished that his wife and his father-in-law had not pushed him into becoming Jerusalem's Chief Rabbi. Try as he would, his muddled brain would not give him the proper answer regarding what action to take next. One thought was uppermost in his mind—this time he must not fail! Jesus must die! But how could he possibly arrest Jesus, try him before the Great Sanhedrin and have the Romans crucify him, all before the beginning of the Passover, which was only thirty hours away?

It was an impossible task! There were rabbinical laws against arresting a Jew at night and there were rabbinical laws requiring the exact corroboration of the testimony of two witnesses against the accused person; and there were other rabbinical laws forbidding the execution of a con-demned person within twenty four hours of his condemnation. And finally he faced the very difficult task of obtaining the Roman Governor's approval of ordering the execution of Jesus.

The Chief Rabbi's head was in a whirl. The more he thought about his problems, the more insoluble they became. He needed help and he needed it badly. There was only one person who could give him that help and that person was his father-in-law, Rabbi Annas. Biting his lip in frustration, Chief Rabbi Caiaphas finally decided to stifle his pride and go to his father-in-law's house and ask him for the help he needed.

When the old rabbi was informed by a servant that his son-in-law wished to see him, he frowned and sighed heavily. He knew that only a weighty problem could bring his son-in-law to his house at this time, and there was little doubt in his mind what the problem was—something concerning the rebel Galilean. Rabbi Annas knew that his son-in-law had seriously botched the job of handling the problems created by Jesus, and consequently, many Jews criticized the temple rabbis and even spoke of them with contempt. As these thoughts pulsed through his brain, Rabbi Annas reflected how unfortunate it was for Jerusalem that one so inept as his son-in-law should be the Chief Rabbi of Jerusalem during such a crisis as now faced their nation. Somehow, he must help salvage what he could from the mess his son-in-law had created.

When Chief Rabbi Caiaphas entered the room, Rabbi Annas quickly put aside all his doubts about his son-in-law and cordially greeted the younger rabbi as though he were the most welcome guest. After their formal greeting was over, Chief Rabbi Caiaphas said, "Father, I have something very important to tell you."

Rabbi Annas courteously replied, "Make yourself comfortable, son, and tell me all about it."

The Chief Rabbi quickly told of his meeting with Judas and of the men he had sent to spy upon him. When he had finished, he said uncertainly, "My first thought was to have the Galilean killed tonight when he comes out of the home where he is eating his Passover supper; but then I remembered you said that no Jew must kill him. So, instead of having him killed, I just sent two guards to follow him and report his whereabouts back to me."

Rabbi Annas slowly replied, "Good, son; so far, very good. Very good indeed."

Chief Rabbi Caiaphas brightened up perceptibly; seldom since he had become Chief Rabbi could he remember receiving his father-in-law's genuine approval of some action he had taken. He was on the verge of speaking again while he was still basking in the glow of the older rabbi's approval, but a look at the older rabbi's thoughtful face told him to remain quiet. Rabbi Annas absentmindedly stroked his long white beard as he quietly thought over the situation. Otherwise, he remained motionless.

Then he quietly said, more to himself than to his son-in-law, "So the Galilean is having his Passover supper in Jerusalem tonight. Well, well, well. He doesn't travel alone; in fact, he is usually accompanied by a large group of disciples, perhaps ten or twenty of them. Now where could such a group of men gather in Jerusalem for a Passover supper? No ordinary house could hold them all. Where do you think they would have that supper, son?"

The Chief Rabbi answered blankly, "Why, I don't know."

Rabbi Annas asked, "Who in Jerusalem that is friendly toward the Galilean has a house large enough to accommodate ten to twenty persons for supper?"

Before the Chief Rabbi could answer, there was a knock at the door and a servant entered and said to Rabbi Annas, "There is a guard from the temple outside who says that he has an urgent message for the Chief Rabbi."

Rabbi Annas replied, "Let him in."

The temple guard entered and bowed low to both rabbis.

Chief Rabbi Caiaphas turned to Rabbi Annas and whispered, "This is one of the temple guards whom I sent to spy upon the Galilean's informer." Then turning to the guard, the Chief Rabbi pompously said, "I suppose you have come to report to me on the whereabouts of the Galilean's disciple?"

As the guard made no reply, the Chief Rabbi impatiently said, "Speak up, man, what is it?"

The temple guard haltingly answered, "Rabbi, the man you told us to follow went to the marketplace, bought some food and then vanished into the milling crowd."

Chief Rabbi Caiaphas snarled, "You fools! How could two of you lose sight of that man if you were both alert?"

Rabbi Annas put forth a restraining hand on his son-in-law and said in a reassuring voice to the temple guard, "Don't worry about it. We know you did your best. Now, go back to the temple, and don't speak to anyone about this matter."

The guard gratefully bowed low and said, "Yes, Rabbi."

After the guard left, Rabbi Annas said very quietly, "The pieces are all beginning to fit together. There are still one or two pieces missing that we don't know about, but we do know enough to act without delay. There is little doubt that some one or more persons of importance in Jerusalem is supporting this Galilean. Tonight we must find out who it is. That person is possibly a member of the Great Sanhedrin. Who else has a house big enough for about twenty guests? Our job is to keep that person from knowing what we know and then notifying the Galilean of our plans."

The Chief Rabbi asked, "How can we do that?"

Rabbi Annas replied, "If the Great Sanhedrin were to meet immediately and remain in session until after we have arrested the Galilean, wouldn't that solve our problems? Son, call an emergency meeting of the Great Sanhedrin. Once all the members are present in the temple, lock all the gates and allow no one to leave. Which one of our members may be sympathetic to the Galilean, we do not know; but there are times when I suspected Nicodemus and possibly even Joseph of Arimathea; however, I am not sure. Besides, there may be other members of the Great Sanhedrin who may be secret followers of this rebel. In any case, we cannot afford to take any chances. Our motto must be: Trust nobody!"

The Chief Rabbi asked, "But what shall I say to the members of the Great Sanhedrin after they are all assembled here? What excuse shall I give them for locking them up in the temple?"

Rabbi Annas replied, "They won't be locked up in the temple. They simply will be our guests for supper tonight in preparation for a very special trial that will be held after the Galilean is brought in. Surely, no member of the Great Sanhedrin would refuse to be our guests at supper, or wish to be absent during such a very important trial. And, in answer to your question regarding the reason for calling this emergency meeting of the Great Sanhedrin, leave that to me. I will speak to them."

As he started to get up from his comfortable couch, Chief Rabbi Caiaphs looked admiringly at his father-in-law while Rabbi Annas said to him, "Return to the temple at once and summon this emergency meeting of the Great Sanhedrin. I will be over in a few minutes and join you."

The Chief Rabbi hastily returned to the temple and quickly dispatched messengers to all the members of the Great Sanhedrin to attend an emergency meeting of the council. Before long, the members began arriving in the temple grounds where they formed tight little knots of heated discussion groups debating what particular emergency might be sufficient reason for the calling of this special meeting of the Great Sanhedrin just a day before the Passover.

By the time Rabbi Annas arrived all members of the Great Sanhedrin were present and all the great doors of the temple were locked shut. While the members of the Great Sanhedrin were unaware of the fact that they were virtual prisoners in their own temple, they sensed the fact that some particularly special event was in the making.

Quietly the members of the Great Sanhedrin all waited for the Chief Rabbi to inform them of the reason for this special meeting. Rabbi Caiaphas said: "You all know of the vicious attacks that the Galilean rebel has made upon our faith since the death of his cousin, John the Baptist. With each passing day his accusations against us become more vicious and inflammatory. The stupid masses who listen to him and follow him are becoming larger and larger, until now they threaten our very existence. We can no longer afford to waste time with this dangerous man." Nicodemus then rose and very quietly asked, "What do you propose to do?"

The Chief Rabbi blurted out, "Let us arrest and kill him."

After a long silent pause, Rabbi Annas rose and said, "Members of the Great Sanhedrin, I am sure that you all know that we are faced with a very grave crisis. Since the time of Moses, God has infused His spirit into the hearts of many of our people, and those men have been our prophets and have kept us in the paths of righteousness. Unfortunately, we Jews have also been cursed at times by agents of the devil, and these impostors have brought nothing but shame and sorrow to our people. Such is the case now. There is a dangerous Galilean rebel amongst us who claims not only that he is a prophet of God, but that he is actually the Son of God."

From all the members of the Great Sanhedrin, came a deafening roar, "Kill him! Kill him! Kill the Galilean rebel!"

Rabbi Annas motioned for silence and then continued, "I agree with you that this man must die, but again, I must caution you that no Jew must kill him.

"This man is obviously not afraid to die and become a martyr, which is proven by the fact that he dared risk riding a donkey into Jerusalem several days ago at the head of a howling mob. And only yesterday, he dared drive the merchants and the money-changers from the temple steps, scattering money and sacrificial animals in all directions. Then he publicly defied our Chief Rabbi, and thereby encouraged our people to hold the members of this Great Sanhedrin in disrespect. So let us all fully understand the fact that we face a tough and formidable enemy."

When the old rabbi paused to take a drink of wine from an earthen jug, the council chamber reverberated again with a monotonously deafening roar, "Kill the rebel! Kill him! Kill him!"

Raising his slender white hands in a motion of silence, Rabbi Annas continued, "We have called this emergency meeting of this council because we have information that leads us to believe that in order to deceive us, he will eat his Passover supper in Jerusalem tonight, rather than eating it as he should tomorrow night on the first day of the Passover. We hope to arrest him some time during the night and bring him here for trial. For that reason, we ask you to be patient and be our guests for supper this evening, because we want you to try him as soon as he arrives.

"We will have our witnesses ready for the trial and if the verdict is in agreement with our findings, we expect you to condemn him to death immediately. Then tomorrow morning we shall all go in a body to the Roman Forum and demand that the Roman governor carry out the verdict of this council and execute this rebellious blasphemer before our sacred Passover begins."

Nicodemus hastily stood up and said, "Rabbi Annas, isn't this whole procedure extremely irregular? How can you justify the arrest of this Galilean at night with our rabbinical regulations? And more important than that, how can you justify having him executed a few hours after his trial? Have all of our rabbinical safeguards for the protection of our people been suddenly revoked?"

Rabbi Annas quietly replied, "Our rabbinical regulations recognize the fact that during periods of emergency, our rules for the protection of the individual can be waived in the interest of the safety of our nation. Such an emergency now exists and therefore, we must act decisively and quickly. As for the rabbinical requirement that a twenty-four-hour interval elapse between the time of condemning the accused and the time of his execution—that provision is a requirement for us. However, since we do not intend to carry out the death sentence, but plan to have the Romans carry out the execution, our rabbinical regulations will not be involved."

Nicodemus stood up again and said, "But the Romans have no reason for killing this Galilean."

"No," replied the old rabbi, "they don't, but as I said at our last meeting, we will give them a reason for executing the Galilean and not just one reason, but several; any one of which will require the execution of this guilty man by the Romans. Are there any other questions?"

As no one spoke, the old rabbi continued in his softly persuasive voice saying, "Gentlemen, I regret as much as any of you do the necessity for executing this man. I do not deny that he speaks with great sincerity and that he has the best of intentions. However, the pathway to hell is paved with good intentions. Unfortunately it is true that this Galilean is an ever-present source of danger to us, to our religion and to our nation. Therefore it is better that this one man should die rather than to have Judaism itself destroyed by internal dissension. I say again, I greatly regret the necessity for this action.

"While we are waiting for the Galilean to be arrested, we would like to ask all of you to make yourselves as comfortable as you possibly can until he is brought in for trial. Meals will be served to you whenever you wish. My son and I thank you very kindly for your patience and your cooperation in this matter. Now relax and do as you wish until the trial begins. Just one thing more, please do not leave the temple grounds until after this trial is over, because we want to be sure that all of you will be present when the trial of the Galilean begins."

Matt. 26 (19-30) John 13 (1-35) John 16 (1-33) Ps. 22 (1-11
Mark 14 (16-26) John 14 (1-31) John 17 (1-26)   14-16
Luke 22 (13-23) John 15 (1-27)   18-19)
Ps. 41 (9)

Chapter 34

The Last Supper

After Judas left the temple, he hurried to the market place to buy the necessary food, spices and wine required for their Passover supper that night. He was already very late and he knew that Peter and John would severely reprimand him for delaying their supper. However, by this time he was beyond caring what any of the disciples said or thought about him. His only thought now was to get the Passover supper over with as quickly as possible so that he could return to the temple, betray Jesus and collect the reward of the thirty pieces of silver.

Hurriedly, he made his purchases of lamb, bread, figs, wine and various spices with the minimum amount of haggling. Quickly he arranged his purchases into a manageable load and slung it over his shoulders. As he trudged wearily down the street toward the house of Nicodemus, he concocted various excuses to explain the lateness of his arrival.

Meanwhile at the home of Nicodemus, Peter and John fretted and fumed as they discussed the many possible causes that might have delayed Judas' arrival so long. Each took repeated trips outdoors peering in the direction of the market place. Finally, John saw Judas coming down the street and ran out to meet him and help him into the house with his heavy burden.

Breathlessly, John asked, "Where have you been so long? Our Passover supper is going to be awfully late."

Judas nonchalantly shrugged his shoulders and said, "Oh, there were tremendous crowds in the market place and all the prices were sky-high, so I had to bargain for hours before I could buy the things we need for our supper with the little money that I had."

By this time, Judas and John had entered the house where Peter was impatiently waiting for them. Peter removed the bundle of food from Judas' shoulders and angrily said to him, "So help me, if it wasn't for the master's daily example of kindness and forgiveness, I would clout you across both ears."

Judas walked insolently up the stairs, resolved to close his mind to all the insults that Peter and John might hurl at him. Once inside the guest chamber where Peter and John had made their preparations for the Passover supper, Peter critically checked each item of food. With his sharp eyes and practiced hand, he examined the lamb and immediately knew that it was lean and tough. Peter grunted, "As usual, the same old goat." John picked up the jug of wine, took a quick swig and immediately spit it out saying, "This stuff is so old it has turned to vinegar. About all it's good for is to soften up that tough old goat."

Peter said nothing more, but disgustedly reached into the market bag and took out a large bunch of figs that he barely glanced at. Then he reached into the bag again and drew out two large round loaves of bread. Blazing with anger, he turned to Judas and said, "Bread? Bread? Leavened bread on the Passover? You cursed idiot! Do you mean to tell me that you expect us to celebrate the Passover supper without unleavened bread? I'll break every bone in your body."

Crouching low behind the long heavy table, Judas defiantly replied, "Well, what did you expect, my noble lord, perfumed matzoths? How much money do you think we have? The matzoths were priced at five times their real value, while the bread was marked down special because no one was buying it. Besides the disciples need something far more nourishing to eat than matzoths."

Peter angrily replied, "The master would prefer that each of us ate one small matzoth for our Passover supper than all of this bread."

Judas sneeringly replied, "Who said this is the Passover? Don't forget that the Passover doesn't start until tomorrow night."

Peter shouted back, "That makes no difference. For us, the Passover begins tonight. Why buy a sacrificial lamb for our supper if we must eat leavened bread with it?"

Judas sarcastically answered, "Why are you making all this fuss about eating leavened bread before the Passover even begins? Since when have we become so strict in the observance of the Mosaic laws? We have broken the Sabbath and the Scriptural laws so many times that I have lost count of the many occasions."

John said, "He sounds like a temple rabbi to me."

Peter growled, "He sure does. I still think I should break every bone in his body. But, what's the use? Let's get on with the supper. John, light that fire."

While Peter and John were still in the midst of their preparations for the supper, Jesus and the other disciples arrived. The newly arrived disciples joined Peter and John in their hasty preparations for their Passover supper and soon all the many small tasks were completed and Jesus and the twelve disciples sat down to eat. Jesus rose and said a short prayer, which the disciples ended with hearty amens.

If Jesus noticed the absence of unleavened bread, he made no mention of it. As for the disciples, they were too hungry and too accustomed to the nonobservance of ritualistic Jewish customs to raise any objections about eating the nourishing bread.

They quietly ate their supper in a state of subdued uneasiness. The eating of the Passover supper one day early, which at first had appeared like such a clever scheme to out-wit the Chief Rabbi, did not seem quite so clever now. This was still Jerusalem and the power of the temple rabbis was very great. Eating in Jerusalem for Jesus and his disciples was a far different matter than eating supper in Bethany. In Bethany they could eat their food with an air of relaxation among friends; in Jerusalem, they gulped their food quietly and fearfully, as they felt the enveloping hostility of the temple authorities.

The people of Jerusalem, who had greeted them so exuberantly a few days before, were now all safely back in their homes. The city itself was full of rumors of planned raids upon the various places where Jesus had been known to visit. Spies were everywhere; suspicion was rampant; and one neighbor feared to speak to another because of the possibility of being implicated in the struggle between the temple rabbis and Jesus.

Up until this time, the disciples had always managed to save Jesus when he was in danger from the wrath of the temple rabbis. This time, however, there was an added factor of danger which hung heavily over all of them, because they sensed it, rather than knowing what it was. Jesus, who felt the depressed mood of the disciples, stood up when they had finished their supper and said, "Let not your hearts be troubled. As you believe in God, also believe in me. In my Father's house there are many mansions which can accommodate all of you. I shall go there before you and prepare a place for you."

Thomas spoke up and asked, "Lord, we don't even know where you are going, so how can we know how to get there?"

Jesus answered, "I am the way, the truth, and the everlasting life. No one reaches God, except through me. Those who have known me, know my Father. Therefore, from now on, you do know my Father and you have seen Him."

Philip said, "Show us your Father, Lord, and we shall be satisfied."

Jesus answered, "Philip, have I been with you so long without your knowing who I am? He who has seen me, has seen my Father. So, why do you say, 'Show me your Father'? The words that I speak to you are not my words, but those of my Father, who dwells in me. It is my Father who speaks and acts through me. Don't you believe that I am in my Father and that my Father is in me?"

Peter said, "Of course we do, Lord."

Jesus replied, "He who believes in me shall be able to do my Father's work, because soon I shall be with my Father, and then whatsoever you ask in my name, you shall receive. I am the true vine and you are the branches. No branch can blossom and grow unless it is attached to the vine. So it is with you. If you abide in me, you will produce a bountiful harvest. If you do not abide in me, you will produce nothing; and those branches which produce nothing shall be cut off from the vine and be thrown into the eternal fire.

"If you love me, keep my commandments and I will ask my Father to send you another comforter, who will abide with you forever. That comforter will be the Holy Spirit whom my Father will send to you in my name. He will teach you everything and remind you of the things that I have taught you. Only beware of the hypocritical rabbis who will throw you out of their synagogues and kill you. Yes, the day will come when these rabbis will persecute you and kill you in the name of the Lord.

"However, if you keep my commandments, as I have kept my Father's commandments, you will abide in my love as I have abided in my Father's love. This is my last commandment to you, that you shall love one another as I have loved you. Greater love hath no man than this—that a man shall lay down his life for his friends."

Jesus now took off his outer garments, wrapped a towel around his waist and filled a basin with water. As the disciples watched him, they realized that they were witnessing a very special event in their lives and a very special event in the life of Jesus. Then Jesus knelt down and began to wash the feet of each of his disciples. When he reached the place where Peter sat, Peter said to him, "Lord, are you going to wash my feet?"

Jesus answered, "Yes, I am. You do not understand what I am doing now, but you will later on."

Peter quickly drew his feet up under him and said, "Lord, you will never wash my feet."

Jesus quietly replied, "Peter, if I do not wash your feet now, you will not share the Kingdom of Heaven with me hereafter."

Peter now quickly stretched forth both his feet, his head and his hands and said, "Forgive me, Lord. In that case, wash not only my feet, but my head and my hands as well."

Jesus replied, "He who is clean, need only wash his feet in order to be thoroughly clean. You are clean, Peter; unfortunately, that is not true of all of you."

Then turning to all the disciples, Jesus said, "Do you know what I have done to you, you who call me Lord and Master? If I, your Lord and Master, wash your feet, it is also fitting and proper that you should wash one another's feet. I have given you an example of proper behavior; now you go and do for others what I have done for you."

Thomas now stood up and said to Jesus, "Master, a little while ago you said that we are not all clean. What did you mean by that?"

Jesus answered, "There is a passage in the Psalms that says, 'My friend in whom I trusted, and who ate my bread, has lifted up his heel against me.' The Scriptures must be fulfilled, and so now I say to you that one of you will raise up his heel against me and betray me."

Jesus' somber prediction added to the disciples' dejected mood. In alarm and consternation they looked at one another searchingly, wondering who the culprit might be. John, who was sitting next to Jesus, dropped his head in sorrow; Peter, who was sitting across the table from him, leaned over and whispered, "Ask the master to tell us who the traitor is."

Before John could ask this question, several of the disciples crowded around Jesus, saying, "Lord, is it I?"

Ignoring their questions, Jesus said, "He who dips his bread with me in this cup will betray me."

While he was speaking, Judas slowly shuffled around the room until he stood next to Jesus. Then when Jesus dipped his bread into his wine cup, Judas slyly dipped his bread in with Jesus' and whispered, "Lord, is it I?"

Jesus replied in an undertone that no one could hear but Judas, saying, "Yes, it is you. Now go and do what you must do and do it quickly."

Judas' face reddened with embarrassment and shame. Quickly he left the table and went out of the house and into the night on his cowardly mission. None of the disciples heard the exchange of words that took place between Jesus and Judas. When the disciples saw Judas leave the room, they thought that Jesus had simply sent him on some errand.

After Judas left, Jesus took a loaf of bread, blessed it, broke it and gave each of the disciples a piece of it saying, "Take this bread and eat it for this is my body."

Then he filled his cup with wine and passed it to each of his disciples saying, "Drink you all of it, for this is my blood which is shed for many persons for the remission of their sins. Do this in remembrance of me."

Solemnly, all the disciples ate their pieces of bread and drank from the cup of wine that Jesus had passed to them. Jesus then said, "And now before we leave, let me quote a prophecy from the psalms of David:

> " 'My God, why hast thou forsaken me?
> Why art thou so far from helping me?
> Avoid me not, for trouble is near
> There is no strength or power in me.
> They have pierced my hands and my feet,
> And all of my bones are out of joint.
> They have divided up my garments,
> My enemies cast lots for my cloak,
> Be not far from me,
> Oh my strength, hasten thou to help me.' "

When Jesus stopped speaking, there was a long silent pause. Then Peter said, "Let us thank our host for allowing us to enjoy our Passover supper in his home tonight and then let us all leave as quietly as possible by the back door one at a time."

John left the room, soon returned and said, "Peter, I have just spoken to one of the house servants and he says that his master has not yet returned from the meeting of the Great Sanhedrin at the temple."

Peter said, "That probably means that the Great Sanhedrin is in session and that can only mean trouble for our master. So let us leave immediately. I will lead out and the rest of you follow after me in the usual order. Each one of you keep in sight of the man ahead and behind you. We will use our regular signals, one short, sharp whistle for a quick halt, and two low whistles means all clear. The last man, who will be

John, will keep a sharp eye out for any one who may be following us. If for any reason we get separated, continue on as best you can through the Fountain Gate to the Garden of Gethsemane, provided that you are not being followed. If you think you are being followed, go to the home of Lazarus in Bethany. Are there any questions? If not, let's go."

Matt. 23 (37-39) Luke 22 (31-46)
Matt. 26 (36-45) John 13 (36-38)
Mark 14 (26-41) John 18 (1-2)
Luke 13 (34-35)

Chapter 35

The Garden of Gethsemane

Once he was outside the home of Nicodemus, Peter crouched low behind the garden wall and remained there until his eyes were accustomed to the lights and the shadows of the night. As soon as his eyes could see in the darkness and his ears were attuned to the sounds of the night, he moved silently down the dark winding street, being careful to remain in the shadows of the buildings. One by one, each of the disciples followed him, being careful to observe the same precautions that Peter did. In spite of their cautious method of travel, they proceeded with considerable speed.

Soon, they arrived at the Fountain Gate, where they found that even at this late hour, pilgrims from many faraway places were still streaming into the city. Peter and the other disciples mixed in with the pilgrims so that they had no difficulty in slipping through the gate unnoticed. Once they were beyond the walls of Jerusalem, the disciples quickened their pace and soon arrived at their favorite hiding place in the Garden of Gethsemane.

Peter arrived first and motioned to each disciple to sit down close beside him as he kept count of each arriving disciple. After Jesus arrived, Peter noticed there were only eleven disciples present. Quietly addressing the disciples, and noting the absence of Judas, he asked. "Have any of you seen Judas Iscariot?" All blankly replied, "No."

John said, "The master sent him on some errand and it probably has delayed his arrival."

Jesus, who was sitting apart from the disciples, heard their conversation and said in a voice full of bitter disappointment, "When I said at supper tonight that one of you would betray me, I was referring to Judas Iscariot. I did not send him on any errand. He left to betray me to the temple rabbis."

Peter angrily said, "I had heard rumors that the Chief Rabbi had offered thirty pieces of silver to whoever would lead the temple guards to our hiding place, but I never imagined that any one of us twelve disciples would be so loathsome as to betray you. However, I have always suspected that filthy Judaean!"

"Unfortunately," Jesus replied, "we must face the fact that the temple rabbis will leave no stone unturned to prevent me from preaching in the temple after the Passover begins. They are afraid to arrest me in the daytime, so they will make every effort to arrest me tonight." Pausing for a few seconds, he asked, "Peter, if we are attacked during the night, what weapons do we have to protect ourselves with?"

Peter replied, "We still have the two swords we brought with us from Galilee and in addition, each disciple has a club."

Jesus answered, "That will have to do. Now, Peter, set up a night watch so that we will have someone on duty during all hours of the night."

Peter said, "I have already decided to separate the night into five two-hour watches, with two disciples on duty during each watch."

Jesus answered, "Good." The silence that followed indicated everyone's worried mood. Then Jesus said, "My children. I shall be with you only a little while longer, and as I said yesterday, you will look for me but you will not find me because where I go, you cannot follow."

Peter asked, "Lord, why can't I go where you are going?"

Jesus answered, "First, Peter, your dedication to God must be strengthened."

Peter vehemently replied, "Lord, my dedication to God is already strong enough to enable me to follow you wherever you go. If need be, I will follow you to prison, or even to death."

Jesus answered in such a low voice that it seemed as though he were speaking to himself, rather than to Peter, saying, "Would you really follow me to prison and to death, Peter? The fact is, that before the cock crows twice tomorrow morning, you will deny three times that you ever even knew me."

Peter indignantly replied, "Even though I should die for it, I shall never deny that I am one of your disciples."

Jesus quietly answered, "I am glad to know how you feel toward me, Peter; but I also know that the devil would like to own you. Never underestimate the power of the devil. However, I have prayed long and hard for you, and I have prayed that you will not lose your faith in me or your faith in God. I know that my prayers shall be answered and that your faith shall be strengthened. After that, you must help strengthen the faith of others and then you can follow me." Peter slowly nodded his head and said, "Yes, Lord."

The other disciples now crowded around Jesus and added their assurances to Peter's that they would forever remain loyal to him. Jesus looked at them all quietly and kindly, as though they were all children, and then said, "So let it be. In times past, I have sent you out on long journeys to distant places without money, without food and without extra clothing, and yet did you ever lack for anything?"

Peter answered. "Never, Lord."

Jesus said, "Now I say to you that when you face the world and travel, take money, take food and take clothing with you. And what is more, take a sword with you. And if you don't have a sword, sell whatever you have and buy one. Now, get all the sleep that you can tonight, because tomorrow will be a trying day. Goodnight."

Peter turned to the disciples and gave them their instructions for being on guard duty during the night. This duty is noteworthy because it is the first time there is any record of Jesus planning to resist arrest. After Jesus had withdrawn to a secluded place in the garden, he dropped to the ground with his arms out-stretched and prayed, "Father, help me in this hour of trial when my heart is heavy in expectation of death. All things are possible to You, and if it is possible to take this cup of sorrow away from me, please do so. However, let it be as You will, and not as I will."

As Jesus prayed, the intensity of his prayers caused the perspiration to flow so freely that it splattered on the ground like large drops of blood. When he had completed his prayers, he rose and returned to the place where the disciples were resting. He found them all fast asleep, so he wakened Peter and said, "Peter, couldn't you stay awake for just one hour?"

Peter jumped up in great embarrassment and said, "I am sorry, Lord, James and John told me that they would stay awake and I thought that I could close my eyes for just a few seconds. I will call Matthew and Andrew now. I am sure that they have had enough rest so that it won't happen again."

Jesus looked silently at Peter and again withdrew to pray alone. About an hour later, Jesus returned and again found all the disciples fast asleep. Once more Jesus wakened Peter and impatiently said, "Peter, can't you stay awake for a single hour?"

This time, Peter was so tired that he staggered up on his feet and apologetically replied, "Forgive me, Lord. I am afraid that I was far more tired than I realized."

Jesus quietly said, "You have spoken truthfully, Peter. The spirit is willing, but the flesh is weak."

Peter answered, "It is now time for the third watch and all of the disciples have had over four hours rest, so I can assure you it won't happen again."

Jesus looked skeptically at Peter and once again withdrew to pray alone. About an hour later, Jesus again returned to find Peter and all the other disciples fast asleep. In complete resignation, Jesus said, "Sleep on. Take your rest. The moment when the Son of God will be betrayed into the hands of the evil sinners is almost here. O, my Father, if I must drink this bitter cup of sorrow that lies before me, then Thy will shall be done."

Jesus walked out of the garden into an open clearing where he could see the dim outline of the temple towers above the darkened skyline of Jerusalem and said, "O, Jerusalem! O, Jerusalem! You stone your prophets and kill those who are sent to save you. How often have I tried to gather your children together and protect them, just as a hen gathers and protects her chicks under her wings, but you would never let me do it. Soon you shall be left alone, desolate and friendless. Then your enemies will come and destroy you. Sorrowfully, I say to you, that you will not see me again until you shall say, 'Blessed is he, who comes in the name of the Lord.' "

Matt. 26 (46-58)(69-75)
Mark 14 (43-54)
Luke 22 (47-53)

Chapter 36

Judas Betrays Jesus

Judas left Jesus and his eleven disciples at their Passover supper in raging anger. He had never shared in the comradeship that was part of the daily lives of the other disciples, but he had always felt that, no matter what happened, he could always depend upon the sympathy and the love of Jesus. When Jesus coldly told him at the Passover supper, "Now, go and do what you must do, and do it quickly," he could feel the cool contempt that Jesus felt for him.

He strode down the dark, narrow, dirty streets of Jerusalem in blind, sullen resentment. His temper smoldered increasingly, as his mind sifted over each of the little bitter hurts that he had suffered from the other disciples during his association with them. Before long, he felt completely justified in betraying Jesus to the temple authorities. Then his thoughts turned to a far pleasanter subject—his reward of the thirty pieces of silver. Upon this subject his mind could deliberate happily and endlessly. Having grown up poor and lived through the hardships and privations as a disciple of Jesus, his prior experiences included no practical limitations regarding the happiness and the material benefits that thirty pieces of silver could buy for him.

Suddenly Judas' imaginary mental wanderings were abruptly interrupted by some drunken revelers, who reeled across his path and almost knocked him down. He was now very late for his appointment with the Chief Rabbi and he knew from his brief encounter with the man that he was an impatient, short-tempered individual.

Before long he was standing in front of the huge, locked gate of the temple. Timidly, he walked up to the heavy wooden door and lightly knocked upon it. As he received no answer, he boldly knocked again, more loudly than before. This time the huge door slowly swung open and Judas quickly recoiled as he saw a spear pointed at his stomach. The guard inside the gate gruffly asked, "What do you want?"

In fear and trembling, Judas answered, "I want to see the Chief Rabbi."

The guard shouted, "Who are you?"

Before Judas could answer, Captain Shama came running up to the gate and said, "Let him in."

Turning to Judas, Captain Shama curtly said, "You are very late and the Chief Rabbi will be very angry with you. Where have you been?"

As Judas started to answer, Captain Shama interrupted, saying, "Never mind! Tell it to the Chief Rabbi. He is the one who will want the answers. Be quiet and follow me."

Captain Shama rapidly crossed the Court of Solomon and went into the private chambers of Chief Rabbi Caiaphas with Judas following close behind him. The Chief Rabbi was in a towering rage; just the thought of dealing with this miserable wretch of humanity made his blood boil. And then on top of it, to be kept waiting by this sniveling disciple of the blasphemous Galilean was something he felt that no self-respecting individual should be asked to bear. After Judas entered, the Chief Rabbi kept striding back and forth across the room, too mentally upset to speak. Suddenly, he turned angrily upon Judas, who seemed to have shrunk to half his size and shouted at him, "Where have you been, you filthy scum? You promised to be here one hour after sundown, and it is now more than three hours after sundown."

When Judas started to answer, the Chief Rabbi screamed at him, "Do you want your reward or don't you? Do you think we are going to pay you a fortune just to have a look at that blasphemous master of yours?"

Judas finally managed to say, "Rabbi, I got here as quickly as I could."

The Chief Rabbi shouted back, "That's not quick enough. There are a great many things that must be done this night before we put an end to that master of yours."

Judas asked, "But you don't plan to kill him, do you? You promised me you wouldn't do that."

Chief Rabbi Caiaphas sarcastically answered, "No, we don't plan to kill your precious master. We just plan to see to it that he never opens his mouth again."

While the two men were still talking, Rabbi Annas slipped unobtrusively into the room, walked over to Judas and said in a reassuring tone of voice, "Of course, we don't intend to kill your master, my dear man. We only want to reason with him. Naturally, he will be tried by the Great Sanhedrin; and as you undoubtedly know, the Great Sanhedrin gives every one a fair trial."

Judas doubtfully asked, "But what *will* happen to my master?"

Rabbi Annas soothingly replied, "Well, of course, we don't know what the result of the trial before the Great Sanhedrin will be. If your master is found innocent of the charges brought against him, he will, of course, be set free. On the other hand, if he is found guilty, there are many possible penalties that may be imposed upon him."

Chief Rabbi Caiaphas growled, "Enough of this nonsense! Let us get on with the job of capturing that rebel Galilean before it is too late to do anything to him."

Judas stubbornly said, "Before I go, I want a definite promise that my master will not be killed."

Rabbi Annas hesitatingly answered, "Well, I am only one member of the Great Sanhedrin, so I cannot speak for all the others; but I suppose that if the Great Sanhedrin finds your master guilty of a mortal offense, that the logical thing to do would be to turn your master over to the Roman authorities to receive whatever punishment they deem proper."

Judas asked. "What do you suppose the Romans will do to my master?"

Rabbi Annas evasively replied, "Who can tell what those foreigners will do? They are a very strange people. They are pagans and heathens, who have only a smattering of civilization. They kill each other in a game and call it a sport. However, as you know, the most serious charge that we have against your master is that of blasphemy, and you know that the heathenish Romans would not consider that a grave offense."

Chief Rabbi Caiaphas abruptly said, "We have wasted too much time on this nonsense already. Let us get on with the arrest of the Galilean. Captain Shama, call in Captain Jakan from King Herod's palace."

After Captain Shama left, the Chief Rabbi turned to Judas and said, "How many men does your master have?"

Judas answered. "There are eleven disciples with the master."

The Chief Rabbi asked, "What weapons do they have?"

Judas replied, "Peter and John have swords, but Peter is

the only one who is hotheaded enough to use his sword."

Rabbi Annas asked, "Do they have any other weapons such as knives, spears or staves?"

Judas answered, "All the disciples have staves, but they only use them for walking."

During this conversation, Captain Shama returned with the Herodian, Captain Jakan. The Chief Rabbi turned to the two captains and said, "This man will lead you to the hiding place of the Galilean. There are eleven men with him and they are armed with two swords and staves. We only want you to arrest the Galilean. Avoid a fight at all costs, unless it becomes necessary to defend yourselves, or unless there is some danger that the Galilean might escape. Captain Jakan, take twenty to thirty soldiers with you. I will send several of our temple rabbis with you who know how to use a stave and they will be accompanied by about a dozen temple servants. With forty to fifty men under your command, you should easily be able to overwhelm the Galilean and his men without a fight."

Captain Shama asked, "How will we know which one of the twelve men is the man that we want in the dark?"

Judas said, "I will point him out to you. The man whom I embrace will be the man that you want."

Captain Jakan said, "Good, I'll get my men ready in the Court of Solomon. Meet me there."

Rabbi Annas spoke up and said, "Before you go, captain, let me emphasize to you again that there are two outstandingly important things necessary to make this night's work successful. The first is to capture the Galilean, the second is to do so without creating a disturbance. If there is a disturbance involving either our own people or the Romans, your mission will have failed."

Captain Jakan replied, "I understand, rabbi. I will instruct my men accordingly."

Chief Rabbi Caiaphas added, "Good. One thing more.

Bring the Galilean to my home first. I want to question him before the trial begins."

Captain Jakan answered, "Yes, Rabbi."

The two captains left, but Judas remained standing motionless and hostile. Chief Rabbi Caiaphas impatiently turned to him and said, "What are you standing there for? Get out and lead our men to your master's hiding place."

Quietly, but firmly, Judas replied, "You haven't paid me yet."

With an angry snort, the Chief Rabbi replied, "And you haven't led us to the Galilean yet."

Rabbi Annas quietly said to Judas, "I promise you full payment of the thirty pieces of silver as soon as your master is delivered to us."

Judas replied, "Very well, I will take *your word* for it."

After Judas left, Chief Rabbi Caiaphas summoned Rabbi Ahab and said to him, "Quick, follow those soldiers. Take all the temple and palace servants with you that can be spared. Make sure you keep your eye on that blasphemer's disciple named Judas Iscariot. He may try to trick those two captains, who wouldn't know the Galilean from a Gentile. Quick, follow them!"

Rabbi Ahab respectfully answered, "Yes, rabbi."

After the rabbi left, Rabbi Annas turned to his son-in-law and said, "There is still much work that must be done this night before our job is completed. I think I will go to your house and get a little sleep."

The Chief Rabbi replied, "Good. I will meet you there in an hour or so, after I have drilled the witnesses on the testimony they are to give at the Galilean's trial."

Rabbi Annas said, "Drill them thoroughly, because we have several members in our council who will insist upon exact corroboration of the testimony of the witnesses in accordance with the precepts of our Mosaic laws."

The Chief Rabbi answered, "Yes, father. I will drill the

witnesses thoroughly myself. However, it does seem like such a waste of time to go through with this trial when everyone knows all the facts in the case."

Rabbi Annas added, "I agree with you, son; but we must follow the procedural laws of the Great Sanhedrin, or else we will lose face with our own people."

Chief Rabbi Caiaphas answered, "Yes, father. Now go to my house and get some sleep. You must be well rested before the trial of the Galilean begins."

The two rabbis bade each other farewell and Rabbi Annas hurried out the temple gate on his way to the home of Chief Rabbi Caiaphas for a few hours of well-earned rest.

Meanwhile, Judas was leading King Herod's soldiers, the temple guards and the temple rabbis carefully, but quickly, toward the house of Nicodemus. When they arrived at the high garden wall encircling the house, Judas silently slipped through the garden gate, while the soldiers and the guards surrounded the house. Within a few minutes, Judas returned and said to the two captains, "The master and his disciples have already left."

Captain Shama said, "What do we do now?"

Judas replied, "They left this house about two hours ago. There are only two places where they could have gone, either to the Garden of Gethsemane or to Bethany."

Captain Jakan said, "If they have gone to Bethany, I am afraid we can't arrest the Galilean in time to accomplish our job before the night is over."

Captain Shama said, "We must arrest the Galilean tonight, no matter how late it is."

Judas interrupted, saying, "Follow me. We shall go to the Garden of Gethsemane first."

Once again, Judas led out with the soldiers and the temple personnel following closely behind him. Quickly, they passed through the Fountain Gate and took the road that led to the

Mount of Olives. As soon as they were out in the open, Captain Shama urged Judas and his men into a slow trot. When Judas stopped trotting and began walking forward slowly and cautiously, Captain Jakan instructed his men with arm signals to advance in a wide-spread V formation. At the entrance to the Garden of Gethsemane, Judas stopped and Captain Jakan motioned to his soldiers to completely encircle the garden.

When the soldiers were all in position, Judas walked into the garden past the sleeping bodies of the disciples and stopped when he came to Jesus. Captain Jakan advanced to Judas' side and flashed the light of a lantern into Jesus' face. Startled and blinking dazedly from the light of the lantern, Jesus woke up and asked, "What do you want?"

Captain Jakan said, "We are looking for Jesus of Nazareth."

Jesus answered, "I am he."

Not knowing whether or not Jesus spoke the truth, Captain Jakan looked from Jesus to Judas for confirmation or denial of Jesus' statement. But Judas suddenly seemed to have lost all power of speech and motion as he stood there staring blankly ahead.

Again, Jesus asked, "Who are you looking for?"

Captain Jakan replied, "We are looking for Jesus of Nazareth."

Jesus said, "I have told you that I am Jesus of Nazareth. If I am the one that you want, then let these others go."

Captain Jakan again turned to Judas for confirmation of Jesus' statement, and Judas now advanced toward Jesus, embraced him and started to kiss him. Jesus withdrew from him and said, "Judas, would you betray the Son of God with a kiss?"

Before Judas could answer, Peter, who was now fully awake, jumped up, drew his sword and swung it at the person nearest to him, who happened to be Malchus, the personal servant of Chief Rabbi Caiaphas. The blow cut off Malchus's left ear. Jesus turned to Peter and said, "Peter, put up your sword. All those who take up the sword shall perish by the sword. This is the cup that my Father has given me to drink and I shall drink all of it."

Rabbi Ahab and his men now rushed to the side of Jesus and tightly bound his hands behind his back. While they were doing so, Jesus turned to Rabbi Ahab and said, "Why have you come upon me like a thief in the night with all these soldiers and men armed with swords and clubs? When I was with you daily in the temple, you stretched forth no hand against me. If you were so anxious to arrest me, why didn't you arrest me in broad daylight in the temple where all the world could see you?"

Rabbi Ahab ignored Jesus' question and with a smug grin on his face, turned to Captain Shama and said, "At last, we have captured this Galilean rebel. Now let us rush him to the home of the Chief Rabbi."

As Captain Jakan's men quickly surrounded Jesus and pushed him between them toward the walls of Jerusalem, Jesus quietly said, "This is the hour of the devil."

Chapter 37

Peter Denies Jesus

When the soldiers and the temple rabbis arrested Jesus, all the disciples fled except Peter, who followed after them as close as he dared. Suddenly, he was startled to find that he had been joined by a strange young man who greeted him cordially. Peter did his best to ignore the stranger, but the young man persisted and said to Peter, "Don't you recognize me? I am Mark, the son of Nicodemus."

Peter said apologetically, "Forgive me. I didn't recognize you in the dark. Our master has been arrested by those soldiers ahead of us and I am following after them to find out where they are taking him. Do you want to come along?"

Mark answered, "I'll be glad to. I am sorry about your master's arrest. I knew there was something strange going on tonight when my father failed to come home from an emergency meeting of the Great Sanhedrin. Never before that I know of has there been an all-night meeting of the Great Sanhedrin. I checked with some of the families of the other members of the Great Sanhedrin and their fathers have not returned either."

Peter solemnly replied, "I am afraid that this special meeting of the Great Sanhedrin was especially called to condemn my master to death."

Mark replied, "I hope not. I know my father will do all he can to prevent it."

"I hope so," Peter replied, "but I'm afraid the temple rabbis hate our Lord too much to allow any one person stand in their way."

Abruptly the arresting group came to a halt and Peter and Mark could hear the angry voice of Captain Shama shouting at a sniveling figure beneath him, "Get away from me, you filthy scum! You'll get your thirty pieces of silver, but not from me. I'd give you nothing but thirty lashes of the whip."

The captain swung his torch at the cringing figure before him and Peter and Mark clearly saw the bearded, frightened face of Judas recoil in terror as the flames from the burning torch singed his matted beard. Judas fell to the ground uttering whimpering sounds that more closely resembled those of an animal than those of a man. The entire group marched past the fallen body of Judas, before he dared rise again.

Peter swore under his breath and said, "I knew that Judaean scavenger was up to something evil tonight when he came back with the supplies for our Passover supper, long past the hour that he was due. Then he argued with me about it. I remember now that, when he left our Passover supper tonight, our Master spoke to him in a voice so low that none of us could hear what he said. Our Lord must have known then what he was up to and yet the master made no move to stop him. None of us could imagine the evil errand that he went out to accomplish. If I could only put my hands around his throat for a minute, I would squeeze the last evil bit of breath out of him."

Even in the dark of the night, Mark could see the powerful muscles of Peter's body tighten with anger and frustration.

The soldiers and the temple personnel continued on their cautious way until they arrived at a luxurious home enclosed by a high garden wall. One of the soldiers tapped lightly on the barred gate, which was quickly opened by a maid, and the entire arresting group entered the garden.

Mark whispered, "This is the home of Chief Rabbi Caiaphas. Wait here while I go in. If I think it is safe for you to enter, I'll come back and call you."

In a little while, the gate was opened by a maid and Mark stepped out and called Peter. As Peter came out of the shadows into the light of a lantern, the maid said to him, "Aren't you one of the disciples of that rebel Galilean?"

Peter indignantly replied, "No, I am not!"

Mark jokingly said, "Now you know, girl, that I wouldn't be a friend of one of the disciples of the Galilean."

The maid looked skeptically at Peter and said, "He sure looks like the man that I saw in the temple with the Galilean."

Mark and Peter laughed boisterously in an attempt to cover up their embarrassment. As they walked away, Peter said to Mark in a low undertone, "That certainly was a tight squeeze. I didn't think that anyone would recognize me in the dark. Well, anyway, why is there a maid at the gate?"

Mark answered, "I don't know, but it seems to me that among the mob following your master, there were most of the Chief Rabbi's servants. It could be that for tonight, they replaced their regular male guards with female servants."

Peter quietly answered, "Well, thank you very much for your help. I see some soldiers ahead gathered around a fire. I may be recognized again, so we had better separate before they recognize me. There's no use involving you and your father in this matter."

Mark whispered, "Very well. I'll go into the house and see what I can find out about their plans for your master and then I'll rejoin you later."

While Mark walked briskly toward the main building, Peter walked nonchalantly towards the fire and sat down at the edge of the group, covering his face as much as he dared, without attracting attention to himself. As the fire was beginning to burn down, one of the soldiers picked up some logs and threw them on the fire. Peter inadvertently peeked from beneath his cloak to watch the flames leap upward. Another soldier, who saw the outlines of Peter's face lighted up by the flames, asked, "Aren't you the disciple of the Galilean who drew his sword against us tonight?"

Peter indignantly replied, "No, I am not!"

Peter's denial was so emphatic that the soldier let the matter drop. However, the silence that followed seemed to emphasize the suspicion that had been aroused by the soldier's accusation of Peter.

Meanwhile, inside the house, Rabbi Annas was grilling Jesus, without success. The fertile, wily brain of the crafty, old rabbi, that had so successfully proved its superiority against others, could make no progress against the straightforward, truthful mind of Jesus. Rabbi Annas became so annoyed with Jesus' calm serenity that he petulantly asked, "What is this doctrine that you teach our people? Tell me, I want to hear about it."

"Whenever I have preached," Jesus answered, "I have done so openly, whether I preached in the temple in Capernaum, or in the temple in Jerusalem. At all of my meetings, I always noticed your spies were present. Why don't you ask them what I preached?"

The words were barely out of Jesus' mouth before Captain Jakan struck him several resounding blows across the face that started a trickle of blood flowing from his nose and mouth. Angrily, the captain said, "Is that the proper way to speak to our revered rabbi?"

Through bleeding lips, Jesus replied, "If I have spoken evil, you can bear witness against me for the evil that I have spoken. But, if I have spoken the truth, why do you strike me?"

Before Captain Jakan could answer, Rabbi Annas interrupted and said, "Never mind, captain. Take this rebel blasphemer to the temple. We will see what he has to say before the Great Sanhedrin. I will follow after you in a few minutes."

Captain Jakan, Captain Shama and Rabbi Ahab surrounded Jesus and led him out the building toward the group of soldiers in the courtyard huddled around the fire. The soldiers quickly left their warm places and formed a solid formation around Jesus, leaving Peter alone sitting next to the fire. Rabbi Ahab glanced toward the fire and seeing Peter, walked over to him, scrutinized him very closely and said, "Didn't I see you with the Galilean tonight in the garden of Gethsemane?"

Peter jumped up, cursed and swore indignantly saying, "I don't know what you're talking about. I never saw that Galilean in my life before. This is the third time tonight that I have been falsely accused and mistaken for someone else."

Rabbi Ahab eyed Peter coldly and said, "You're a liar. Your speech betrays you, you are a Galilean."

Peter replied, "Can I help it if I'm a Galilean? All of us Galileans aren't the Galilean's disciples."

Rabbi Ahab turned to Captain Shama and said, "I am sure that I am right, but never mind now. We have more important matters to attend to. Let's go."

As Jesus was being led through the garden gate by his captors, a cock crowed loudly twice announcing the dawn of a new day. The crowing of the cock shook Peter out of the reverie into which he had fallen. In his guilty frame of mind,

the crowing of the cock sounded to him like the accusing
voice of a prosecutor, as he vividly recalled Jesus' forewarning that he, Simon Peter, would deny knowing his master
three times before the cock crowed twice that morning. In
deep remorse, Peter jumped up and ran out the gate after
Jesus, sobbing and weeping like a lost soul.

Matt. 26 (57-68)   Luke 22 (63-71)
John 18 (24)
Mark 14 (53-65)   John 18 (12-14)
Deu. 13 (1-5)

Chapter 38

The Great Sanhedrin Condemns Jesus to Death

As soon as Rabbi Annas arrived at the temple, Chief Rabbi Caiaphas became a dynamic center of human activity, sending servants and temple guards scurrying in all directions throughout the temple on numerous detailed errands. As a matter of precaution, the Chief Rabbi checked all the temple gates in order to reassure himself that they were all locked and guarded.

Then he went to his private chambers and summoned ten of his most trusted servants and informed them that they were to be the witnesses against Jesus at his trial that night. The Chief Rabbi divided his servants into five pairs of witnesses and drilled each pair repeatedly on the testimony they were to give. After hours of patient and impatient coaching,

Chief Rabbi Caiaphas found to his consternation that his servants could not follow his simplest instructions. He emphasized his instructions with bitter sarcasm, but the end result was hopeless frustration, angry resentment and utter confusion. The inability of his servants to repeat his carefully selected accusations against Jesus created within him a paroxysm of fury. The more he bellowed, glared and cursed, the more confused and frightened his servants became.

The Chief Rabbi's normally short temper was on the verge of an explosion. It didn't seem possible that any one body could contain so much heat, fury and nervous tension without something inside of it bursting or breaking down. For once, he was extremely tired. He had been on his feet for over twenty hours and every minute of it had been under high pressure. Now he was surrounded by a group of servants who seemed determined to exasperate and torment him.

The Chief Rabbi was in a nervous sweat. He felt dreadfully alone. Inside in the council chambers, the members of the Great Sanhedrin conversed nonchalantly, apparently indifferent to the tremendous problems that faced their Chief Rabbi. Several hours passed and his witnesses were no more ready for the trial than they had been when he began drilling them. It was already too late for the Chief Rabbi to go to his home and grill Jesus with Rabbi Annas. In the distance, the Chief Rabbi heard the first faint crowing of a cock announcing the dawn of a new day. In despair, he looked out the windows and saw the first gray streaks of dawn lighten up the countryside.

Chief Rabbi Caiaphas was in a state of panic. Mumbling to himself, he thought, "Shall I fail again?" The very thought sent the Chief Rabbi into a renewed frenzy of activity. He tried to quiet his nerves momentarily by thinking of the cool, calm face of his father-in-law; and for a few minutes, his nervous activity quieted down and his tense face relaxed. But not for long. It was useless. The forced relaxation was more trying on his frayed nerves than his normal nervous, frustrated activity. He was no Rabbi Annas and he knew it.

Once again, a cock crowed and the Chief Rabbi despondently looked out the window and this time his heart sank with fear as he saw King Herod's soldiers and the temple guards crossing the Court of Solomon with Jesus in their midst. For the Chief Rabbi, this should have been a moment of triumphant exultation. Instead, it was a moment of fear and self-recrimination, because he realized he had failed completely to prepare his witnesses for the trial.

Chief Rabbi Caiaphas' body became rigid as his gaze remained fixed on the courtyard below, where he saw the pathetic figure of Jesus moving serenely among his captors. Jesus' face was bloody and his arms were tightly bound behind his back; but otherwise, he moved with quiet composure and proudly, as though he were the master of the group, instead of the prisoner in it. The Chief Rabbi clenched his teeth as he muttered to himself, "Who would think that that skinny bit of humanity could cause me so much grief and anxiety and defy me before the entire world? Why, I could crush him with my bare hands. I swear that he shall not escape me this time. By one means or another, he shall die."

Captain Shama entered the Chief Rabbi's chambers and said, "Chief Rabbi Caiaphas, we have the Galilean outside in the Court of Solomon. What shall we do with him?"

The Chief Rabbi answered, "First, wash off his face and clean him up as much as you can. This blasphemer has friends everywhere and we don't want any of our council members wasting any sympathy on him. After you have cleaned him up, take him to the council chambers. Tell Rabbi Ahab to tell the council members that the Great Sanhedrin will be in session in ten minutes."

Chaptain Shama replied, "Yes, rabbi."

The Chief Rabbi continued, "Did Rabbi Annas come with you?"

The Captain answered, "No, rabbi, but he did say that he would follow soon after us."

Chief Rabbi Caiaphas gave a long relaxed sigh of relief as he said, "Good."

Temple servants were soon scurrying into all parts of the temple rounding up the seventy members of the Great Sanhedrin. In the midst of all the hustle and bustle, Rabbi Annas arrived, looking as fresh and chipper as though he did not have a care in the world. Quietly he asked the Chief Rabbi, "What kept you from coming home and grilling the Galilean with me?"

The Chief Rabbi lamely answered, "Oh, it took me longer to drill the witnesses than I expected."

Rabbi Annas replied, "I thought it would. Do you have your witnesses ready?"

The Chief Rabbi lied, "Yes, father."

Rabbi Annas said, "Good. We will need them, because I could make no progress in breaking down the Galilean."

These cold words gave the Chief Rabbi a sinking, guilty feeling as he reflected on how poorly he had prepared his witnesses for the trial. As he contemplated these facts, a servant entered the room and announced that all the members of the Great Sanhedrin were assembled in the council chambers, waiting for the trial to begin. Rabbi Annas looked apprehensively at his son-in-law, and said to him in a voice filled with deep concern, "Don't you feel well? Try to relax, son. It will all come out all right."

The Chief Rabbi looked gratefully at his father-in-law, but remained silent as he walked rigidly into the council chambers. Both rabbis were greeted warmly by the members of the Great Sanhedrin as they walked toward the rostrum. Jesus and his captors were already waiting on the raised dais. Rabbi Annas walked up to the rostrum and opened the trial by saying, "Fellow members of the Great Sanhedrin, I know that you are all as fully aware of the gravity of this hour as I am. Our beloved nation is threatened today as it has not been threatened in many centuries. We have fought off foreign invaders, and at times we have even suffered foreign invasion, as we do now; but, through all these misfortunes, with occasional unfortunate exceptions, we have remained a united people.

"Now, we are again threatened by an enemy who has always proven in the past to be the most dangerous of all our enemies—an internal enemy. This internal enemy is the Galilean rebel who stands before you. Pathetic and weak as he appears, he still threatens the very foundations of our nation with civil war.

"I must ask that you set aside your natural sympathies for a sincere and well-intentioned man and concentrate your thoughts upon the safety and the future of Judaism. That must be the overwhelming consideration and the only consideration in the mind of every member of this great council at this time. There is now no room for maudlin sentiment.

"I have one other request to make of you and that is that you forgive us, my son and me, for keeping you up so late. However, since the time remaining before the beginning of our sacred Passover is very limited, we ask your forbearance and your cooperation in bringing this trial to a speedy conclusion. My son and I wish that we could have had more time to prepare our charges against this determined enemy of Judaism, and I must admit that our entire case is far from perfect. However, I am sure that you will all agree that the transgressions of this Galilean, corroborated by two witnesses in each case, justify the guilty verdict of death. Thank you very much for your patience, gentlemen; this trial will now begin."

As Rabbi Annas left the rostrum, he was greeted with a hearty round of applause. Chief Rabbi Caiaphas then stood up and walked over to the rostrum with an ancient scroll in one hand and a heavy parchment in the other hand. Placing the parchment on the rostrum, the Chief Rabbi said, "You

have all heard the introductory remarks made by our revered
Rabbi Annas, and I wish to say that I heartily endorse every
one of Rabbi Annas' statements. Before I make my charges
against the rebel Galilean, I wish to read to you the advice
and the warning that Moses gave to our forefathers many
centuries ago about such a man as this rebel Galilean."

Caiaphas slowly unrolled the scroll and read, "If some
dreamer arises amongst you and makes some prophecy that
happens to come true; or, even if he performs some deed that
appears like a miracle to you, and then says, 'Let us go and
worship other gods and serve them,' you must not listen to
the words of that false prophet. Remember, the Lord, your
God, is testing you to determine whether or not you love your
God with all your hearts and with all your souls. You must
always obey the Lord, your God, and fear Him and serve
Him and keep His Commandments. As for that false prophet,
you must put him to death, because he has taught rebellion
against the Lord, your God."

After laying aside the scroll, Caiaphas said,

"You have heard the words of the Lord, your God. Now,
cherish them and keep them as your guide in this trial. The
break of dawn is already upon us. So, I will make my charges
against this blasphemer as brief as possible:

"1. He claims he is the Son of God and the King of the Jews.
"2. He claims our temple will be destroyed and that he can
     rebuild it in three days.
"3. He claims he can resurrect the dead.
"4. He claims he has the right to break the laws of Moses.
"5. He claims he has the authority to rewrite the Mosaic
     laws according to his own ideas.

"Now I will call in our witnesses who will prove to you that
each of these claims is false."

Unfortunately for the Chief Rabbi, the testimony of the

first two witnesses was so conflicting that even a jury as biased as the Great Sanhedrin listened coldly and skeptically to them. In great embarrassment, Caiaphas dismissed them and called in his next two witnesses. Once again, these witnesses failed miserably to corroborate each other's testimony, as had the previous pair.

In rapid succession, Caiaphas called his third, fourth and fifth pair of witnesses, all of whom tried desperately to repeat the charges fabricated for them by Caiaphas, but their obvious efforts betrayed them. In the agonizing silence that followed the false testimony, the Chief Rabbi looked desperately around the room until he saw the reposed face of Jesus. Its very calmness caused him to rail angrily at Jesus, shouting, "What do you have to say about these charges? Are you a mummy? Say something!"

Annas quickly rose, walked over to his son-in-law and quietly said, "Caiaphas, you have presented your case against this blasphemous rebel exceptionally well. Do you mind if I speak to him?"

Caiaphas looked blankly at his father-in-law and gratefully mumbled, "No."

Turning to Jesus, Annas said, "I ask you to swear to tell us by the living God, if you are the Messiah, the Son of God."

Jesus answered, "Yes, I am the Son of God and one day you shall see me sitting in Heaven on the right hand side of my Father."

Before Rabbi Annas could say another word, Caiaphas bounded up from his seat, ripped his cloak wide open in the traditional Jewish manner, indicating he had heard a blasphemous statement made and that he, the Chief Rabbi, vigorously protested that statement with all his heart and soul. From the depths of his hulking body, he exultantly shouted, "He has spoken blasphemy! Now you have all heard it yourselves. Council members, what is your verdict?"

From all parts of the council chamber came a deafening roar: "Kill him! Kill him! Kill him!"

The Chief Rabbi danced an exuberantly happy, elephantine jig and then sank back into his seat in utter exhaustion, overcome with joy and emotional relief. From the very jaws of defeat, he and Rabbi Annas had snatched a great victory and his sworn enemy had finally been condemned to death. As soon as the din in the council chamber subsided, old Rabbi Annas again advanced to the rostrum, motioned for silence and quietly said, "Fellow members, please remember that at this meeting all we have done is to condemn this Galilean to death and this is only the initial step to rid ourselves of this very dangerous enemy. There still remains the final step that must be taken to complete our task and that is the actual execution of this blasphemer.

"There now remain barely twelve hours before the beginning of our sacred Passover, and if we are to avoid defiling this great religious day with the death of this rebel Galilean, he must be dead before sundown today. In order to get this deed done, there are still several important steps that must be taken. As soon as the Roman governor is awake, we must take the Galilean to the Forum and accuse him of certain crimes against Rome. My son and I shall bring the necessary charges against him.

"You members of this council will still have a very important duty to perform in order that our death verdict of the Galilean is carried out. When you leave here, we want you to go directly to your homes and get all the members of your families and all your servants together and whoever else you can command and bring them to the Forum an hour after sunrise. Then, when the Roman governor asks the mob for a verdict for the Galilean, as I am sure he will, have your group shout, 'Death to the Galilean!' If need be, we want our people to be prepared to riot unless the Roman governor approves the death verdict for the Galilean. Now, go to your homes quickly and quietly, and arrive at the governor's palace with your group promptly at the appointed hour."

As the council members slowly filed out of the council chambers, Captain Shama and Captain Jakan led Jesus out to the Court of Solomon and turned him over to Rabbi Ahab and his men for safe keeping. When Rabbi Ahab gleefully told King Herod's soldiers and the temple servants that the Great Sanhedrin had condemned Jesus to death, they received this news with joyful shouts. Quickly they proceeded to heap every indignity and sadistic torment upon Jesus their evil minds could conceive. They began their torment by striking and spitting at Jesus, while they hurled vile epithets at him. Rabbi Ahab watched this brutality for awhile and then said to Jesus' tormentors with a sardonic leer, "Stop! Don't you know who this Galilean is? He is the great prophet who can see with his eyes shut and foretell the future. Look, let me show you."

Then, taking a piece of cloth, he blindfolded Jesus and said to his tormentors, "Now each of you strike him in turn and than ask him who it was that struck him."

The soldiers and the temple personnel happily joined in this sadistic game, and before long Jesus was bleeding profusely from his nose and mouth. Since Jesus absorbed this punishment unflinchingly and without protest, his tormentors soon tired of this senseless brutality.

When Rabbi Ahab saw that the soldiers and the temple servants were tired of their cruelty, he devised a new game to add zest to their bestiality. So, with mock severity, he said to Jesus' tormentors, "Stop! You are not playing this game properly. You see, you are not putting the powers of this great prophet to the proper test. You must bear in mind that he *foretells* the future. Therefore, you should say to him, "Prophesy, Galilean, who is it that is going to strike you next?' Then, after you have asked him to prophesy, strike him and see whether or not he has prophesied correctly."

With this new incentive added to their sadism, they once again struck Jesus unmercifully, until he was on the verge of collapse. When Rabbi Ahab saw that the tormentors of Jesus were again tiring of their game, he said to them, "That's enough. Apparently, the Galilean isn't prophesying today." Then he added with a bitter laugh, "And he won't be prophesying tomorrow either."

Chapter 39

Judas Repents

After Judas received his reward of the thirty pieces of silver, he walked hurriedly down the street toward the Golden Gate. When he saw several temple guards and Roman soldiers lounging there, he reduced his pace to a slow nonchalant walk until he was well beyond the walls of the city. Once he was out in open country, where he felt sure that no one was watching him, he quickened his pace, until he arrived in the hilly country east of Jerusalem.

His mind throbbed with innumerable plans of the various uses that he would make of his money. But right now, the immediate problem before him was to put his silver into a safe place until he could decide how to make the best use of it. He walked uncertainly oveer the sandy hills, seeking a readily identifiable hiding place for his treasure and yet one that would be safe from discovery by prowlers.

Finally, he found a depression in the sand hills that was out of sight of casual passers-by and yet identifiable as to its location. The spot he selected was in line with two of the temple towers and also in line with the battlements of the Roman fort. Sighting along these two lines with considerable deliberation, he chose their exact point of intersection and carefully marked this point with a cross.

Withdrawing the money bag from under his cloak, Judas carefully opened it and slowly counted the thirty silver pieces. He ran his fingers lovingly over each shiny silver piece and then tested each one for its toughness with his teeth. When he felt satisfied that all the silver coins were sound, he reluctantly placed the silver money back into the bag. Next, he dug a deep hole at the exact spot that he had marked on the ground with a cross and carefully placed his bag of silver into it. He quickly filled the hole, tamped the ground over it and spread the remaining loose soil in an irregular manner so as to remove all signs of human activity.

Triumphantly Judas rose and surveyed the area around him. He was now a man of means which made him a man of considerable importance. As he made his way back into Jerusalem, he let his mind wander freely over the many things that he would do with his new-found wealth. He was so immersed in his day-dreaming that he was unaware of the fact that the first gray steaks of dawn were already lighting up the sky. He walked idly and aimlessly through the streets of Jerusalem without noticing where he was going. Subconsciously, but irresistibly, his footsteps led him back toward the temple. Suddenly, his day-dreaming was brought to an abrupt end as he listened in horror to the bantering conversation of two temple guards.

One of them said, "Well, they finally caught up with that blasphemous Galilean." The other guard replied, "Yes, and what's more he won't be around to blaspheme much longer. The vultures are certainly going to have a good Passover supper tonight."

While the two guards laughed uproariously, Judas' heart almost stopped beating. His mind kept repeating that they couldn't be talking about his master because the Chief Rabbi and Rabbi Annas had repeatedly promised him that they would not kill Jesus—surely the guards must be talking about someone else; maybe it was Peter they were talking about, because he was the one who had drawn his sword and cut off the ear of Malchus, the servant of the Chief Rabbi. However, Judas' sinking heart told him something else, and that something else was too frightening for his mind to think about.

At all costs, he realized, he must find out immediately who it was the guards were talking about. Gone was the bitterness and the anger of the previous day; all that he could feel now was a deep personal anxiety for the safety of Jesus. Fearfully, he rushed up to one of the guards and taking hold of his cloak, asked in a tearful voice, "Who is it that will be the Passover supper for the vultures tonight?"

The guard drew back repulsively and said with considerable irritation, "Take your hands off of me, you filthy bumpkin; or you, too, will be feeding the birds tonight along with that cursed Galilean."

Judas cried out, "Which Galilean? Which one?"

The guard yelled back, "Which Galilean? Which one? There is only one Galilean worth crucifying and that's that blasphemer, Jesus of Nazareth."

Judas dropped to the ground in a pathetic, helpless heap, crying his heart out in remorse and despair. In that one awful moment, the veil of deceit with which he had cloaked his betrayal of Jesus was torn away from his warped mind and he saw himself as he was—a contemptible traitor. Forgotten now were all the little hurts and the corroding bitterness over the imaginary insults that he had built up in his own mind to justify his treachery. Now his heart and his mind begged and sobbed for forgiveness. The master had forgiven the worst of repentant sinners. Could not there be forgiveness for him too? There must be!

Fiercely determined to right the grievous wrong he had

committed, Judas quickly rose to his feet and dashed out of the temple grounds to the Golden Gate. Abandoning all thoughts of caution, he madly retraced his steps to the place where he had carefully buried his silver treasure. Sighting quickly along the lines formed by the temple towers and the embattlements of the Roman fort, he hastily dug a hole at the imaginary point of intersection.

Anxiously he dug deeply into the sand expecting to uncover his buried treasure with each scoopful of sand. Failing to find his hoard of silver, he dug deeper and deeper. When his digging failed to uncover his bag of silver, he worriedly sighted again on his lines of reference and chose a new point of intersection. Once again, he dug desperately and deeply into the sand.

When the second hole failed to uncover his silver hoard, he frantically dug one hole after another without reference to any point in particular. All the holes revealed nothing but sand and stones. Judas viewed the barren scene around him with shock and dismay! Now the dreadful thought entered his mind that perhaps his silver treasure had been stolen! The very thought sent him into a frenzy of furious digging, all without result. Exhausted from his desperate activity, he dropped flat on his face, crying and sobbing without restraint. With his arms outstretched, his fingers clawed fiercely into the ground and suddenly touched something soft and velvety. It was the bag of silver!

In a few minutes, Judas dug out the leather bag and sped with it toward the city walls of Jerusalem without making any attempt to conceal the treasure he carried. As he ran, he could see the first red streaks of dawn lighting up the blue-black sky. Without slackening his pace, Judas ran through the city gate, and up to the temple grounds and unceremoniously knocked loudly on the huge gate. He was still breathing hard when the gate opened and the temple guard looked at him contemptuously and said, "You, again?"

Judas blurted out, "Yes, and now let me in to see the Chief Rabbi, right away."

The guard drew back in wonderment at the audacity and determination shown by this little man who a short time before had been a cringing, sobbing wreck of humanity. While the guard pondered uncertainly whether or not he should allow Judas to enter the temple grounds, Judas sped past him and ran across the Court of Solomon to the entrance of the council chambers.

The trial of Jesus had just been completed and the members of the Great Sanhedrin were slowly sauntering out, excitedly discussing the dramatic conclusion of the trial of Jesus. Judas hurried past the elegantly dressed rabbis, until he spied the Chief Rabbi. The Chief Rabbi and Rabbi Annas had their arms around each other laughing and congratulating themselves upon the successful termination of a very difficult trial. Judas dashed up to the Chief Rabbi, tugged his sleeve vigorously and said, "I have something very important to say to you."

The Chief Rabbi looked indulgently at Judas and thinking that he might have some additional important information to give him, said in a gay, carefree manner, "All right, come on inside."

Then turning to his father-in-law, Chief Rabbi Caiaphas smilingly said, "The Galilean's betrayer says he has something very important to tell me. Let us go to my private chambers and find out what he has to say."

Rabbi Annas cheerfully replied, "Good. Let us go."

Turning to several of the other council members, the Chief Rabbi also invited them to join him. After the Chief Rabbi and his guests had made themselves comfortable in the Chief Rabbi's private quarters, Judas remained standing in the center of the room, cringing and fawning upon the great men around him. The Chief Rabbi condescendingly said to Judas, "What is it, my man? What is this important matter that you want to tell me about? Do the Galilean's disciples think that perhaps they can rescue him?"

All the rabbis except Rabbi Annas laughed uproariously at Chief Rabbi's oafish humor. Instead of replying, Judas bowed low, drawing his head from side to side as though he were seeking to shrink his frail body into a smaller and smaller space. Then in a weak, wheedling voice, he said, "Honorable Chief Rabbi, honorable rabbis of the Great Sanhedrin, forgive me for I have sinned greatly against a just man. I have betrayed the blood of my innocent master; however, I have repented and I ask for your forgiveness. You have given me thirty pieces of silver to betray my master to you, and now I return all that money to you. Ask anything of me that you will, and I will do it for you. Beat me, if you will, but I beg of you, please let my master go."

The Chief Rabbi and the other council members listened with open-mouthed amazement at Judas' statements. As soon as they had gotten over their initial surprise at his request, the rabbis, led by Chief Rabbi Caiaphas, broke out into loud peals of laughter that made their bodies shake with merriment. When the laughter had partially subsided, the Chief Rabbi turned to Judas and laughingly said, "So, you have repented, eh? Well, isn't that a beautiful sentiment?"

Judas dropped to his knees, prostrated himself before the Chief Rabbi and pleaded, "Please, Chief Rabbi, please listen to me. Jesus of Nazareth is a good man. He means no harm to anyone. Please let him go."

Chief Rabbi Caiaphas drew away in disgust, kicking Judas as he did so, saying, "I made a contract with you to pay you thirty pieces of silver to lead us to the Galilean and you led us to him and I paid you. The contract is completed. Take your remorse some place else. We have no use for it here. Now, get out!"

Judas cried, "But Chief Rabbi, you promised me that you would not kill my master."

Chief Rabbi Caiaphas shrugged and said, "Who is killing your master? Not us."

Judas sobbed, "No, but you are going to get the Romans to kill him."

The Chief Rabbi answered, "We have no control over the Romans. Who can tell what the Romans will do? Those Gentiles will kill each other just for sport."

Judas insisted, "But you promised me. . . ."

The Chief Rabbi angrily interrupted, "Promises, promises, promises; every other word you say to me is what I promised you. All I promised you is thirty pieces of silver and that we wouldn't kill the Galilean. Now we gave you the thirty pieces of silver and we are not going to kill your precious master. Now get out, before I have you thrown out."

Judas rose up with the pent-up fury of a trapped animal. Taking the bag of silver, he threw it at the Chief Rabbi saying, "Then take your dirty blood-money and may you all choke on it." He ran from the room, crying and sobbing until it seemed that his frail body would burst. After he was gone, the rabbis carefully searched every corner of the room until they had recovered all thirty pieces of silver. All eyes now turned expectantly toward the Chief Rabbi as he placed the bag of silver on the table before them.

He was obviously in a quandary. The return of the money required making an important decision because the money was unquestionably tainted and defiled. Scratching his head indecisively, Caiaphas turned to his father-in-law and asked, "Father, what do you think we should do with this money?"

Rabbi Annas remained silent a few minutes and finally said, "This money is truly blood-money. Therefore, we cannot return it to the temple treasury because it will defile our temple. Nor can we allow any Jew to derive any benefit from it or else he, too, will be defiled."

The Chief Rabbi asked, "What then, shall we do with this money?"

Rabbi Annas spoke very slowly as he replied, "There are now many Gentiles living amongst us in Jerusalem and there is no adequate burial ground in which to bury them when they die. We can't allow them to be buried in our cemetery, lest they defile it. I recommend we use this money to buy a burial ground for the Gentiles."

This recommendation was so unusual it caught the Chief Rabbi by surprise. In his bewilderment, he looked around the room into the faces of all the other rabbis for guidance before replying to his father-in-law's novel suggestion. When he saw general approval in the eyes of all the other council members, he quickly recovered his composure and said, "That's a splendid idea. Yes, that's what we'll do. We'll spend this blood-money for a burial ground for the Gentiles; and since we are paying for the cemetery, we should name it. I recommend we call it The Blood-Money Cemetery."

This heavy-handed humor brought a faint smile to the faces of several of the assembled rabbis, but Rabbi Annas glared at his son-in-law contemptuously and quietly said, "There are a great many things we must do this day before our work is done. So let us go to our homes and get what rest we can so that we can get our individual tasks done before our sacred Passover begins."

Matt. 27 (1-2)   Luke 23 (1-7)
Matt. 27 (11-14)   John 18 (28-38)
Mark 15 (1-5)

Chapter 40

Pontius Pilate and the Rabbis

After all the members of the Great Sanhedrin left the temple grounds, Chief Rabbi Caiaphas turned his pent-up energy upon the temple staff. While the Chief Rabbi had serious mental and spiritual deficiencies, his physical energy seemed unlimited. While others around him dragged their feet for lack of sleep, the Chief Rabbi bounded from place to place, showing no indication of the fact that he had had no sleep or rest for the past twenty-four hours. His reserve stamina seemed inexhaustible.

This was the Chief Rabbi's greatest hour and he intended to make the most of it. He knew the other rabbis considered him an incompetent successor to his very capable father-in-law, but now he intended to show them how competent he could be in a crisis. Calling Captain Shama, Captain Jakan and Rabbi Ahab to his side, he said to them, "As soon as the Roman governor is awake, we will take that rebel Galilean to

the Roman Forum and ask the Roman governor to execute
him. Since the Romans do not understand the crimes that the
Galilean has committed against Judaism, and as he has committed no crime against Rome, Pilate will be reluctant to
order his execution."

Pausing for a moment to get his thoughts together, the
rabbi continued, "In circumstances such as these, where the
Roman authorities are faced with a difficult decision, they
refer the decision to a mob and that custom they call democracy. Therefore, when Governor Pilate asks the mob to decide the Galilean's fate, it is your job to be sure that the mob
before the governor's balcony today consists only of temple
personnel and those persons who are unquestionably loyal to
our temple. In order to perform your job properly, each of
you shall be responsible for half the area in front of the governor's balcony. Captain Shama, you shall be responsible for
the east half of the forum; Captain Jakan, you shall be responsible for the west half of the forum. Are there any questions so far?"

Both captains shook their heads, so the Chief Rabbi continued, "Each of you will have about fifty men. With these
men, form a ring around the governor's balcony. Captain
Shama, place your first man about fifty paces east of the balcony. Then place your next man two paces south of him until
you have thirty men in a line due south of the balcony. Then
place your next man two paces west and continue doing so
until your last man will be in line with the center of the
balcony. Captain Jakan, you repeat the process, beginning at
a point fifty paces west of the balcony until you have completed the ring joining with Captain Shama's men.

"Once your ring is formed, allow no one to pass through it,
except recognized servants or members of the households of
the Great Sanhedrin or of King Herod's palace or known
Judaeans who are loyal to the temple. Allow no Galileans or
Gentiles through your line. There will be a sufficient number

of rabbis around to help you identify those persons who are loyal to the temple."

Captain Jakan asked, "Supposing there are some persons inside our ring when we first form it. What about them?"

The Chief Rabbi replied, "Rabbi Ahab will have a group of temple rabbis and servants who will check on those few persons who may be standing about the Forum at this early hour of the morning. However, their number should be small. In any case, before you allow any persons through your ring, check with Rabbi Ahab to make sure that the area has been thoroughly checked before allowing anyone through your line."

Captain Shama asked, "What about members of the Roman household and perhaps even Roman soldiers?"

The Chief Rabbi answered, "I am almost certain that all the Roman soldiers are now within Fort Antonia, so I don't believe there will be any of them about. If any members of the Roman household or their servants try to come through your lines try to persuade them to go around you. However, in no case, create a disturbance."

Captain Jakan asked, "What weapons shall we carry?"

The Chief Rabbi answered, "Equip your men with clubs or short pieces of chain. Whatever they carry must be easily concealed beneath their cloaks."

Captain Shama asked, "How soon do you want us to form this ring?"

The Chief Rabbi answered, "The sooner, the better. The sun is now rising and the Roman governor should be up within an hour. So the sooner you form your ring, the fewer will be the loiterers who will be gathered in front of the Forum."

Captain Jakan asked, "How long shall we maintain this ring?"

The Chief Rabbi answered, "Hold your line until the Roman governor has confirmed the death penalty of the Galilean. This is the most important reason for your ring of men. Not only must you allow only loyal temple persons within your ring, but once they are gathered there, no one must be allowed to leave until Pilate has approved the crucifixion of the Galilean.

"It may even be necessary for your men to demonstrate, shout and start a riot if Pilate becomes stubborn and refuses to confirm the death sentence. But whatever it takes to accomplish our purpose to get the Galilean killed, we intend to do it."

Captain Jakan asked, "What shall we do in the event that the Roman governor refuses to execute the Galilean?"

The Chief Rabbi snarled, "In that event, incite your soldiers and all the people around you to riot and create a tumult that will threaten the life of the Roman governor himself."

Captain Jakan asked, "Won't that be rather dangerous?"

The Chief Rabbi replied, "I don't think so. The Roman governor arrived in Jerusalem only a few days ago from his headquarters in Caesarea. He obviously expects no trouble to develop here on this visit, because he came with only a small detachment of men. Therefore, I feel sure that it is safe for your men and the people to riot at will without fear of serious punishment from the Romans. In any case, the most important action before us now is to kill the Galilean before sundown today and let the consequences be what they will."

Captain Jakan asked, "If we incite our people to riot, how can we exercise any control over them after the riot starts?"

The Chief Rabbi's jaw jutted out and his dark tense face became purple with rage as he blurted out between clenched teeth, "In that event, there will be no need to exercise any control over our people. Let the power of the mob take over. The Galilean is our prisoner and we will only turn him over to the Romans for execution. If the Roman governor refuses to execute him, then we want our people to riot, take the Galilean from the Romans and stone him to death. One way or another, the Galilean shall die before sundown today!"

Captain Jakan slowly replied, "I understand, rabbi. Are there any other orders that you want to give us?"

The Chief Rabbi's face relaxed somewhat as he answered, "There may be. For that purpose, there will be temple rabbis scattered throughout the crowd, who will act upon signals from me and who will convey my instructions to you."

Captain Jakan answered, "Very well. I will do my best to carry out your orders."

In the meantime, Rabbi Annas was at home peacefully sleeping in bed. One of the secrets of Rabbi Annas' strength was his great ability to completely relax physically and mentally at a moment's notice wherever he might be. In circumstances where lesser men would burn up their energies in useless physical exertion and mental worries, the old rabbi was as relaxed as a family cat beside its own fireplace. After Rabbi Annas had several hours' rest, a servant awakened him and the rabbi got up and ate a quick, light breakfast. Soon he was on his way back to the temple.

As Rabbi Annas walked contentedly through the narrow streets, he carefully reviewed his past experiences with the Romans, cataloguing and selecting those arguments which he believed would be the most effective in getting the Roman governor to approve the death penalty for Jesus and rejecting those reasons which he knew the Romans would consider inconsequential. He knew that none of the reasons used to obtain Jesus' death sentence before the Great Sanhedrin would have any effect upon the Roman governor.

Rabbi Annas had visited Rome as the representative of the Jewish nation on several occasions and he had earned the respect of the Romans as a shrewd negotiator. On his first visit to Rome, Rabbi Annas had obtained two very important concessions for the Jews from the Roman emperor: that the Jews could worship God as they wished, and that no Jew need serve in the Roman army.

On another occasion, Rabbi Annas had journeyed to Rome to protest to the Roman emperor the placing of the Roman emblem within the walls of the temple in Jerusalem by Pontius Pilate. The Roman emperor had agreed with Rabbi Annas that the Roman emblem was an offense to the Jewish people and Pilate was compelled to remove the offending emblem. These diplomatic victories had earned for Rabbi Annas the respect of the Roman emperor and the resentment of Pontius Pilate.

In addition to the diplomatic prestige that Rabbi Annas had gained from his voyages to Rome, he had also acquired an excellent understanding of the strength and the weakness of Rome. The strength of Rome, he knew, lay in their excellent military operations and in the tolerance of their rule over subject people. But the tremendous success that had resulted from the Romans' excellent military and civilian administration had spread their limited troops thinly over widely scattered areas of the world connected only by the most primitive forms of travel and communication; while their tolerant rule over subject people required their entrusting important police powers to local authorities.

Rabbi Annas felt that the greatest weakness of the Romans lay in their system of democracy. To him, it seemed inconceivable that a powerful nation would subordinate its legal authority to the whims of a mob. Today, he planned to use that Roman policy of democracy to carry out the will of the Great Sanhedrin—the execution of Jesus.

Rabbi Annas walked briskly and confidently toward the temple. The early morning air was cold, raw and humid, and it made him feel considerably colder than it actually was. But his walk and his manner were full of confidence, because he could now visualize the final end of a wary foe of his cherished religion. When Rabbi Annas entered the temple gate, he found his son-in-law and a group of rabbis impatiently waiting for him to arrive. In an attempt to hide his irritation, Chief Rabbi Caiaphas greeted his father-in-law with unusual cordiality. Rabbi Annas returned his son-in-law's cordial greeting and then smiled complacently as he greeted the other rabbinical members of the temple.

A short distance away from the rabbis, Jesus stood in a corner of the temple grounds with his hands still tightly bound behind his back, guarded by Rabbi Ahab and a group of temple servants. After greetings between all the rabbis had been completed, Chief Rabbi Caiaphas turned to Rabbi Ahab and said, "Follow closely behind us on the way to Fort Antonia."

Chief Rabbi Caiaphas then led the way to the Roman fort, walking briskly ahead of his party. As he entered the Forum around the governor's balcony, he noted with pleasure that Captain Shama and Captain Jakan had done their work well. The soldiers from King Herod's palace and the soldiers and servants of the temple had encircled the Roman governor's balcony to a point where the encircled area could hold well over 1,000 persons. Inside the encircled area, the Chief Rabbi happily noted that there were present only persons who were loyal members of the temple or of King Herod's household.

When the rabbis reached the entrance to Fort Antonia, they informed the sentry they wished to see the Roman governor. Within a few minutes, Captain Ditalo, the captain of the Roman guard, appeared and invited the rabbis to enter and make themselves comfortable in the governor's private chambers.

Rabbi Annas replied for the rabbis, saying, "Thank the Governor very kindly for his courtesy, captain, but our religious regulations forbid us from entering a Gentile building today. At sundown, our most important religious festival begins. If we should enter a Gentile building now, we would be defiled and we could not cleanse ourselves before sundown; therefore, we could not celebrate our religious Passover tonight. Thank you again very kindly, but we will wait out here and speak to your governor when he comes out on the balcony."

Consequently, the rabbis remained standing outdoors, tired, cold and impatient, while Captain Ditalo went into the fort to give Pontius Pilate the rabbis' message. After an unusually long delay, Pontius Pilate appeared on the balcony, looking stern and unfriendly. There was no friendship, or even the superficial semblance of it, between Pontius Pilate and the temple rabbis. So the Roman governor bluntly and gruffly asked, "What do you want?"

Before Rabbi Annas could answer with one of his typically diplomatic replies, Chief Rabbi Caiaphas pompously advanced toward the balcony and pointing to Jesus, bluntly said, "We want this man executed."

Pontius Pilate raised his eyebrows in surprise and asked, "Why? What has he done?"

The Chief Rabbi blurted out, "What has he done? He is an evil-doer, who is perverting our people. He is a rebel and a fanatic. Do you think we would ask that he be executed if he were not an evil man?"

The Roman governor looked coldly at the Chief Rabbi and said, "Is that the only charge that you have against this man in justification for his execution?"

Chief Rabbi Caiaphas knew that he had made a poor presentation of the case against Jesus from the Roman viewpoint, but being unable to back down gracefully said, "This man says he is a prophet of God, while actually he is a son of the devil. He has obtained many followers by his skillful talk, dividing our people into opposing groups."

Pontius Pilate shrugged his shoulders nonchalantly as he answered, "Rabbi, that is a religious matter and not one that concerns Rome. This is a case for your people to decide. Take this man away and judge him yourselves in accordance with your own religious laws."

Rabbi Annas pushed his son-in-law determinedly aside and said, "Honorable governor, before you go, allow me to say a few words. This man not only claims to be the Son of God, but he also claims to be the King of the Jews. Therefore, he is not only a rebel who endangers our nation, but he is also a rebel who endangers your nation. Our council, the Great Sanhedrin, has given him a fair trial and found him guilty of various offenses and condemned him to death. However, since we are not permitted to carry out the death penalty, we ask that you carry out this execution for us."

Pontius Pilate looked skeptically at the two rabbis and then slowly said, "Send that man up here to me. I want to speak to him myself."

After Jesus had been led into the Judgment Hall of the Roman Fort, Governor Pilate went in and said to Jesus, "Do you really claim to be the King of the Jews?"

Jesus answered, "Is that your own idea or has someone else suggested it to you?"

Governor Pilate replied, "How would I know? Am I a Jew? It is your own people and your own chief rabbis who have arrested you and delivered you to me. They are the ones who bring these charges against you."

Jesus said, "They are hypocrites and liars."

Pilate asked, "But what have you done that makes them demand your execution?"

Jesus replied, "As you are a stranger in my country, I am afraid that you will not understand. However, I will say this to you, my kingdom is not of this world; because if it were, my servants would fight so that the rabbis could not have arrested me. You see, my kingdom is in heaven."

Pilate asked, "Are you a king, then?"

Jesus answered, "In the Kingdom of God I am a king. The reason for my birth and the reason for my coming into this world is to bear witness to the truth of God's will. Therefore, everyone who believes in the truth listens to the message I bring to them from God."

The Roman governor thoughtfully bowed his head and said, more to himself than to Jesus, "What is the truth?"

Slowly walking out to the balcony, Pontius Pilate said to the assembled rabbis, "I have questioned this man whom you want executed and I can find no fault in him at all."

The Chief Rabbi's clenched fist shot upward in trip hammer fashion and the temple rabbis scattered throughout the crowd repeated this action until it reached the outermost group of temple demonstrators. There followed first a rumble and then a mighty roar of derisive shouts. When the roar had subsided, Chief Rabbi Caiaphas sarcastically asked, "Do you hear the voice of our people? This rebel is stirring them up from Jerusalem to Galilee and yet you say that you can find no fault in him at all? What kind of a governor are you?"

Governor Pilate asked, "Did you say that he was stirring up the people in Galilee?"

The Chief Rabbi roared back, "Yes, I said in Galilee."

Pilate asked, "Is he, then, a Galilean?"

The Chief Rabbi angrily answered, "Of course, he is a Galilean. What other Jew would show such disrespect for our Mosaic laws?"

Pontius Pilate's face now relaxed into a sigh of relief as he answered, "Well, in that case, he comes under the jurisdiction of King Herod Antipas, the King of Galilee, who fortunately is in Jerusalem right now to celebrate the Passover. I shall immediately send this man over to King Herod Antipas and let him decide what action should be taken in this matter."

Before any of the rabbis could raise any further arguments, the Roman governor quickly turned on his heel and bolted back into the fort. As Pontius Pilate reentered the reception chamber, he saw his wife, Claudia, peering intently at Jesus through a narrow slit in the heavy curtains. Crossing the room to where his wife stood, the Roman governor said, "Claudia, what are you doing here?"

His wife answered, "I just had to see that man. I just had to see him. I dreamt about him last night."

The Roman governor solicitously replied, "Now, Claudia, you know you shouldn't be in this part of the fort where it is chilly. Besides, you haven't been feeling well lately. Come, let's go and have a bite to eat."

His wife softly answered, "Yes, dear."

Meanwhile, outside the fort, Chief Rabbi Caiaphas and Rabbi Annas were so stunned at this unexpected turn of events that they were shocked and speechless. This was one event that even the wily brain of crafty old Rabbi Annas had not anticipated. In their frustration, the temple rabbis angrily blamed their Chief Rabbi for his failure to obtain the Roman governor's approval for the execution of Jesus. As usual, Rabbi Annas remained discreetly silent and calm, while the angry voices around him buzzed loudly like so many angry hornets. The one thing that did alarm him was the fact that he noticed that the mob that had been so carefully planted before the governor's palace was beginning to disintegrate, as the people felt themselves leaderless. Rabbi Annas spoke sharply to the Chief Rabbi, saying, "Quick, give orders to your rabbis and your soldiers to hold their places here. This day is not yet over!"

Luke 9 (7-9)
Luke 23 (7-12)

Chapter 41

Rabbi Annas, King Herod and Jesus

As soon as Rabbi Annas had recovered from his initial surprise at the unexpected turn of events created by Pontius Pilate's sudden decision to send Jesus to King Herod, his reactions were prompt and decisive. Turning to his son-in-law, he said, "Remain here and see to it that all these people hold their places before the governor's balcony. I am going to see King Herod Antipas before the Romans arrive to persuade him that he must refuse to accept responsibility for the fate of the Galilean."

The Chief Rabbi dutifully answered, "Yes, father."

As Rabbi Annas hurried toward the king's palace, he thought of the strange circumstances that twice within five days required him to visit the two licentious brothers, both of whom were named Herod, and both of whom he strongly detested. Combined within the old rabbi was a strong feeling of family pride and a strict dedication to his religion. His personal pride rebelled at asking favors of an evil person, but his sense of dedication to his religion compelled him to override his personal feelings and speak to the adulterous kings. While Rabbi Annas hurried toward the palace, his normally calm features became frozen into the stern pattern that people adopt when they are faced with a necessary, but painful duty. How he wished that this ugly matter of the execution of Jesus could be quickly accomplished and forgotten, so that he could contentedly enjoy his Passover supper and resume his study of the ancient Scriptures.

When he arrived at the palace of King Herod, he told the guard that he wished to see the king. Before long, an embarrassed servant came to the gate and asked the rabbi to be seated. It was obvious from the unusual quietness that the king's household had not yet begun to stir. Stifling his pride, Rabbi Annas said to the servant, "Take me to your king immediately. It is urgent that I see him at once."

The servant airily replied, "But, rabbi, the king never rises before noon."

Rabbi Annas sternly said, "Tell the king that I am here on a matter of life and death and that his own life depends upon the action that he takes."

The awed servant answered, "Yes, rabbi. I will go and waken the king, but it may cost me a severe flogging."

The servant returned after a long wait and led the rabbi through a series of darkened halls to the king's bed chamber. The room was so dark that the rabbi could barely see. As he paused at the doorway, adjusting his eyes to the semi-darkness, he heard the king's hoarse, sleepy, drunken voice calling out to him, saying "Come in, rabbi, come in. Sit down. What brings you here in the middle of the night?"

Rabbi Annas moved forward cautiously so as not to stumble over any of the numerous objects scattered over the floor of the disarrayed room. Then he said quietly, but firmly,

"Sire, it is not the middle of the night. In fact, it is almost the middle of the day. Within a few minutes, there will be Roman soldiers arriving here with the rebel Galilean."

The king vacuously replied, "Roman soldiers coming here with the rebel Galilean? Why? I thought it was our soldiers who went out to capture the Galilean. What happened?"

Rabbi Annas patiently answered, "Many things have happened, sire. I urge you to dress quickly and have something to eat, while I tell you what has happened during the past twelve hours."

The king lightly replied, "Oh, I never eat anything at this hour of the day. It is very bad for my stomach."

With great effort, the king got out of bed, filled a tumbler full of strong liquor and quickly drank it down. Now, apparently wide awake, he turned to the rabbi and said, "Go ahead and tell me your story while I dress."

With an air of resigned martyrdom, the old rabbi turned his head away to avoid watching the king dressing and replied, "Our soldiers arrested the Galilean last night and took him to the temple where he was tried and condemned to death by the Great Sanhedrin. Early this morning, we took him to the Roman governor to have the death sentence carried out. Instead of approving our death verdict, the Roman governor decided to send this rebel to you for final disposition because he is a Galilean."

King Herod suddenly straightened up and cheerfully said, "Well, isn't that nice of the Roman governor? It's about time he finally recognized my authority over my own subjects."

Rabbi Annas spoke slowly, but with intense feeling, as he replied, "Sire, this Galilean is one subject over whom you must *not* exercise your authority."

The king tartly replied, "And why not?"

Rabbi Annas slowly answered, "Because, sire, he is a very dangerous man, a much more dangerous man than John the

Baptist was, and you know how much trouble his followers created after his death."

The king recoiled at the words "John the Baptist" as he visualized again the defiant staring eyes in the bloody, bearded head of the renowned evangelist. Quickly recovering himself, he said, "But, I have been told that this Galilean is the reincarnation of John the Baptist."

Rabbi Annas patiently replied, "I am afraid, sire, that you have been misinformed. This Galilean was born only a year or so after John the Baptist. Therefore, he cannot possibly be the reincarnation of his cousin."

The king petulantly said, "Well, come to the point, rabbi. What is it that you want me to do? You have the habit of always correcting me and speaking to me as though I were a child."

The normally calm, gray face of Rabbi Annas reddened perceptibly as he struggled to remain courteous to this wastrel king. Speaking slowly and dispassionately to avoid betraying his contempt, the old rabbi replied, "Sire, when the Romans bring the Galilean to you, have nothing to do with him. Send him back to the Roman governor with your compliments and regrets. If you execute this Galilean, our own people may rise up against us. The resentment over the execution of another so-called prophet by your men or ours may incite our people to rebel against us."

With a carefree toss of his head, the king said, "Oh, I have no reason for wanting to execute the Galilean; in fact, I would like to meet him. They tell me he is quite a magician. I would like to see him perform some of his magic tricks."

Rabbi Annas answered with an air of great resignation, "Sire, the Galilean is probably here now. Of course, if you wish to see him perform some of his feats of magic, you may do so. But I must remind you that this man is under sentence of death by the Great Sanhedrin and that sentence must be carried out before sundown today when our Passover begins, in order that this holy day shall not be defiled by this man's death."

Obviously impressed, the king asked, "How can I help?"

The rabbi replied, "The Romans pride themselves upon their democracy, which is nothing more than mob rule. They make a special fetish of it at their games and on all those occasions when their officials have an unpopular decision to make. We can expect the Roman governor to allow the fate of this Nazarene to be determined by the shouts of the mob. That is the time when we will want as many of your soldiers and servants to be present around the governor's balcony to scream and shout with our temple rabbis for the execution of the Galilean."

Nodding his head, the king answered, "Very well, I will immediately order every soldier and servant I can spare to join your rabbis before the governor's palace. Now will you please go, so that I can speak to the Galilean?"

Rabbi Annas quietly said, "Yes, sire, you shall see him. But please remember to return him to the Roman governor as quickly as possible?"

With great irritation, the king replied, "Yes, yes and a third time, yes. Now go!"

Rabbi Annas made no attempt to conceal his disgust as he left the king's bed chamber. After the rabbi left, the king went to the reception chamber, where the Roman soldiers were already waiting for him with their prisoner. When the king entered the room, the Roman officer, Captain Ditalo, respectfully saluted the king and courteously said, "King Herod Antipas, I deliver this man, Jesus of Nazareth, to you with the compliments of Governor Pontius Pilate. Chief Rabbi Caiaphas has brought a number of religious and civil charges against this man; none of which affect Rome. Since this man is a Galilean, the governor recommends that you pass judgment upon him."

King Herod smilingly replied, "Thank you, captain, and tell the governor for me that I deeply appreciate his courtesy in recognizing my authority over my own subjects."

Captain Ditalo saluted King Herod and quietly answered, "Yes, sire."

After Captain Ditalo left, the king turned toward Jesus with a pleasurable air of excitement. This day was a rare occasion in his life, when both the most revered rabbi in all Jerusalem and the Roman governor acknowledged that he was the King of Galilee. Not only had they both acknowledged that he was the king, but they both sought his kingly favor.

Secretly, the king liked to dabble in feats of magic, and he hoped that Jesus would show him some special tricks of the magician's art. Little wonder that the king turned toward him with a pleasurable air of excitement and said, "I have heard so much about your magical powers that I have been looking forward to meeting you for a long time. You see, I've been delving into the art of magic myself and I have been anxious to meet someone like you, who is a master of the art, to teach me some of its basic tricks. Won't you please show me how you perform some of your simpler tricks of magic?"

Jesus stared stonily ahead, as though he were wholly unaware of the king's presence. Again and again, the king spoke to him, using his most persuasive powers of speech, but Jesus completely ignored him. Finally, in a soft, wheedling voice the king said, "Come on, Galilean, you don't have to be so stand-offish with me. I'm not like those stiff-necked temple rabbis. Just perform one simple little bit of magic for me and I'll be satisfied." After a brief pause, the king added, "Remember, I have the power to set you free."

Jesus still gave no indication that he had heard a single word the king had spoken. Finding himself completely ignored, Herod became thoroughly irritated and shouted, "Have you lost your tongue, Galilean? Can't you speak? You know I can have you stoned to death or even beheaded?"

In spite of the king's angry threats, Jesus remained silent and motionless. Since neither superficial friendliness nor angry threats had any effect upon Jesus, King Herod tried a new approach—mockery. The king's manner and voice suddenly changed to one of banter and ridicule as he said, "They tell me that you claim to be the King of the Jews. Is that right? If you are, when do you plan to take over my throne?"

As Jesus continued to completely ignore him, King Herod became impatient with his unresponsive prisoner and summoned his servants. When they arrived, he said to one of them, "This man claims to be the king of the Jews. Bring me one of my purple robes so that we may dress his royal majesty in garments befitting his kingly station."

The king's juvenile remark brought forth gales of laughter from the palace servants, who had crowded into the room. While they were still laughing at the king's humor, a servant returned with a beautiful purple robe with the royal emblem embroidered upon it. Herod took the robe and with mock humility placed it around Jesus' shoulders, then turning to his servants, he said, "Salute and bow to the new king. Hail, Jesus of Nazareth, King of the Jews!"

King Herod bowed low before Jesus and then each of his servants imitated him in turn and saluted Jesus with the same mocking words and false air of humility. Finally tiring of his childish game, Herod sarcastically said, "Return this dumb Nazarene to the Roman governor with my compliments and tell him I have no reason for punishing this stupid Galilean."

One of the servants asked, "What shall we do with your robe, sire?"

"Oh let the Galilean keep it. He'll need it where he's going."

Chapter 42

The Rabbis' Victory

As Rabbi Annas left King Herod's palace, he cast his experienced eye upon his shadow on the ground and quickly estimated it was about two hours before noon. Less than eight hours now remained before sundown to get Pontius Pilate's approval of the execution of Jesus and have him crucified and killed. The old rabbi knew that he must hurry to get both of these important tasks done in such a short time.

For the first time in his life, Rabbi Annas actually trotted. It was more of a jog than a trot, but unquestionably the old rabbi was moving at a fast pace for an old man. When he arrived back at Fort Antonia and saw many of the palace and temple servants away from their allocated places before the governor's balcony, he became livid with rage. He strode over to his son-in-law, who was idly chatting with several of the temple rabbis, and for the first time the long strain of his prolonged persecution of Jesus told upon the old rabbi. Angrily facing his son-in-law and the temple rabbi, he said, "Get back to your places, you fools! And get all the soldiers and servants back around the governor's balcony immediately. The Galilean will be here at any moment."

Chief Rabbi Caiaphas' dark face reddened with embarrassment as he lamely replied, "Yes, father. We were just resting until you got back. We will get everyone back into place immediately."

Meanwhile, back at King Herod's palace, Jesus was led out through the palace gate surrounded by a detachment of King Herod's soldiers. Jesus' arms were still tightly bound behind him, so now they felt numb and lifeless from his shoulder blades to his finger tips. King Herod's resplendent purple robe that was jauntily cast over his slender shoulders, emphasized his drawn palid features. He had been without food, sleep or rest for over thirty hours and now, in the midday sun with the heavy robe hanging over his shoulders, he moved slowly and dizzily. When he hesitated for a moment, one of the soldiers booted him sharply saying, "Keep moving, king. The buzzards are waiting for you."

Out of the depths of his physical and spiritual resources, Jesus found the strength to move ahead at the fast pace set for him by the king's soldiers. When he came in sight of the mob around the Roman governor's balcony, they set up a terrific clamor of derisive shouts. Reluctantly, the crowd opened a narrow pathway to the entrance of Fort Antonia for Jesus and his guards to pass through. Those persons nearest Jesus mocked, threatened and spit at him. Finally, Jesus obtained temporary relief from his tormentors when the gates of Fort Antonia opened up and quickly closed behind him.

Upstairs in the dining room of the fort, Pontius Pilate and his wife were having their mid-morning meal when they heard the wild howling of the angry mob. Anxiously, Claudia said to her husband, "Just listen to the inhuman screams of that awful mob."

Governor Pilate answered, "It makes my blood run cold."

While Pontius Pilate and his wife had been talking, Captain Ditalo entered the room and said, "Governor, King Herod's soldiers have returned the prisoner with a message from the king saying that he returns the Galilean to you with his compliments. However, the king states that he has no reason for punishing this prisoner."

Pontius Pilate frowned, paused and said, "Where is the prisoner now?"

Captain Ditalo answered, "In the reception hall, sir."

The governor asked, "Where are the rabbis?"

Captain Ditalo replied, "They are in the Forum below your balcony anxiously waiting to see you."

Claudia said to her husband, "Please, dear, don't approve the death penalty for that man from Galilee. I never saw him before in my life until the rabbis brought him here this morning, and yet I saw him clearly in my dream last night. He looked at me so long with those sad, sorrowful eyes that I wanted to get up and scream, but I just couldn't move. Please, dear, don't let the rabbis kill him?"

Pontius Pilate gravely answered, "I promise you, Claudia, that I will do everything in my power to save this man's life, but these Jews are a very excitable people about religious matters. Now they are celebrating one of their very special religious holidays and they are stirred up to fever pitch. This man has offended them in some way or other and nothing but his death will satisfy them."

Again from outdoors came blood-curdling yells that reverberated strangely through the ancient stone walls of the fort. Claudia shuddered and said, "Their howling sounds weird and unnatural. Please, Pontius, do what you can to save that man."

The governor quietly answered, "I'll try my very best, Claudia, but if the rabbis incite their people to riot, I have only a handful of troops in Jerusalem with which to control them."

He walked slowly and reluctantly to the balcony facing the Forum, and as he stepped out he was met by a derisive roar from the mob below. The rabbis had ample time by now to coach the mob with a few simple hand signals, so that their responses to the rabbis' instructions was like that of a well-drilled chorus. When the governor saw the sea of angry, snarling faces before him, he knew that he would have a very difficult time to pacify these excited people. What he didn't know was that it was actually impossible to placate the hatred that lay in the hearts of the temple rabbis, who had incited the mob to fury.

So, unknowingly and innocently, Pontius Pilate tried to do the impossible—save Jesus from death. When the noise of the mob subsided, Pontius Pilate said in a very conciliatory tone of voice, "Your temple rabbis brought this prisoner to me this morning charging him with certain crimes, and demanded that he be executed. I carefully cross-examined this man myself, and I could find him guilty of no crime. Normally, I would release such a prisoner immediately. However, since your rabbis have argued so vehemently that this Galilean is guilty of certain crimes, I sent him to King Herod of Galilee for judgment. King Herod also interviewed this man and he has now returned him to me with the statement that he could not find him guilty of any crime. Under these circumstances, it is obvious that this man should go free. However, I am aware of the fact that he has caused considerable disturbance among you, so he cannot be wholly blameless. Therefore, I shall have him flogged as punishment for creating this disturbance and then set him free."

As soon as the governor stopped speaking, the Chief Rabbi's hands signaled a peremptory message to the rabbis near him, who relayed his instructions to the other rabbis throughout the crowd, and this time the reaction from the mob was almost instantaneous. Again, there was a low rumble of subdued voices and then a mighty roar of jeers and howling. Some of the more belligerent men in the center of the mob threw rocks into the air which, from the balcony, appeared to be aimed directly at the governor.

In order to get away from the noise and the insults of the angry Jews, Pontius Pilate turned and walked back to the reception chamber where Jesus was standing between two soldiers. Pilate walked up to him and said, "Why do the Jews hate you so much? Who are you, anyway?"

Jesus remained silent, so Pilate asked, "Why don't you answer me? I am trying to help you. Don't you realize that I have the power to crucify you and I also have the power to set you free?"

Jesus quietly answered, "You would have no power over me at all unless you had received that power from heaven. Therefore, those who delivered me to you have the greater sin."

Pilate looked sympathetically at the resolute man before him and decided he must try once again to save the life of this dedicated man. He returned to the balcony and again addressed the angry mob with a pacifying speech that he hoped would soothe their angry temper. But the blood-thirsty mob, sensing their power, responded with louder and angrier shouts of derision. During a brief lull, Rabbi Ahab shouted, "Why do you protect this man who is urging our people to revolt against Rome? This rebel claims he is King of the Jews and anyone who claims he is King of the Jews is an enemy of Caesar; so, if you let him go, you are no friend of Caesar's."

Pilate knew these charges were monstrous lies, but he also realized that the enraged rabbis were insensible to reason.

Still unwilling to admit the hopelessness of the situation, he returned to the council chamber and asked Jesus to follow him out to the balcony.

It was now almost noon and the bright sun shining on Jesus' pale face gave it a pathetically ascetic glow. Pointing to Jesus, the governor addressed his humanitarian plea for mercy directly to the common people by saying, "People of Judaea, look at your king. Here is a real man!"

Pilate got no further as the rabbis nearest the balcony yelled, "Take him away! Crucify him! Crucify that rebel!"

Pilate asked in exasperation, "Shall I crucify your king?"

Chief Rabbi Caiaphas yelled back, "We have no king but Caesar."

Ignoring this obvious lie, the governor, urged on by the memory of his wife's piteous plea, said in his most conciliatory tone of voice, "It is the Roman custom that upon the celebration of an important festivity such as the Passover, I shall release to you one prisoner. At this time, I ask you which of two Jewish prisoners shall I release to you, the murderer Barrabas or Jesus of Nazareth?"

This was one event that the temple rabbis had anticipated and prepared for, because it had been the custom of Roman governors to free one prisoner to the Jews each year during the Passover festival. Therefore, the temple rabbis had been instructed that when the Roman governor offered to release a prisoner to them, they should shout for the release of any prisoner but Jesus. Soon, the well-drilled mob was yelling in unison, "Barrabas! Barrabas! Barrabas!"

In bitter frustration, Pontius Pilate yelled back, "What then am I to do with Jesus of Nazareth?"

The mob roared back, "Crucify him! Crucify him! Crucify him!"

Governor Pilate pleaded, "Why? What evil has he done?"

Ignoring his question, the mob repeatedly roared, "Crucify him! Crucify him! Crucify him!"

The roar of the crowd beat upon the brain of Pontius Pilate with unremitting relentlessness. The pack of human wolves were now in full cry in pursuit of their prey. In one last desperate attempt to save Jesus, Pontius Pilate said, "If you crucify this innocent man, his blood will be upon your heads and upon the heads of your children and your grandchildren for generations to come."

Chief Rabbi Caiaphas yelled back, "Let his blood be upon our heads and upon the heads of our children from now to eternity, but crucify the Galilean!"

Pontius Pilate yelled back, "Then take him yourselves and crucify him, because I find no fault in him at all."

Turning his back upon the blood-thirsty mob, Governor Pilate walked sorrowfully into his private chambers, where he took a basin and filled it with water. Upon returning to the balcony, the governor held the basin high over his head for every one to see, and placed it on the top of the balustrade. Carefully dipping his hands into the water, Pilate looked down upon the rabbis beneath him and holding his wet hands high over his head, said, "I am innocent of the blood of this righteous man. The blame for his death rests upon you."

From the temple rabbis came an answering defiant shout, "Let his blood be upon our head and those of our children and grandchildren, but crucify the Galilean!"

Slowly and solemnly, Pontius Pilate replied, "So shall it be!"

In deep despair, Pontius Pilate turned to Captain Ditalo and ordered him to release the prisoner named Barrabas and crucify Jesus. When Chief Rabbi Caiaphas heard the Roman governor give this order, he embraced Rabbi Ahab and danced wildly around the Forum with him in unrestrained joy. Soon all the other temple personnel, except Rabbi Annas, followed their example, so that before long the entire Forum was filled with the unusual sight of bearded temple rabbis, dressed in their long black robes, joyously whirling and dancing, in celebration of their great victory.

Meanwhile, Rabbi Annas walked out of the far side of the Forum slowly and dejectedly.

And so Jesus died on a Friday, probably in the first week of April in the year A.D. 30. All four of the evangelists agree on the exact time of the day that Jesus died, which was the ninth hour, and as the Jews counted hours from the time of sunrise, the ninth hour would correspond to three o'clock in the afternoon of our time. As Jesus was born in the latter part of December of about 6 B.C. he was probably about thirty-five and a half years old at the time of his death. After Jesus was pronounced dead by the soldier who thrust his spear into his side, Captain Ditalo looked up at the cross and said, "Truly, this man was the Son of God."

Chapter 43

The Burial

The four soldiers who had crucified Jesus now gathered up his clothing and, in accordance with the custom of their times, claimed it for themselves. Jesus had little more than the barest minimum of clothing, but he did have a fine cloak woven without seam from top to bottom.

All four of the soldiers wanted the cloak more than any other garment that Jesus wore. So, when they tried to divide the clothing into four equal parts, they could not agree on any equitable division. Finally, one of the soldiers said, "This cloak is worth more than all the other garments put together. We can never reach an agreement on the division of the clothing unless we set the cloak aside and divide the remaining clothing into four equal parts."

Another soldier said, "That can easily be done, but who is going to get the cloak?"

The first soldier replied, "I suggest we throw dice for it and let the winner take the whole garment." The other soldiers nodded their heads in agreement and so the clothing of Jesus was divided by lot and by the throw of the dice. Meanwhile overhead the buzzards swooped lower and lower, waiting for the people clustered around the crosses to move away so that they could feast upon the bodies of the three dead men. Among the spectators were Mary, Jesus' mother, John, Mary, the mother of James, Mary Magdalen, Nicodemus and Joseph of Arimathaea.

Joseph said to Nicodemus, "Let us see to it that Jesus has a decent Jewish burial."

Nicodemus asked, "Where can we bury him at this late hour of the day?"

Joseph replied, "I have a tomb nearby that I had dug for myself and my family. It has never been used. We can bury him there."

Nicodemus answered, "Good, but do you think the Roman governor will allow us to remove his body?"

Joseph said, "I think so. At least we can try. I will go to see the Roman governor myself, while you go into the city and buy the cleaning fluid, the spices and the aromatic spirits that we need for the burial. On my way back, I will buy a bolt of linen."

Nicodemus replied, "But Joseph, you don't intend to expose yourself to the wrath of the Chief Rabbi by openly going to see the Roman governor, do you?"

Joseph replied, "No, I don't. As you know, I have been on friendly terms with the Roman tribune, Captain Ditalo, for a long time. I feel sure that he will get me into Fort Antonia through the guards' entrance."

Nicodemus answered, "It's still risky, but at least it is better than being seen going into the main gate of the fort by one of the temple rabbis."

Joseph replied, "While we are gone, we will need someone

to watch the body of Jesus. Those buzzards overhead have smelled death and they are circling lower and lower. If Jesus' body is left alone for just a few minutes, those buzzards will tear it to pieces and he won't be fit for a decent burial."

Nicodemus said, "There is a group of his family and friends here. We can ask them to watch Jesus' body and keep the buzzards away until we get back."

"Good," Joseph replied. "Let us go and speak to them."

John and Jesus' mother, and Mary Magdalen readily agreed to watch Jesus' body while Nicodemus and Joseph were away on their respective errands. When Joseph arrived at Fort Antonia, Captain Ditalo met him at the guards' entrance and guided him quickly into the governor's reception chamber. When Pontius Pilate entered, Joseph said, "Honorable governor, I request your permission to remove the body of Jesus of Nazareth from the cross for burial."

Governor Pilate answered, "But it is not possible that he is dead yet. The Chief Rabbi was here only a few minutes ago asking me to hasten his death by having his legs broken."

Joseph sadly replied, "I know, governor, but Jesus of Nazareth is dead. I saw him die myself shortly after the Chief Rabbi left Golgotha to see you. He was so weak that he died on the cross before the soldier arrived to break his legs."

Still incredulous, the governor turned to one of his servants and asked, "Has Captain Ditalo returned from Mount Calvary yet?"

The servant replied, "Yes, sir, he has just returned."

Pontius Pilate said, "Tell him to come in."

When Captain Ditalo entered, the governor asked, "Has Jesus of Nazareth died yet?"

Captain Ditalo answered, "Yes, sir. I just returned from Golgotha to report his death to you."

Turning to Joseph, the puzzled governor said, "Very well. You may take the body of the Galilean for burial."

Joseph hurried out of Fort Antonia to the central market

place, where he bought a bolt of fine linen. With the linen tucked under his arm, Joseph hurried down the street through the Gennareth Gate to Mount Calvary. There he met Nicodemus and the members of Jesus' family. Together, they gently lowered the body of Jesus from the cross and carried it to the entrance of the tomb of Joseph of Arimathea. A huge round rock protected the entrance to the cave, and the men laboriously rolled it back. After Jesus' body was laid on a large flat slab, the women thoroughly washed it with the cleansing fluid and then carefully wrapped it with linen which they liberally sprinkled with aromatic spirits to keep the body sweet-smelling as long as possible. When the women had completed their work, the men placed the body in one of the burial niches and closed the entrance of the tomb by rolling back the huge rounded carved rock.

That night Rabbi Caiaphas went to bed in high good humor as he happily reviewed in his mind all the events of the preceding day culminating in the crucifixion of Jesus. However, in spite of the fact that the day had ended happily, he did not sleep well. All night long he fidgeted and tossed in his bed as he saw Jesus in his dreams calmly preaching in the temple, in the synagogues and in many foreign lands. By the time he woke in the morning, he had a splitting headache and he was in a black, sullen mood.

This was the Sabbath, the first day of the sacred Passover, and the Chief Rabbi should have felt supremely happy because his great enemy was dead. However, instead of being happy, he fretted and fumed at his servants, saying his breakfast was cold and tasteless. Suddenly he stopped his fretting and fussing as he recalled Jesus' prophecy that on the third day after his death, he would rise again from the dead.

Now he felt sure that he knew the meaning of his troubled dreams. It was a forewarning that Jesus would be resurrected in accordance with his prophecy. The Chief Rabbi suddenly felt weak, cold and depressed. Fearfully, he told himself that the Galilean must never rise from the dead. He knew he could never again face those calm, brown eyes that pierced right through his hard brutish exterior. Nervously, the Chief Rabbi summoned Rabbi Ahab and said, "Send messengers to all the members of the executive committee of the Great Sanhedrin to meet me here two hours before high noon."

Rabbi Ahab looked at the Chief Rabbi incredulously and said, "But, rabbi, this is the Sabbath of the Passover!"

The Chief Rabbi angrily roared, "You fool! Don't you think I know what day this is? Do as I tell you!"

Rabbi Ahab looked at Chief Rabbi Caiaphas dubiously, wondering if his superior had suddenly lost his senses. Shaking his head in bewilderment, he walked off to carry out the Chief Rabbi's orders. Two hours before high noon, all the members of the executive committee of the Great Sanhedrin arrived at the home of Chief Rabbi Caiaphas audibly grumbling their displeasure at being summoned out of their homes on the Sabbath of the Passover.

When they were all comfortably seated, the Chief Rabbi apologetically said, "I deeply regret calling you out to another emergency meeting on this Sabbath Day of our sacred Passover, but the great danger that we face from the Galilean is not over yet. We all know that he is dead. I witnessed his death myself and many of you were with me, there at Golgotha when he died. But now we are faced with another danger which is even greater than the one we faced before his death. And that danger is the possibility of his resurrection."

This statement was met with such a round of unconcealed scornful sneers that Rabbi Annas felt compelled to protect his son-in-law by saying, "Please, gentlemen, please let us give Rabbi Caiaphas an opportunity to tell us what he has on his mind."

The assembled rabbis glanced contemptuously at the Chief Rabbi and then settled back into their chairs with undisguised impatience. The Chief Rabbi continued, "I know that many of you believe, as I do, there is no resurrection. But what we believe and what we think is not the point in question now. The important thing is, what do the people believe? We all know that there are a great many of our people who believe in resurrection, and prior to his death the Galilean predicted that he would be resurrected the third day after his death."

With an obviously bored air, one of the rabbis said, "What has this got to do with your bringing us here on this day of all days—the Sabbath of our Passover?"

Flustered and embarrassed, the Chief Rabbi replied, "Last night, I dreamt that the Galilean rose from the dead. I know that you will say that this is something I imagined, but I am only telling you what I saw in my dreams, and in my dream I saw the Galilean alive as clearly as I see you now."

Another rabbi sarcastically said, "So, in your dreams you saw the Galilean rise from the dead. So what? Maybe you have too great an imagination, or maybe you ate too much last night and you have an upset stomach. Is this any reason for bringing us here on the Sabbath Day of the Passover?"

"I know how you feel about resurrection," Caiaphas lamely replied, "and I agree with you. Still I am confident that my dream is a forewarning of trouble. Maybe it would mean that the Galilean's disciples plan to steal his body from the sepulchre and then claim he had risen from the dead. For us, the results of such an act would be disastrous."

Rabbi Annas quietly asked, "What do you plan on doing about this, Caiaphas?"

The Chief Rabbi answered, "I recommend that we all go see the Roman governor and demand that he seal the tomb of the Galilean and place a guard over the tomb night and day for at least three days after the time of his death. Then, if nothing happens, we can prove to our people that the Galilean's prophecy of his resurrection was false, and thereby undermine all their beliefs in his prophecies."

This unusual suggestion was followed by a deep silence that plainly indicated that while no one wanted to contradict the Chief rabbi, neither did anyone agree with him. To these traditionally orthodox Jews, the idea of breaking the Sabbath of the Passover by pleading with the Roman governor was extremely repugnant. The fact that this recommendation came from the Chief Rabbi made its acceptance that much more difficult. In their quandary, the rabbis inevitably turned their heads toward old, reliable Rabbi Annas. When the old rabbi saw that all eyes were focused on him, he slowly said, "Let us do what Caiaphas recommends and all go together to see the Roman governor."

Reluctantly, the rabbis rose with muffled grumbles and went to Fort Antonia to see Pontius Pilate. This time they were glad to be ushered into the Roman governor's reception room as they were anxious to avoid being seen by their people openly breaking the Passover Sabbath. When Pontius Pilate was told who his visitors were, he strode stiffly into the reception room and coldly said, "What is it this time?"

The Chief Rabbi meekly answered, "Honorable governor, we have just remembered that the impostor from Galilee predicted before he died, that three days after his death that he would rise again from the dead. We all know that this is impossible, but many of that man's followers are very gullible and we are afraid that some of his disciples will go to his sepulchre at night, steal his body and then tell our people that the Galilean has risen from the dead."

Pontius Pilate stared stonily at the Chief Rabbi and coldly replied, "What is that to me?"

The Chief Rabbi answered, "Honorable governor, if our people should believe that the Galilean has been resurrected, they will probably riot and try to kill all of us. The resulting conflict would be worse than the conflict that would have developed if we had not condemned him to death in the first place. Now, we can easily prevent this disastrous event from happening if you will place a guard over the Galilean's sepulchre night and day for three days. Then we can prove to our people that the Galilean's prophecy regarding his resurrection was false."

Pontius Pilate shrugged his shoulders with an air of indifference and said, "You have your own men. If you want to place a guard over the sepulchre of Jesus of Nazareth, use them. Now, get out."

The temple rabbis left Fort Antonia dejected and frustrated. As they walked toward the temple, they argued and debated among themselves how they could persuade any of their guards to work on the Sabbath of the Passover. Finally, Rabbi Annas said to his son-in-law, "There is only one way to do it and that is to use temple guards for this unpleasant duty. My son, you will have a hard time explaining this breaking of the Passover Sabbath to the temple guards, but that is the only way out now."

The other rabbis quickly agreed with Rabbi Annas and soon the Chief Rabbi found himself all alone on his way back to the temple to provide the necessary guard at the tomb of Jesus. Now he wished that he had never brought the matter up because he could see no way out of the unpleasant predicament that he had gotten himself into. As soon as he arrived at the temple, he summoned Captain Shama and explained to him the duty required of him and the temple guards.

When Captain Shama started to protest, the Chief Rabbi flew into a rage and shouted, "Be still! These are trying days. More trying upon me than they are upon you or anybody else. The most important duty before us now is to prevent the disciples of the Galilean from stealing his body from the sepulchre. Take two men with you and seal the tomb of the Galilean and leave those two men on duty to guard the tomb.

Replace them as often as necessary, so that there will always be two men on duty at the tomb day and night until three days after the time of the Nazarene's death. Now go!"

"But, Rabbi," the Captain protested, "how can I explain this flagrant breaking of this Passover Sabbath to my men, when we have always been so strict with them about ordinary Sabbath Days?"

The Chief Rabbi growled, "That is your problem. We all have extraordinary things to do in extraordinary times, and these are very extraordinary times. Now, go, before those crazy disciples of the Galilean steal his body from the sepulchre."

With a deep sigh of resignation, Captain Shama disgustedly answered, "Yes, rabbi."

Matt. 27 (5)   Luke 24 (1-53)
Matt. 28 (1-20)   John 20 (1-31)
Mark 16 (1-20   John 21 (1-25)

Chapter 44

The Resurrection

After Jesus was buried, his mother, John, and Mary Magdalen started on their way back to Jerusalem. The sun was setting fast, casting long shadows of their figures before them. As they walked past the crosses occupied by the bodies of the two criminals, they quickly turned their heads away to avoid seeing the horribly mutilated remains of the two men. The vultures had eaten away the soft fleshy portions of their bodies, leaving the head, hands and feet virtually intact. Other muscular portions next to the bones had been partially eaten away, so what remained on the cross was a repulsively gruesome composite of flesh and bones.

Mary shuddered as a vulture circled low over her head and she impulsively huddled closer to John. When she walked past the shadow of Jesus' cross, she broke into a fit of uncontrolled sobbing. John put a protective arm around her shoulder and did his best to comfort her. As they walked through

310

the Gennareth Gate toward the Via Dolorosa, a hulking figure stepped out of the shadows, walked silently beside them
for a short distance and whispered, "John, have you seen any
of the other disciples?"

Immediately recognizing Peter's husky voice, John answered, "No. Have you?"

Peter replied, "No, I haven't. Let's look for them in the
morning and then decide what to do next."

John said, "Good. Where shall we meet?"

Peter answered, "Let us meet at daybreak in the Mount of
Olives."

John replied, "I'll be there."

Peter quickly disappeared again into the shadows of the
night and John continued walking homeward with Mary and
Mary Magdalen. The following morning was a gloomy, misty
day with clouds covering the earth like a shroud. Peter arrived early at the Mount of Olives, but found it impossible to
locate the disciples' usual meeting place, with all its familiar
landmarks obliterated by the fog. He wandered about aimlessly for awhile and then began shouting into the enveloping
mist. His voice sounded hollow and weird, as he stumbled
forward uncertainly. Suddenly, he was startled to feel a hand
clasped on the back of his shoulder, and he turned to see
John standing beside him.

"I heard you shout," John said, "and I tried to follow the
sound of your voice, but it seemed to come from many different directions. Then I came across the imprint of your big
feet, and all I had to do was to follow them. So, here I am."

Peter replied, "Thank goodness you are here. Even though
we have been here many times before, I feel as though I were
in a lost world. It seems as though heaven is ashamed of the
sight of earth and is trying its best to hide it from view."

John quietly answered, "These past few days are ones
which the world will forever remember with shame and
sorrow."

As the two men talked, they walked slowly toward the Garden of Gethsemane, carefully noting each rock, tree and mound as possible guides to their favorite hiding place. After they had traveled cautiously for a while, John said, "There's one good thing about this heavy mist and that is, while it is difficult for us to see, it is just as difficult for others to see us."

"That's the truth," Peter answered. "In fact, it won't be safe for anyone of us to be in Judaea for a long time to come."

Suddenly, John grasped Peter's arm and said, "Look!"

Peter looked straight ahead, but with his poorer eyesight, could see nothing. He groped forward uncertainly, and said, "I don't see a thing."

John turned Peter's head toward a grotesquely misshapen tree, beneath which, a man seemed to be floating through the air. Pointing toward the tree, John shouted, "Look! Look there! Right ahead of you!"

Peter slowly advanced toward the tree and saw that the man who seemed to be floating beneath it was actually hung from the tree by a cloak. It was Judas! Peter quickly drew back and said in a voice filled with bitterness, "Let him be! He belongs to the vultures."

John looked quietly at the angry grief-stricken face of Peter and said, "No, Peter. The master wouldn't have it that way. Remember, I told you how the master forgave the criminal on the cross; and, before he died, he even forgave those who crucified him. The fact that Judas committed suicide proves that his tormented soul cried out for mercy and forgiveness for the evil deed he had done. I am sure our Lord has already forgiven him. We can do no less."

Peter covered his face with his two huge hands and sobbed, "Master, forgive me. Up until now, I could think of nothing but vengeance."

John, quietly said, "Come on, Peter, let us cut Judas down and bury him as best we can."

Reluctantly, Peter helped John lower the body to the

ground and with their bare hands, they dug a shallow grave, placed Judas' body into it and covered it with as many stones as they could find.

After they had buried Judas, John said, "Do you have any idea where the other disciples may have gone?"

Peter replied, "No, but I thought that we might start looking in the Garden of Gethsemane and then in Bethany and finally at the homes of our friends in Jerusalem. Anyway, I thought it best that we search for them on the Sabbath, when there won't be so many people around."

As the two men talked, they walked slowly toward the Garden of Gethsemane. Finding no one there, they went to Bethany where they found Andrew, James and Thomas, and the five of them returned to Jerusalem where, after careful search, they found the remaining six disciples. During a brief discussion, the disciples agreed to meet the following day at the home of the Judaean friend, where Mary, Martha, Mary Magdalen and John were staying.

The following morning, Mary Magdalen and Martha left early for the sepulchre to place some aromatic spirits on Jesus' body. In the foggy, dusky dawn of daybreak, the two women picked their way carefully as they walked past Golgotha. While approaching the tomb, they wondered whom they could find to roll back the great stone at the entrance of the cave. Suddenly, the two women stopped short in amazement and fear when they found themselves before the tomb with the great stone of the sepulchre rolled back, with two soldiers lying in front of it fast asleep.

Stepping gingerly around the bodies of the sleeping soldiers, the two women tiptoed cautiously into the tomb. Because of the enveloping darkness of the dank cave, they moved forward very slowly until their eyes became accustomed to the dim light. Suddenly, they saw before them a young man dressed in a long, shiny, white robe sitting next to the empty burial niche where Jesus had been laid! Seeing their look of shocked amazement, the young man calmly asked, "Are you looking for Jesus of Nazareth?"

The two women were so speechless with fear that they just nodded their heads in agreement, so the young man said, "As you can see, he's not here; he has risen from the dead. Go and tell Peter and the other disciples that he will meet them later as he promised he would."

Frightened beyond control, the two women ran out of the sepulchre as fast as they could. In their haste they stepped on the bodies of the two sleeping guards, who quickly woke up and looked in the direction of the fleeing women. Stretching their cramped arms and legs, they yawned, rose and rubbed their blinking eyes. When they looked toward the sepulchre, they were amazed to see that it was wide open. Hesitatingly, they walked into the tomb until their eyes became accustomed to the darkened gloom. Suddenly they saw the figure of the young man in the long white robe, sitting next to the empty burial niche. Fearing they were seeing the ghost of Jesus, the frightened guards turned and fled out of the tomb as fast as they could back to the temple. When Captain Shama saw the two guards running into the temple grounds, still panting from their long run, he demanded an explanation from them for deserting their post at the tomb. The two guards shamefacedly told Captain Shama that they had seen the ghost of Jesus.

Captain Shama scoffed at their story but decided it would be best to have them tell it to the Chief Rabbi. When the captain and the guards entered the private chambers of the Chief Rabbi, he was gloomily discussing the unexpected turn of events with his father-in-law. Irritably looking up at the captain, Caiaphas asked, "What is it?"

Captain Shama apologetically answered, "Rabbi, these two guards were on duty at the Galilean's sepulchre last night and they have something very important to tell you."

Chief Rabbi Caiaphas looked up at the two guards and curtly said, "All right, get on with it. Tell me your story."

The two guards shifted uneasily from one foot to the other, hardly knowing where to begin. Each made a false attempt at clearing his throat, hoping meanwhile that the other guard would tell the unpleasant story of their flight from the sepulchre. In angry irritation, the Chief Rabbi said, "Come on, tell us your story. We don't have all day to wait."

Rabbi Annas said soothingly, "Be a little patient, son. Don't you see that these men are still out of breath?"

Then, turning to the guards, the old rabbi said, "Now, take your time, men. Rest easy and tell us the whole story in your own way."

The bolder of the two guards answered, "Rabbi Annas, we were on the last watch at the sepulchre last night and all was well and everything was quiet. Suddenly, I felt an overpowering desire to sleep. I struggled against this feeling as hard as I could, particularly when I saw that my companion here had already fallen fast asleep. That is the last thing that I can remember, just trying to stay awake. The next thing I knew, I felt someone running over me and then I heard the scared screams of two women running away from us in frenzied panic."

The guard paused for a moment to see what reaction his story had upon the two rabbis and when he saw the gentle, nodding face of Rabbi Annas, he continued a little more boldly, saying, "By that time, I was fully awake and so was my companion. Then we turned toward the sepulchre and we found to our surprise that it was wide open with the great stone rolled back. We walked into it, just stopping long enough to get our eyes accustomed to the inner darkness. Then when we walked further into it, we saw a young man sitting beside the burial niche, dressed in a long shining white robe; but the burial niche was empty!"

Again, the guard paused and Chief Rabbi Caiaphas irritably said, "Go on, go on! Finish your story."

The guard lamely continued, "Well, we were both so scared by this apparition, which we felt sure was the ghost of the Galilean, that we both turned and ran out of the cave as fast as we could and came back to the temple."

The Chief Rabbi sneered, "Fine guards! Such brave guards! The very thing we feared the most has now happened. Now the Galilean's disciples will claim that the prophecy of their master is true and that he was resurrected the third day after his death. Oh! What cowards you are! You should both be stoned to death!"

The Chief Rabbi glowered at the two cowering guards as though he would crush them both with his bare hands. In frustration and anger, he tugged and pulled at his long, black beard as though he intended to yank it out by the roots. With each motion, he kept muttering, "Such fools! Such idiots! We are undone! Soon the whole world will be told about the miraculous resurrection of that rebel Galilean."

Meanwhile, Rabbi Annas remained quiet, while his mind sought the solution to another difficult problem. Completely ignoring his upset son-in-law, he said quietly to the two guards, "Be seated, men. Make yourselves comfortable. Captain, send the servant for a jug of wine. These men are very tired and cold after their long duty last night and they need to be refreshed."

Captain Shama was so startled by this unusual request of Rabbi Annas, that he went out to fetch the jug of wine himself. When he returned with the wine and some cups, Rabbi Annas said to the two guards in an overly cheerful tone, "Drink up, men. It's a cold morning. You must revive your spirits."

Both the guards took a long drink of wine and before long, they were smiling happily as though they were the heroes of the night. When the old Rabbi saw that the two guards were in a relaxed, jovial mood, he said to them, "Now let's see. Let us review the events of last night very carefully. You say that while you were on guard duty last night at the sepulchre, you both fell into a deep and powerful sleep, even though you both tried very hard to stay awake. Isn't that right?"

Both guards eagerly nodded their heads and the old rabbi slyly continued, "Drink up, men, refresh yourselves. Since you were both overwhelmed by an irresistible desire to sleep, I imagine it means that your wine was drugged. Isn't that so?"

The two guards, who had brightened up amazingly under the influence of the wine and the sympathetic prompting of the old rabbi, eagerly answered, "That's it. Our wine must have been drugged."

Rabbi Annas' crafty face now hardened slightly as his piercing bright eyes drilled through the dulled eyes of the two guards as he said, "Then, while you were in your drugged sleep, some men rolled back the great stone of the sepulchre and stole the body of the Galilean. Isn't that the way it happened?"

The two guards stuttered and stammered as their faces showed their disbelief in the old rabbi's story. Noting their skeptical reaction, Rabbi Annas reached into his voluminous robe and took out a handful of silver and carefully divided it into two equal parts and pressed the silver coins into the palm of each guard. Looking intently into the eyes of each man, he slowly said, "Think carefully, men, haven't I told last night's events the way it happened? Maybe I left out some minor detail, but you agree with me about the main part of my story, don't you?"

The bolder of the two guards answered, "Rabbi Annas, I know I can speak frankly to you. Both of us will tell the story of last night's events exactly as you have told it to us. But what will happen to us if the Roman governor finds out we were lying?"

"You leave the Roman governor to me," Rabbi Annas replied. "I promise to protect you against any punishment that he may order against you. Now, go and tell your story to as many persons as possible, before the disciples of the Galilean try to delude the people into believing that the Galilean has been resurrected."

Pocketing their money and nodding knowingly, both guards respectfully, said, "Yes, Rabbi."

That night, the eleven disciples met with the mother of Jesus, Martha, and Mary Magdalen behind locked doors in the home of their Judaean friends. Mary and Mary Magdalen excitedly and repeatedly told in detail all the events that had occurred in the sepulchre. However, the questions and the doubts in the minds of several of the disciples were so great that they repeatedly questioned the two women over and over again regarding each minute detail of their experience in the tomb. Finally, Thomas rose and said, "I'll never believe that our master has risen from the dead until I can see him with my very own eyes."

Vehemently, Mary Magdalen replied, "But we saw the angel with our very own eyes, and he told us that Jesus was resurrected."

Doubtfully, Thomas asked, "*Whom* did you actually see?"

With considerable irritation Mary Magdalen answered, "I told you, we saw the angel in a shining white robe, just like the one that Jesus wore."

Stubbornly, Thomas reiterated, "I'll never believe that the master has been resurrected until I can see him and t-t-touch him." His last words sounded so strange that Mary Magdalen looked over at him apprehensively. She noticed that his eyes were glazed and his body seemed abnormally rigid. Then Mary Magdalen felt her own body become tense and her vision became blurred. She tried to shake her head vigorously and only gradually did her vision return to normal. Then she saw Jesus standing beside Thomas!

Turning to Thomas, Jesus said, "Put your finger into these holes in my hands."

In great awe and consternation, Thomas put his finger into the hole in each of Jesus' hands. Jesus continued, "Now, put your hand into this hole in my side."

With a look of wonderment and fright, Thomas did as he was told. As the realization of the truth of Jesus' resurrection dawned upon him, Thomas' mouth dropped open, his eyes became glassy and his entire body became rigid. Dropping to his knees, he clasped Jesus around the waist and pleadingly said, "My Lord, and my God, forgive me."

After a long pause, Jesus answered, "Hereafter, have faith in me."

With one hand on Thomas' head and with the other out-stretched, Jesus said, "Blessed are those who have faith with-out proof. Now all of you go forth and teach the people of all nations the commandments I have taught you. Teach them to love God above all else in the world. Tell them to love their neighbors as themselves and to repay hate with love. Teach every one to become as a child before God, because only those who are pure in mind and pure in spirit, will enter the Kingdom of Heaven.

"Baptize all repentant sinners in the name of the Father and of the Son and of the Holy Ghost. Remember that God is a Spirit and that you carry Him within you everywhere you go. May God be with you always. Farewell."

And so, ended Jesus's ministry on earth. His betrayal, con-demnation and crucifixion did nothing to minimize the message he brought to the world. Never again would injustice, brutality and selfishness be acceptable as rules of conduct for the people of the world. While Jesus did not create a miracle of converting all mankind to beneficial acts of brotherhood, he did create a standard of living by which all mankind would thereafter be judged.